To Mi
with best wishes

AKA

SHAKESPEARE

AKA

SHAKESPEARE

A Scientific Approach to the Authorship Question

PETER A. STURROCK

AKA SHAKESPEARE: A Scientific Approach to the Authorship Question
Copyright © 2013 by Peter A. Sturrock
Published by Exoscience
Place of Publication: Palo Alto, California 94301

ISBN-13: 978-0-9842614-5-1 (Color Paperback edition)
ISBN-13: 978-0-9842614-1-3 (B&W Paperback edition)
ISBN-13: 978-0-9842614-2-0 (Color ePub ebook edition)
ISBN-13: 978-0-9842614-3-7 (Color Kindle/Mobi edition)

Printed in the United States

Cover photograph: Quill pen in hand on paper background by
iStockphoto©Cimmerian
Book design by DesignForBooks.com
Editing by EricksonEditorial.net

www.exoscience.org

For Martita

Contents

APPENDICES

REFERENCES

PLATES

Preface

*H*ow did this book come about? Purely by chance! In writing my memoirs (*A Tale of Two Sciences*) a few years ago, I recalled that during my youth (when I was very green in judgment), I attempted to compose poetry (with minuscule success). The only poem that I could remember was a parody of Shakespeare's most famous sonnet, "Shall I compare thee to a summer's day?" My parody began, inevitably, "Shall I compare thee to a winter's night?" This recollection prompted me to reread the famous sonnet, which led me to read the neighboring sonnets, and soon I was reading the entire sequence.

I was not the first person to find the sequence puzzling, nor shall I be the last. One cannot read these sonnets without facing three big questions: *Who wrote them? To whom were they addressed?* and *What were they all about?* Assuming that the answer to the first question is *William Shakspere* (his preferred spelling) of *Stratford-upon-Avon,* I could see no sensible answers to the other two questions. Nor did I find satisfactory answers in books written by some of the great Shakespeare scholars.

So I learned that there is an *Authorship Question!* Although most scholars—notably those in academia—do not question that Shakspere (from Stratford-upon-Avon) and Shakespeare (the great poet and playwright) are one and the same person, there are many independent scholars who sincerely doubt it.

In the course of my long (69 years and counting!) scientific career, I have had occasion to study a number of science-related problems concerning which scholars inside academia and scholars outside of academia disagree. I have concluded that neither group has a monopoly on either wisdom or truth. I have not found that academic scholars are always right—but neither have I found that they are always wrong.

Many arguments are presented by both the Shakspere-Is-Shakespeare advocates, and the Shakspere-Is-Not-Shakespeare dissenters. I did not find any one argument, either way, to be conclusive. Eventually, I realized that the question could best be resolved by weighing and combining many different pieces of evidence. It happens that weighing and combining scientific evidence is something I have thought about for many years, and I could see no reason why the relevant tools could not be brought to bear upon the Authorship Question.

My goal was then clear-cut: to approach the Authorship Question from a scientific perspective. But how could I make the scientific procedures I had in mind comprehensible to non-scientists? And how could I make the process interesting?

My answer (the success of which remains to be seen) has been to develop the book as a dialog. My four characters have different skills and different perspectives. Beatrice is an academic scholar who initially harbors no doubt that Shakspere and Shakespeare are one and the same person, but Claudia is a rebel who instinctively challenges authority. Martin is a statistician skilled in the weighing of evidence, and James is a scientist—a worldly one—who serves as the benevolent master of ceremonies. With that plan, writing was a pleasure rather than a pain: I did not need to think about what to write—I simply had to listen to my actors talking and arguing with each other. This book is my record of their spirited conversations. It is also a record of Martin's processing of Beatrice's and Claudia's judgments to arrive at their overall assessments concerning three candidates—Shakspere, de Vere, and an enigmatic "Somebody Else."

It is a pleasure to again thank Kathleen Erickson for her critical but supportive collaboration as Editor, and to again thank Michael Rohani for his skill and creativity in designing this book. It is also a pleasure to thank Margaret (aka Peggy) Rathmann for producing the sketches of our four actors. Now we know exactly what they look like! I also thank Bill Busse and John Wick for their skillful assistance in preparing the graphics.

I am indebted to many colleagues and other friends for encouragement and support. Two of my scientific colleagues have played crucial roles: Jeff Scargle, an astrophysicist at the NASA Ames Research Center and a renowned expert in statistical analysis, has helpfully critiqued my numerical analysis; and Martin Hellman, Emeritus Professor of Electrical Engineering at Stanford University and a world leader in cryptology, has helped me evaluate the significance of messages that can be found in the Inscription to the Shakespeare Monument and in the Dedication to the Sonnets. These analyses are built upon the seminal work of David Roper (concerning the Inscription) and of Jonathan Bond (concerning the Dedication). I am also indebted to Diana Price for her insightful and helpful comments on an early version of this book; to Jonathan Bond, Gerhard Casper, Marty Cawthon, Richard Martin, Marsh McCall, David Roper, and Rich Wolfson for helpful suggestions; and to Richard Adams, Sherry Blair, Elvia Faggin, Pierre Kaufmann, Adele Langendorf, and Tita McCall for their interest and encouragement.

Prologue

Why another book about the Shakespeare Authorship Question?
Because the identity of the author we know as "Shakespeare"
remains an open question. Most scholars of English literature
maintain that he was a gentleman of that or similar name who
was born and died in the small town of Stratford-upon-Avon
in the County of Warwickshire in England. However, there are
a growing number of independent scholars who dispute that
contention. The scholastic community has not persuaded the
independent scholars to see the error of their ways. But neither
have the independent scholars persuaded the orthodox scholars
to see the error of their ways. The Authorship Problem therefore
remains unresolved.

What are my credentials for this undertaking? A love of
literature and a fondness for attempting to solve problems—be
they in mathematics, physics, electrical engineering, astrophysics, or what are euphemistically referred to as "anomalous
phenomena"—coupled with a conviction that scientific thinking
need not be restricted to scientific problems. It has been a happy
adventure to try to bring scientific thinking to bear upon this
great problem of literature.

I have written this book in such a way that any reader can
examine the Authorship Question for himself or herself, and

hopefully arrive at his or her own answer to the four-centuries-old mystery—Who precisely was the greatest writer in the English language, a possibly super-brilliant but only lightly schooled gentleman from the provinces who never left England, or a brilliant, exceedingly well-schooled and well-traveled obscure nobleman who was controversial during his lifetime and remains controversial today? Or somebody else?

If there is any single argument that yields a conclusive answer to this mystery, the genius who has discovered that argument has kept it to himself or herself. Each side of the debate has many arguments to present—no one of which is conclusive. This means that one must deal with a number of separate items and then, to get a final result, find a way to combine the results of these investigations. The procedure adopted in this book is designed to meet these requirements. As is typical of scientific research, the procedure involves some "number-crunching." However—peace to the Reader—you will not need to do any crunching yourself. The book's website contains a friendly wizard (affectionately known as *Prospero*) who will make all the calculations for you.

You may just read the book, or you may participate by expressing your considered opinions concerning the various questions that arise, which you will find set out in a series of "charts." You will be asked to express your opinions in terms of "weights." Suppose, for instance, that a certain question has just two possible answers. If you have no preference concerning the possible answers, you would give them equal weights (1 and 1, or 10 and 10, etc., . . . only the ratio of the weights is significant). If you were sure that one answer is false, you would give that answer a weight of zero, and the other option any weight other than zero. But if in your opinion one answer is ten times more likely to be correct than the other, you would give the options weights of 10 and 1 (or 20 and 2, or 100 and 10, etc.).

Since the goal of research is to arrive at a consensus, you might consider working in a small group—perhaps a book club.

It would be interesting to identify points of common agreement and points of contention.

When you have finished expressing your opinions in terms of weights, *Prospero* will reduce all of your judgments to just three numbers:

The opinions you have expressed lead Prospero to conclude that

1) The probability that the author was the gentleman from Stratford-upon-Avon is X;

2) The probability that the author was the Earl of Oxford is Y; and

3) The probability that the author was somebody else is Z.

After we have received input from one hundred or more readers, we plan to publish a summary of their results, such as *95% of respondents consider that the author is most likely to be XXX*; etc. We hope to be able to compare the thinking of orthodox and unorthodox scholars to see where and why they differ.

Now if you are ready to begin your journey, Beatrice, Claudia, and James await you at the Buena Vista Café in Sausalito in California.

But before you set out, Prospero—like Polonius—offers some *precepts for your memory.*

Prospero's Precepts[1]

All beliefs in whatever realm are theories at some level.

Do not condemn the judgment of another because it differs from your own. You may both be wrong.

---

1. Prospero is quoting from Stephen Schneider; Dandemis; Francis Bacon; Peter Medawar; Arthur Conan Doyle; Francis Crick; Richard Feynman; Charles Darwin; Mark Twain; Thomas Jefferson; and Arthur Schopenhauer.

Read not to contradict and confute; nor to believe and take for granted; nor to find talk and discourse; but to weigh and consider.

Never fall in love with your hypothesis.

It is a capital mistake to theorize before one has data. Insensibly one begins to twist facts to suit theories instead of theories to suit facts.

A theory should not attempt to explain all the facts, because some of the facts are wrong.

The thing that doesn't fit is the thing that is most interesting.

To kill an error is as good a service as, and sometimes even better than, the establishing of a new truth or fact.

It ain't what you don't know that gets you into trouble. It's what you know for sure that just ain't so.

Ignorance is preferable to error; and he is less remote from the truth who believes nothing, than he who believes what is wrong.

All truth passes through three stages. First, it is ridiculed, second, it is violently opposed, and third, it is accepted as self-evident.

Online Database and Calculator—
AKA Prospero

Readers of *AKA Shakespeare, A Scientific Approach to the Authorship Question*, are invited to participate in the resolution of this question, carrying out your own research by answering the same questions we discuss in this book. This involves three steps:

1. You consider each specific item of evidence in turn, and enter your judgments concerning the relevant questions. This step requires no mathematical skill.

2. You then enter your judgments into the online database and processor which we call *Prospero*.

3. Prospero carries out the necessary calculations and returns your final probabilities for the candidate authors, based on all the information you have provided.

You may access Prospero at www.aka-shakespeare.com. Clicking on *Prospero* will prompt you for a password to verify that you are a reader of this book.

The password is: bayes

You may then create your personal account that enables you to interact with Prospero.

Prospero will process your inputted information and return your final probabilities.

Summaries for each of the individual items of evidence will be displayed to users.

Summaries of the final probabilities for the Shakespeare candidates will be displayed for public access.

Dramatis Personae

Plate A. JAMES MONROE, highly intelligent with an open and inquiring mind, grew up in a small college town in Oregon and moved to Southern California for his graduate education in physics. A successful scientist and engineer who holds several lucrative patents and is skillful in managing people, he created and sold three electronics companies in Silicon Valley. However, he has misread his interest in nature and his love of the outdoors to become a somewhat less successful vintner in Carmel Valley. (Sketch by Peggy Rathmann)

Plate B. CLAUDIA CARTWRIGHT MONROE spent some of her early years in the Middle East, where her father advised multinational companies on the intricacies of the United States tax code and the hazards of the Foreign Corrupt Practices Act. With a natural gift for languages, she became fluent in Arabic, Hindi, and Urdu, which led to her being recruited by the CIA. She became intrigued with intrigues, and retired from the Company to write detective stories—successfully. Her marriage to James was the second for each of them. (Sketch by Peggy Rathmann)

Plate C. BEATRICE QUINN grew up in an academic community in Vermont, where her mother was a Professor of Psychology and her father a Professor of Latin and Greek. She took to English Literature, and wrote a PhD dissertation entitled *Town and Country: A Comparative Analysis of the Poetry of Geoffrey Chaucer and William Langland* (focusing, of course, on *The Canterbury Tales* and *The Vision of Piers Plowman*). This dissertation so impressed the Dean of the Faculty at Marin State University (who happened to have been born and raised in Langland's county of Worcestershire) that he transferred an empty billet from Russian and Slavic Languages to the English Department, which saw fit to offer the position to Beatrice. Her first book, *Langland's Vision*, has been favorably reviewed in many English-Literature journals, and has established Beatrice as the leading authority on English alliterative verse of the late Middle Ages. Her marriage to an engaging entrepreneur, who proved to be better at engaging than at entrepreneuring, has recently come to an amicable conclusion. (Sketch by Peggy Rathmann)

Plate D. MARTIN ANDERSON came to the United States from Sweden at the not-so-tender age of fourteen. He had a flair for mathematics, and his first degree was in that field. However, he found that mathematics is somewhat removed from the real world and that his skills were unsalable, so he acquired a PhD in statistics, for which there is always a ready market. After broadening his expertise still further to include Decision Analysis, he became a valuable addition to the teaching staff of the Joint Institute for Strategic Analysis in Monterey. A natural athlete, his main—but not his only—sport is tennis. Despite many entreaties to the contrary, he remains a bachelor. (Sketch by Peggy Rathmann)

The Buena Vista Café in Sausalito,
Overlooking the San Francisco Bay

An Intriguing Book Review

It is a puzzlement!

JAMES is in his early sixties. He is not tall, but is strongly built, and has the vibrant complexion of one who spends a lot of time outdoors. After selling his most recent, and most successful, business, he has purchased a house and winery in Carmel Valley, and spends most of his time in the vineyard. He has dark brown hair, gray at the edges, and is wearing casual but expensive light-beige slacks and an open-neck, short-sleeve shirt.

CLAUDIA, James' wife, is in her mid-forties, and she, too, has a strong physique. She writes detective stories. A lifelong redhead, she was once told that women with red hair should never wear red clothing—so she always wears something red or partly red. Today, she is wearing a bright Hawaiian shirt over a flowing, nondescript skirt, and a pair of large sunglasses, through which she peers at each person strolling by the café, on the lookout for a familiar face.

BEATRICE is an attractive brunette in her early forties, a Professor of English Literature at Marin State University. She is wearing a light-blue pants suit, and a matching, large-brimmed hat. She takes off her hat, and sips her gin and tonic with the satisfied air of someone who has just received her first royalty payment from her first book.

JAMES has been reading a newspaper. He suddenly puts it down.

JAMES. This is curious.

BEATRICE. What is so curious that it puzzles a scientist?

JAMES. It is a scientist's job to be puzzled by a new problem. Otherwise, he might be jumping to an unwarranted conclusion.

CLAUDIA. Is somebody jumping to an unwarranted conclusion today?

JAMES. That is the question. This book review suggests that we may all have been jumping to an unwarranted conclusion for the last four hundred years.

CLAUDIA. Ah, yes, James, that must be the review about Shakespeare, and the book must be the one by Bill Bryson. [1] I read the review online yesterday, and it happens that I had quickly skimmed through the book when I was at the airport last week.

JAMES. Then you know more than I do. What did you think of the review?

CLAUDIA. I learned that Bryson—who has written on all sorts of topics in the past, and who can hardly claim to be a Shakespearian scholar—takes the position that what he refers to as "conspiracy theories" are uniformly without merit. The reviewer, on the other hand, came to the conclusion that Bryson had spent too much time being cute, and not enough time doing his homework. From the very little I have read so far, I found the review much more persuasive than the book.

BEATRICE. Really, Claudia! I always thought of you as a highly intelligent person. I know that you have to be speculative and creative in writing your detective stories, but I cannot conceive that you would seriously consider that the Shakespeare plays were not written by Shakespeare! You must have a pretty poor opinion of the intellectual abilities of hundreds of Shakespeare scholars who have now spent hundreds of years studying Shakespeare's work!

CLAUDIA. I am sure that all of those scholars, in whom you have such great faith, were serious and well-intentioned, Beatrice. But were they asking the right questions? Take the first fourteen sonnets. The orthodox interpretation seems to be that they are simply melodic variations on a theme of Paganini. To find an alternative interpretation, one would have to ask some probing questions: Who was the Fair Youth to whom those sonnets were addressed? Who was the young lady whom the poet wanted him to marry? And why was the poet so keen to bring about that marriage? What was in it for the poet?

Frankly, I find it incredible that your Shakespeare scholars are willing to spend so much time analyzing the words and the rhyming schemes, and the meters, and all that, but—as far as I can tell—so little time carrying out a close, serious, and professional examination of the Authorship Question. I have done some reading on this matter, and I do not see that we can be all that sure who wrote all that wonderful material written by someone who was either named *Shakespeare* or chose to write under the name of *Shakespeare*.

JAMES. I can add a short anecdote to this interesting debate. I have not looked into the Authorship Question myself, but I have a friend who is a professor of astronomy at Bradford University, who once became interested in this question. He learned that there were five eminent Shakespeare scholars on the faculty of his university, so he wrote separate letters to all five of them, inquiring about their views on the subject. He got exactly the same response from all five—zero—not even an acknowledgment.

It seems that wherever there is a profession, there is an imminent danger of groupthink. Even scientists, whom we revere as being supremely objective and rational, can behave quite irrationally. Just try mentioning "astrology" to an astronomer, or "cold fusion" to a physicist, and see how rapidly his back stiffens, his eyes dilate, and his face freezes. Or whisper in the ear of a mathematician that you have discovered a simple proof of Fermat's last theorem—but be sure you have an escape route close at hand, in case he or she does not have a sense of humor.

It seems that members of any profession owe it to their guild to do all that they can to maintain the illusion that they have knowledge and insight far beyond the capabilities of all of those poor benighted souls who are not members of their guild.

CLAUDIA. Without wishing to steal my husband's well-deserved thunder, I would like to point out that George Bernard Shaw expressed much the same thoughts somewhat more succinctly. His words were "All professions are conspiracies against the laity" [2].

BEATRICE. Very interesting, ladies and gentlemen, but I would like to point out what should be an obvious fact—knowing the name of the author would not change a single word in any of the plays or poems. I personally have no doubt about the authorship, but I also fail to see that it is consequential. Whatever the answer may be, it can have no influence whatever on our appreciation of what he wrote—assuming, of course, that he was a "he."

CLAUDIA. That is indeed an assumption, Beatrice. One of the candidates for the mantle of Shakespeare is in fact the Countess of Pembroke. Would that be of no interest to you?

BEATRICE. It could come in handy. I am leading a seminar on feminist studies next year.

CLAUDIA. So it might be worth discussing, even though the discovery would not change any of the words that "Shakespeare" wrote. Anyway, Beatrice, you can't say there is no doubt about it. Would you bet your life that the man from Stratford-upon-Avon and the author Shakespeare were one and the same person?

BEATRICE. No, of course not. But I would wager one-hundred-to-one.

JAMES. Actually, Beatrice, odds of one-hundred-to-one are not that impressive for anyone who has had experience in dealing with probabilities—which I have had to do in my way of business. If you were tossing a coin and it came up heads seven times in a row, you would probably be interested, but not greatly impressed. But the odds against that happening are more than one hundred to one. If that represents the strength of your conviction, I would say that you are really not that committed to the Stratford contender—or pretender.

BEATRICE. Well, of course, I am not a betting person, so I am not used to thinking about probabilities.

JAMES. Well, it might be helpful if we were to try to think that way. If we could all—hopefully cooperatively—dissect this problem, and compare notes on each part of it, we might find that—to our great surprise—we could reach a consensus. And if we could not agree, we would at least see just where and why we differ.

CLAUDIA. Thank you for calming the waters, James. That seems to me like an idea worth pursuing.

JAMES. But of course, we would have to agree that we are not looking for absolute truth. We are never going to have the evidence it would take to achieve that—unless someone suddenly finds a chest full of manuscripts and correspondence. Think what that would sell for on the open market! But, in everyday life, we get by without having absolute truth about most things. If I want to go to the bank tomorrow morning, I'll drive to where it is today even though, from a strictly logical point of view, it might not be there. It might have gone up in smoke during the night!

BEATRICE. James, you are sounding very philosophical today. Have you been reading some Socrates or Thomas Aquinas?

JAMES. No—Ambrose Bierce! If I find that I am getting too serious about life, I read a few pages of *The Devil's Dictionary* [3]. But, more seriously, it happens that I am meeting Martin

Anderson for lunch tomorrow. He teaches statistics at the Joint Services Institute for Strategic Analysis down in Monterey, but he has business in Palo Alto. Martin has a healthy skepticism about practically everything. You would think that, with his background in statistics and decision theory and all that, he would know what is believable and what is not. However, he keeps emphasizing how little information we have on many topics that we have to make important decisions about.

CLAUDIA. I sometimes feel the same way. When I see two young people about to get married, I wonder how much they know about each other, and if they know what a challenging project a marriage really is.

BEATRICE. I have first-hand experience of that! After what was supposed to be a romantic sabbatical in Rome, Fabian and I realized that, after twenty years, togetherness is not exactly what it was *come prima*. Characteristics that were once endearing have somehow become irritating. That is why I am now a single lady, and able to spend all the time I want with whomever I want—which I find very refreshing.

CLAUDIA. Congratulations, Beatrice. We think you made the right decision. I am happy to say that James and I have so far managed to steer safely past the rocks and shoals in our marriage. Luckily we hit more shoals than rocks—which helped us survive.

JAMES. Very interesting—but, to get back to the Shakespeare question, I am intrigued that a few apparently rational scholars think that it is a problem. And I must say, Beatrice, that I am also intrigued that it is such a hot-button issue for the mainstream Shakespeare establishment. I personally would be very interested to see just how strong the case is that all those plays and poems were in fact written by a man of humble origins, with very limited educational opportunities, from Warwickshire in the West of England, three or four days from London by horse. (No railway and no public carriages in those days.)

May I suggest that we all read a little, and think a little, to see if there is any way that we could sort out the problem in our own minds—but probably not in anyone else's!

CLAUDIA. Good idea! The question has intrigued me for a long time.

BEATRICE. My guess is that it will be a complete wild-goose chase. But you can count me in. The last time I checked, I still had tenure.

JAMES. Thank you, Beatrice. I am sure that we can rely on you not to let Claudia or me jump to any unwarranted conclusions!

However, I recommend that we involve Martin. He teaches military people how to solve problems (when he is not preparing for his next tennis match). If we can persuade him to meet with us, we can be sure that we shall not spend our time spinning our wheels.

BEATRICE. I can go along with that. I shall be spending the weekend in Carmel in two weeks time. I have to talk up English Literature at the Alvarado School. And while I am in the Monterey area, I also need to talk up Marin State University to some of our wealthy alumni who live on the Nineteen Mile Drive!

You two live only a few miles up the road in Carmel Valley. Let's see if Martin can join us. We can all meet for dinner at the Highview Inn. We can enjoy the wine and the view. If we cannot get any inspiration from the sea-spirits, at least we can get some consolation from their great chef.

CLAUDIA. James and I will be back in San Francisco next weekend.

James, why don't you start our project by reading the Bryson book and giving us your opinion of it? It is short, and it should be easy reading. You can see how he compares with Ambrose Bierce.

JAMES. That sounds manageable. So we all meet again a week from today, same place.

NOTES

1. Bryson (2007).
2. Shaw (1906).
3. Bierce (1911).

The Buena Vista Café

A Closer Look at the Book Review

The puzzlement becomes intriguing.

JAMES. We are happy to see you again, Beatrice. I gather you had a party to celebrate your newest book contract.

BEATRICE. Yes, we had a great celebration. Do you think the cost of a party is tax-deductible?

CLAUDIA. Only if you made some advance sales, and have receipts to prove it.

BEATRICE. I thought as much. Too bad! And how was your week, James? Did you find time to do your homework?

JAMES. Yes and no. I read a short, lively book, but without much enlightenment.

BEATRICE. The Bill Bryson book?

JAMES. Yes—*Shakespeare, the World as Stage* [1]. A statement on the dustjacket reads "vivid, unsentimental, witty, and fast-paced." I approve of his unsentimentality, but I could wish that he had been less vivid, less witty, and taken his time to share some real information about Shakespeare.

BEATRICE. What had you expected?

JAMES. The publisher, in the inside jacket, leads us to believe that Bryson is in the same league as Plutarch, Lytton Strachey, and Samuel Johnson. Publishers always stretch a point, but rarely that far. They quote Strachey, saying that the goal of the series is "to preserve a becoming brevity which excludes everything that is redundant and nothing that is significant." What I found, instead, is much that is redundant and little that is significant.

CLAUDIA. What was so redundant?

JAMES. Much of the book is about England—London, in particular—and the times in which Shakespeare—whoever he was—lived. Most of the rest was speculation. Here is a typical page—page 81—it contains these phrases: "appears to have," "doubtless," "according to tradition," "may well be," etc., etc., and ends with "it is tempting, even logical, to guess . . ."

BEATRICE. He must have found a few relevant facts to include.

JAMES. He tells us that "researchers have found about 100 documents relating to William Shakespeare and his immediate family—baptismal records, title deeds, tax certificates, marriage homes, writs of attachment, court records, etc." He goes on to say "although he left nearly one million words of text, we have just fourteen words in his own hand—his name signed six times and the words "by me" on his will. Not a single note or letter or page of manuscript survives." This strikes me as very suspicious. One interesting fact that I did learn is that Mr. Stratford (meaning the man from Stratford-upon-Avon) seems never to have spelled his name the same way twice in a row. The signatures that survive read as "Wilm Shaksp," "William Shakespe," "Wm Shakspe," "William Shakspere," "Willm Shakspere," and "William Shakspeare." (It is interesting that most of these spellings involved a consonant following the k rather than an e following the k, suggesting that the *short-a* pronunciation—as in "cat" and "hat"—was more common than the *long-a* pronunciation of "wake" and "bake.")

CLAUDIA. A number of people who write on the Authorship Question use the name "Shakspere" for the man from Stratford. We could do the same to avoid assuming that he is the same person as our author "Shakespeare."

BEATRICE. But James, as far as I am aware, we do not have much in the way of records of any other writers at that time, either.

CLAUDIA. Actually, that is not true, Beatrice. You should look at a book entitled *Shakespeare's Unorthodox Biography. New Evidence of an Authorship Problem* [2]. The author is Diana Price, who makes a very careful study of what we know—and, more extensively, what we do not know—about Shakspere.

There is a remarkable table at the end of her book, which she calls a "Chart of Literary Paper Trails," in which she compares Stratford with 24 known writers who lived at the same time. She considers ten items of evidence related to the writing profession. For every writer except Stratford, she finds at least three such items. For Stratford, she finds none. When we meet with Martin, we can ask him whether that difference is what a scientist might term "statistically significant."

Here is another interesting fact about Price's book: Of the 372 "orthodox" works that she consults, 40% are published by university presses, 37% by commercial presses, and the rest appear in journals, etc. By contrast, of the 41 "unorthodox" works that she consults, none is published by a university press, 46% are published by commercial presses, and the rest appear in journals, etc.

JAMES. So what is the inference?

BEATRICE. Maybe that university presses have high standards of scholarship.

CLAUDIA. Or possibly that they are just more conservative—more gun-shy, perhaps.

JAMES. This does raise the crucial question—Where could one turn for unbiased information?

CLAUDIA. Or, if there is no such source, how can one cope with bias?

BEATRICE. We seem to be embarked on a journey here, but I for one am not at all sure about our rationale. We are moving toward steps that may or may not lead us to the identity of Shakespeare, something that I am not really in doubt about at this time. But you may turn up evidence that opens my mind—maybe changes my mind. But what I really question is—What is the point of finding out the true identity of Shakespeare?—assuming for the purpose of argument that it was not Mr. Stratford. Knowing the plays were written by Lord X or Lady Y will not change one word in those plays. So why is it important? What difference would it make?

JAMES. You asked that question before, Beatrice. It is valid question. Let me ask you a question. Have you ever read the Diary of Anne Frank?

BEATRICE. Some time ago—yes.

JAMES. When you were reading that diary, did you pay any attention to the identity of the author?

BEATRICE. Of course I did. The diary was all about Anne and her life and her circumstances.

JAMES. Does it occur to you that the same may be true of Shakespeare's plays and poems—especially the sonnets? The plays are written in third-person terms, but the thoughts are those of the author. He is not expressing himself as directly as he would in confiding his thoughts to a diary. But his thoughts and emotions are probably there all the same. I imagine that if we could relate the plays, for instance, to the author's life story, they might become even deeper, richer, and more significant. Frankly, it baffles me that a scholar such as yourself, who is used to analyzing texts in great detail, should consider that the identity of the author is less important than the meter and the rhyming scheme and such technicalities.

CLAUDIA. James was surprised to hear your comment, Beatrice. But I am not surprised. I have heard that comment before. But—oddly enough—only in relation to Shakespeare. I have yet to hear anyone suggest that symphony and opera programs should not bother to list the names of composers. Imagine the announcement of an opera—it gives the name of the opera, say *Cosi Fan Tutte*, but it does not bother to mention that the music is by someone called Mozart. Wouldn't that strike you as rather odd?

But you must have read Shakespeare's sonnets, haven't you?

BEATRICE. Of course. I teach a regular course on English poetry.

CLAUDIA. Did you ever read them right through, one after the other?

BEATRICE. No—that is not the way I structure the course. We take one poem at a time, and analyze it line by line. There is a wonderful book by Helen Vendler that I use [3].

CLAUDIA. When you listen to a concerto, do you listen to it phrase by phrase?

BEATRICE. Of course not—What I hear is one piece, but with themes and variations.

CLAUDIA. Poems have themes and variations, too. Sometimes it is a sequence of poems that has the theme and variations. I think the sonnets do. Next time you go on a vacation, try reading all one hundred and fifty four sonnets right through, one after the other. Any one poem may seem just like clever and beautiful wordplay. But read the entire sequence, and you may find that the poet is baring his soul—and his agony.

As I read them—and I am sure there are many different ways to read them—the sonnets are the story of two unsuccessful, inappropriate, and unhappy love affairs: one with a "fair youth," and the other with a "dark lady."

Does Vendler not discuss the fair youth and the dark lady, and wonder who they were? If not, why not? Or does she simply read them as the exercises of a wordsmith honing his craft?

BEATRICE. OK, James and Claudia, you have made your points. And yes, Claudia, I'll take that little book with me in the fall, when I go on my Aegean cruise. If I read ten a day, I'll get through them in a fortnight. But by that time, maybe we shall have figured out just who everyone was—the poet, the fair youth, the dark lady— even the rival poet. However, Vendler makes a pretty good case that they were not real people at all—just archetypes.

CLAUDIA. Invented for the pleasure of twentieth-century scholars?

JAMES. When shall we three meet again? Soon, I hope, but preferably not in thunder, lightning, or in rain!

BEATRICE. I shall be spending the weekend in Carmel next week.

JAMES. Yes—we are looking forward to our meeting at the Highview Inn, and—with any luck—Martin will be joining us.

NOTES

1. Bryson (2007).

2. Price (2001). (This book is notable as the first on the Authorship Question to be published in a peer-reviewed series by a mainstream publisher.)

3. Vendler (1997).

A Room at the Highview Inn in
Carmel, Overlooking the Pacific

Enter a Helpful Statistician

Late afternoon. The trio becomes a quartet.

James, Beatrice, and Claudia meet with Martin who, in his early forties, has a strong, Nordic build—tall, straw-color hair, and piercing blue eyes—slow-speaking but fast-moving; author of a standard textbook on Decision Analysis; a local tennis champion whose favorite sport is diving for abalone; single, but not for a lack of female admirers.

JAMES. Thank you for inviting us to the Highview Inn, Beatrice. Were you well and appropriately received at the Alvarado School? Were you able to interest the students in literature?

BEATRICE. It was slow-going—until I mentioned that William Faulkner, whenever he needed a little extra money, would spend time screenwriting in Hollywood. That remark got their attention.

CLAUDIA. Did you have any luck chatting up your wealthy alumni?

BEATRICE. I'm sorry, but I'm not allowed to talk about that— *Company Classified!* But for your information, when I am chatting up alumni I'm not allowed to raise the tawdry issue of money myself. That topic must be raised by the alumnus or alumna or it doesn't come up at all.

JAMES. I am glad your talk went well, Beatrice. But now I want you to meet Martin. We have had some good telephone conversations, so he has a good idea of the project that we are thinking of undertaking.

Martin, I would like you to meet Beatrice, who rather suspects that we are on a wild-goose chase.

MARTIN. Happy to meet you, Beatrice. You may prove to be correct, but I suspect we going to have some very enjoyable conversations all the same.

BEATRICE. Either way, perhaps we shall learn how the spooks in the military go about problem-solving.

MARTIN. We do not train spooks in Monterey. I understand that goes on in Virginia.

JAMES. Martin, you must now meet Claudia—our resident detective.

MARTIN. Happy to meet you too, Claudia. I gather that you have some bones that we can chew on. I hope that our jaws are as strong as *Alice-In-Wonderland's* Father William.

CLAUDIA. I have done some virtual problem-solving in my novels. Now it will be interesting to see how an expert goes about it.

MARTIN. I hope that James has not given you unfair expectations of my abilities. I spend more time giving lectures on statistics than in grappling with real problems involving real human beings.

JAMES. Well, now that we have been properly introduced, how would you like to start, Martin?

MARTIN. Well, since this problem has—or could once have had—legal ramifications, how would we start if we were in a courtroom?

JAMES. The judge would ask the plaintiff to make a brief introductory statement and then ask the same from the defendant.
I guess that Claudia qualifies as the plaintiff, since she's the
one who harbors the most doubts about the authorship of the
Shakespeare corpus. And that leaves Beatrice as the defendant,
since she thinks that our doubts are unwarranted.

MARTIN. That sounds good. Would you like to start, Claudia?

CLAUDIA. This is a tall order. I had not expected to find myself
in a courtroom, so I forgot to bring my brief with me. The difficulty with this problem is that no one argument is conclusive.
One is dealing with a lot of little facts, each of which is "iffy."

JAMES. We all agree with you so far, Claudia.

CLAUDIA. Once you doubt that any of the Shakespeare corpus
was written by the gentleman from Stratford, there are only a few
words that you can be sure that he did write.

BEATRICE. And they are?

CLAUDIA. The few words that are on Shakspere's will. His will
contains three of the six known signatures [1]. I was struck by
how bad the writing was and, even more, by how variable it was.
You would think that someone who had written thousands on
thousands of lines would have developed a standard signature.
One expert (Jane Cox) has proposed that some of the signatures
may have been written by scribes [2, 3]. This poses a big problem.
If they are indeed written by the same person, why was the writing so bad and so inconsistent? And if they were not written by
the same person, does this suggest that Shakspeare could not even
write his own name, and had a clerk do it for him?

However, more basically, what strikes me is not so much what
is in the will, as what is NOT in the will. A writer must have
his equipment—notebooks, records, correspondence, and—one
would expect—some old manuscripts in polished or unpolished
forms, and some new manuscripts that are being—or were

being—worked on. What do we find? Nothing! No letter, no note, no record, no manuscript! To judge from comparisons with known writers of the same time, this is quite rare [4].

MARTIN. I like the possibility of comparison with other authors. That could be very helpful.

JAMES. Claudia—if this were a scene in one of your detective stories, what might the all-seeing detective pick up in looking over the will?

CLAUDIA. The second-best bed! That is what everyone notices and is so puzzled by. It is his only reference to his wife and it was his only bequest to her. One might say "Well, maybe he had had a bad day at the office." But this was his will—his "last will and testament." So I think that Miss Marple, or Lord Peter Wimsey, or whoever, might be wondering what could conceivably be behind it.

BEATRICE. And what do you suggest?

CLAUDIA. It sounds to me, and it looks to me, as if he had a grudge against his wife.

MARTIN. This is getting interesting. How would your detective check out that theory?

CLAUDIA. Well, she might look to see if there is anything odd or unusual about their marriage. And there certainly was [4]. In November, 1582, a marriage license was issued to "William Shaxpere" and Anne Whateley of Temple Grafton, a few miles from Stratford, I believe. But William did not get to marry this lady. The very next day, a marriage bond was posted for "William Shagspere" and Anne Hathaway of Shottery, who was then three months pregnant, courtesy of William. Anne (who may have been a widow, since someone of that name had married a "William Wilson" in 1579) was seven or eight years older than William. So William may have found someone younger and cuter to marry since the time he had tumbled in the hay with Miss Hathaway.

For a long time, it was thought that the clerk had slipped up and spelled the name incorrectly on the first occasion. But there was more to it than that. The bond was for 40 pounds (a very large sum of money—eight years salary for a normal farm worker) to arrange for a rapid marriage. The bond was to indemnify the Bishop of Worcester in the event that there proved to be something illegal about the proposed marriage, which was being arranged at unusually short notice. (No time to publish the bans, it appears.) The bond was guaranteed by two men from Stratford who accompanied William to Worcester for the transaction.

It rather looks as if young William was hoping to marry Miss Whateley, but relatives of Miss Hathaway caught wind of the fact, and made a possibly friendly but definitely firm suggestion to William that he had better marry Miss Hathaway, and quickly, which he did.

This brings me back to the will. Miss Marple suspects that leaving his wife the "second-best bed" may have been a mean-spirited reminder to Anne that she had been his second-best wife—a chill wind from beyond the grave.

BEATRICE. Well, that is a very cute and highly creative comment on the "second-bed" matter, but I fail to see that it has anything to do with the Authorship Question.

CLAUDIA. I agree completely. But "second-best bed" are three of the very few words that can be unambiguously attributed to Mr. Shakspere. All I'm saying is that the most important document we have concerning William is his will, and if the will is giving us any hint of his character, it is not a character that I particularly admire.

However, the presiding judge is giving me a signal that it is time to wrap up my remarks. So let me summarize by just saying that I have enormous difficulty in relating the little factual information we have concerning Mr. Shakspere with the wonderful literary output of William Shakespeare, whoever he may have been. What happened to William between 1582, when he may or may not have been able to write his name, and may or may not have remembered from one day to the next which spelling he preferred, and 1593 when he ostensibly published the first of his two long poems (*Venus and Adonis*) that made him instantly famous? (His second long poem—*The Rape of Lucrece*—came a year later.) Did some goddess wave a magic wand over him, to suddenly fill him with grace, knowledge, and nobility—like Athena leaping fully armed out of the head of whomever's head she leaped out of?

BEATRICE. Brava! You would do well as a Queens' Counsel at the Old Bailey!

MARTIN. I agree—That is a great opener. I guess it is your turn now, Beatrice.

BEATRICE. Well, I wish I could do a Mark Anthony, and bring you all around with the force of my rhetoric and perhaps a little guile. (We can teach a little rhetoric at our university, but we are not supposed to teach much guile.) However, luckily I think I can get by with being plain and simple.

Is it credible that somebody else wrote all of the Shakespeare canon, and then pinned the blame (or, rather, the glory) on a country bumpkin from the West Country? What on Earth would be the motive? And if he had tried to do that, is it credible that all of London (or, at least, all of the writing and acting communities in London) would go along with keeping the information top-secret? Remember, too, that everyone would have had to keep the secret not only up to 1616, when William passed away, but for almost four centuries beyond that date.

There have been thousands of scholars burning many metric tons of midnight oil figuring out just where William of Stratford was, and just what he was doing, throughout his life. Except, that is, for the time 1578 to 1592 when we do lose track of him. These are called "The Lost Years." They are the few years after he left Stratford-upon-Avon (Had he been caught deer-poaching? We shall never know.) and before we pick up his trail in London. Wherever he was during those years, he was obviously very busy—and very productive. By 1593, several of his plays had already been performed— *Titus Andronicus, Henry IV* Parts One, Two, and Three, *Richard III, A Comedy of Errors,* and *The Taming of the Shrew.* It was not the practice, in those days, to list the names of the playwrights, but they were known, in due course, to have been written by Shakespeare (or Shakspere, if you prefer).

JAMES. You have to be careful, Beatrice. It makes a big differ-ence whether you attribute those plays to "Shakspere," the young man from Stratford-upon-Avon, or to "Shakespeare" the enigmatic author, whose identity we are going to try to determine.

Plate 1. Engraving by Martin Droesholt on the title page of the First Folio, 1623. This was certainly not based on a sitting by William Shakspere of Stratford-upon-Avon, who had died in 1616 at the age of 52. What it was based on is unknown. Moreover, the picture has several peculiarities: In relation to the shoulders, the head is larger than normal by 50%, which helps give the impression that the head is floating above the body. Where one expects to see the front of the right shoulder of the doublet, we see the rear of the left shoulder. The extra line by the left side of the face helps give the impression that the face that we see is a mask.

BEATRICE. A good point. I guess I am presenting the ortho-dox, establishment position. I am reminded that, in more recent times, some women novelists have tried to hide their identities (to try to overcome male prejudice), but they could not maintain their cover very long.

However, to my mind there are two incontrovertible "documents" that establish Shakspere as the author: The introductory material of the "First Folio," published in 1623;

and the inscription on the monument to Shakespeare in Holy Trinity Church at Stratford-upon-Avon, installed we believe just a few years after his death in 1616. If the identification of Shakspere as Shakespeare was a myth, it was a myth that was written in stone.

CLAUDIA. Well done, Beatrice. That is an impressive improvisation. However, I do find it a little disconcerting that both of your "incontrovertible" items of evidence were posthumous.

JAMES. An interesting point. But we have now had our two opening statements—one from the prosecution and one from the defense. Both extemporaneous and both impressive!

Are you ready to be an expert witness, Martin?

MARTIN. No, I do not think I can be a witness. I have not yet witnessed anything! My role, I think, will simply be to help organize our thinking and discussion. Maybe we shall learn what to believe. If not, we may simply learn what not to believe.

JAMES. Either way, that would be progress, Martin. The Sun is about to set, and it is a very clear sky. Let us go out on the deck. We may be lucky enough to see a green flash this evening.

NOTES

1. Price (2001), 127.

2. Price (2001), 125.

3. Thomas & Cox (1985).

4. Roper (2008), 55–58.

A Meeting Room at the Highview Inn

First Impressions of the Scope of the Authorship Question

Martin introduces his colleagues to the Reverend Thomas Bayes.

Mid-morning. Beatrice and Martin in tracksuits.

JAMES. So, how was your tennis lesson, Beatrice?

BEATRICE. I learned a lot—including the fact that I am not a natural athlete!

MARTIN. But you did very well, Beatrice. You have good, quick reactions.

JAMES. Having engaged in verbal conflict with Beatrice, I am not surprised. But tell me, Martin, were you always a tennis player?

MARTIN. Not at all. I first chose fencing, and became quite good at it. But it was difficult to find sparring partners, so I switched to tennis. They are very different—In fencing, the essential requirement is to maintain a solid defense, for as long as it takes, until that split second when you can strike. In tennis, at my age, I have to attack early. If an exchange goes beyond six strokes, I am probably going to lose the point.

JAMES. You must study warfare, too, in your line of business. Do you see any similarity with sports?

MARTIN. Absolutely! I could draw all kinds of parallels. For instance, if you want to win a battle, you give the assignment to a genius like Patton. But if you have allies you must work with, you had better find someone like Eisenhower. In the McEnroe tennis family, John was the genius, but Patrick was the better choice as captain of a Davis-Cup team. John was the Patton, and Patrick the Eisenhower!

JAMES. I would like to hear more—but later. To turn to present business, tell me, Martin, what are your impressions so far?

MARTIN. I have done a little reading in preparation for our meeting, and I must say that Claudia and Beatrice reflect quite well the impressions I have formed from what I have read. Claudia makes it quite clear that, if we were not already convinced of the conventional view of the authorship, we would not see a very strong case for attributing the work to the gentleman from Stratford. And Beatrice reflects quite well the standard position that it is up to the challenger to make a case for repudiating the conventional view.

This brings me to my first recommendation. If we are going to look into this problem at all, we must do it without prejudice. We must approach the issue with an open mind. This means that we must treat our candidates impartially.

My second recommendation is that we should adopt some new terminology. We obviously cannot use the same name "Shakespeare" for the author and for the gentleman from Stratford. Some scholars suggest that some of the Shakespearian plays had co-authors, but no one has suggested that the sonnets had a co-poet. (*A Lover's Complaint*, which was appended to the Sonnets is another matter—Some scholars do suggest that it had different, or mixed, authorship.)

The sonnets were published with the hyphenated name "SHAKE-SPEARE." I suggest that we follow this example, but use an asterisk instead of a hyphen, like this "Shake*Speare." The asterisk should remind us that we are dealing with someone whose identity we have not yet decided.

Plate 2. Edward de Vere, 17th Earl of Oxford, Lord Great Chamberlain of England, by an unknown artist, from a lost original, 1575. [http://en.wikipedia.org/wiki/File:Edward-de-Vere-1575.jpg]

BEATRICE. But doesn't "Shake*Speare" sound quite like "Shakespeare"?

MARTIN. I sense a difference. "Shakespeare" has a strong accent on the first syllable. When I say "Shake*Speare," I find I am giving the stronger stress on the second syllable. Admittedly this

Plate 3. Edward de Vere, apparently middle-aged, by Marcus Gheeraedts, circa 1590. [http://en.wikipedia.org/wiki/File:Edward_de_Vere.JPG]

is not a perfect solution. However, we can completely avoid confusion if we use "Stratford" (or "Mr. Stratford") to denote the gentleman from Stratford. And I gather that he was officially a gentleman, since he secured a coat of arms.

CLAUDIA. Yes, indeed, with the motto "non sans droict" (not without right), which Jonson naughtily paraphrased in one of his plays as "not without mustard."

MARTIN. Interesting! In order to treat our candidates equally, I also suggest that we use "Oxford" as an abbreviation for Edward de Vere, Earl of Oxford, the person who seems to be the main other contender as the writer of Shake*Speare's canon.

BEATRICE. That seems fair enough.

MARTIN. A key concept in our deliberations is going to be that of "probability," which we need to discuss a little.

CLAUDIA. As I recall, from conversations with some statisticians, there is more than one school of thought about "probability."

MARTIN. Yes, Claudia, you are quite right. Until recently, the standard interpretation of probability theory is what is known as the "frequentist" approach, which is based on the concept of repeating an experiment many, many times, and looking to see what fraction of the time one gets a particular result. This makes for nice, clean theory, but it is really unrealistic and unnecessarily restrictive. The alternative interpretation, which is now used extensively in science, and which is the one we are going to use, is called the "Bayesian" approach. The "Bayesian" interpretation of probability is, to put it simply, "your best guess." But it is supposed to be your "best guess" based on specified information.

Let us start with the simplest idea of a probability. Suppose we are presented with a closed bag, and are told that it contains 99 white balls and 1 black ball. What can we say about the possible result of drawing a ball from the bag? If that is all the information that we have, we can summarize the information we have by saying "the probability of drawing a white ball is 0.99, and the probability of drawing the black ball is 0.01."

But now suppose we are told "the white balls and the black ball are the same size, but the black ball is cracked." Then, if are allowed to take time to feel the balls in the bag, we may be able to avoid the black ball, so that the probability of drawing the black ball would be less than 0.01. The probability has changed because we have acquired new information.

What this tells us is that the probability we assign to the result of a choice or an event depends on the *information* we have (assuming for simplicity that we are given honest information— that no one is trying to deliberately mislead us).

BEATRICE. I get the general idea. Can you flesh it out a little, without involving us with mathematics?

MARTIN. I can try. Suppose we start out with an estimate of the probability that a certain hypothesis is true. We call this the *prior probability*, since this is our estimate *prior* to acquiring some new information. Now suppose that we acquire some new information. This will change our estimate of the probability to what we call the *post probability*. By how much will it change? That will depend on how surprising that information is. If the new information is not at all surprising (it is more or less compatible with the hypothesis), it will lead to only a slight change in our opinion about the hypothesis. However, if the new information is surprising (it is not something we expected on the basis of our hypothesis), then the post probability will be much bigger than the prior probability.

Bayes' Theorem simply expresses this thought in the form of an equation:

The ratio of the post probability to the prior probability is equal to the ratio of the probability we would assign to the new information if we were told that the hypothesis is true to the probability we would assign to that information if we did not know whether the hypothesis is true or not.

Or—to put it more succinctly—

New information increases the probability of a hypothesis in the same proportion as the hypothesis makes the information more likely [1].

This theorem is named after the Reverend Thomas Bayes, who lived from 1702 to 1761 and was a Presbyterian minister in the lovely little town of Tunbridge Wells in Kent, southeast of London. He was also a mathematician and wrote a long and sophisticated article concerning probability calculations. For some reason, he did not submit his article for publication (times have changed!). But one of his friends came across the article after Bayes had passed away, and forwarded it to the Royal Society. The Society recognized the importance of the article, and published it.

The story is actually a little more complicated than that. The analysis that Bayes wrote up was much longer and more complicated than the neat, simple theorem that now carries his name. Bayes' article implicitly—but not explicitly—implies what we now call *Bayes' Theorem*. Some scholars think that the theorem should really be named after Laplace, one of the greatest scientists of all time, sometimes referred to as "the Newton of France." Laplace (whose full name was *Pierre-Simon, Marquis de Laplace*), was born in 1749 in Beaumont-en-Auge in Normandy, and died in Paris in 1827, at what was then the ripe old age of 77. He contributed to many areas of science and mathematics, and introduced the concept (now referred to as "Bayesian") that probability can refer to a "state of knowledge," rather than the numerical results of a series of experiments. A famous quote from Laplace (relevant to our project) is *Probability theory is nothing but common sense reduced to calculation.*

Since our goal is to investigate the Authorship Question as if it were a scientific problem rather a literary problem, Bayes' Theorem will be the basis for our investigation. However, we shall need to develop a procedure, based on Bayes' Theorem, that is suitable for analyzing more than one hypothesis (it turns out that three will be enough), and can cope with any number of pieces of information. We can take up this development after lunch.

JAMES. Thank you, Martin. We have to rely on you to tell us enough that we can take advantage of the procedures you have in mind, but not so much that we feel lost in a fog.

Talking of fog—You were both lucky to have had a very clear morning for your tennis workout this morning. One is not always so lucky here in Carmel.

And speaking of Carmel—It occurs to me that we could be referred to as Carmelites!

BEATRICE. Especially since we are engaged in a dialog. But let us be sure that this dialog of these Carmelites does not end in us all losing our heads!

JAMES. Let's hope so. On that cheerful note, I suggest we adjourn for lunch.

NOTE

1. The author is indebted to Jeffrey Scargle for this succinct formulation of Bayes' Theorem.

A Meeting Room at the Highview Inn

An Introduction to Scientific Inference

The Carmelites try to decide whether or not Shake*Speare was lame.

JAMES. This has all been very instructive, Martin. As you know, I have been a practitioner of science. But practicing scientists never have to worry about the nature of science. It seems pretty obvious that "science is what scientists do." Now—oddly enough—when I am stepping into a completely different field—Elizabethan literature—I find that I am faced with the question—What is Science?

Knowing of your interest, and in preparation for our meetings, I recently looked to see what books have been written on "scientific inference." The answer is "Not many!" I found one book of that title, by the great geophysicist Harold Jeffreys, published in 1931 [1]. As far as I can tell, there has been no other book by that title.

MARTIN. There is a very good little book, by I. J. Good, entitled *Probability and the Weighing of Evidence*, published in 1950 [2]. It really is about scientific inference, although Good does not use that term in his title.

JAMES. Out of interest, I looked through my university catalog. There are all kinds of courses on all fifty-seven varieties of science—but there is no course on "scientific inference." The nearest

I could find was a course on the philosophy of science in the Philosophy Department!

MARTIN. All this does not surprise me. It seems that scientists are taught how to pick fruit from the tree of science, but not how to tend the roots.

But now that you are thinking about Elizabethan literature, and the Authorship Question, I am curious to hear more of your thoughts about what contribution a scientist—or a pair of scientists—might make to this problem.

JAMES. That is a challenging question. I have to ask myself— What does a one-time practicing scientist and engineer like me have to offer in relation to a problem that is way outside his field of expertise? When I was running a business, if I was faced with a problem outside my field, I would find someone inside that field to consult.

Of course, that is exactly what I did when I first recommended that we engage your services—for one dollar a year, I believe. In general, problem-solving is a skill that scientists have to acquire, but it is not a skill that a professor of English literature has to acquire. Even without getting into the intricacies of probability theory and all that, I can see that a scientist is going to look at the Authorship Question from a very different perspective than would a scholar of Elizabethan literature.

BEATRICE. That admission is very intriguing to a scholar of English literature. Can you clarify, please?

JAMES. Well, I think that Martin is doing the clarifying for us. He is showing us how to separate a big indigestible problem into smaller morsels—edible, if not tasty. And he is showing us how to organize our thinking to make it more productive, and to make it more "consensible." I am an admirer of John Ziman, the English physicist who wrote several books about science [3]. He argued that an important distinguishing feature of science is "consensibility." Scientists try—or are supposed to try—to present a case so clearly and so securely that any other scientist has to accept his case. Not always happily, of course.

CLAUDIA. We are now talking generalities about science—and we know you have been a successful practitioner. And you very wisely brought in Martin, to explain to us how we can organize our thinking about a problem, once we have a reasonably good idea of what that problem is.

Plate 4. Henry Wriothesley, 3rd Earl of Southampton. The two great "Shakespeare" epic poems, *Venus and Adonis* (1593) and *Rape of Lucrece* (1594), were dedicated to Wriothesley. It is widely believed that Wriothesley was the "Fair Youth" of the sonnets. [http://en.wikipedia. org/wiki/File:Henry Wriothesley_1594.jpg]

Beatrice and I realize and accept the roles you think we can play. Beatrice is supposed to be the guardian of the faith (no offense intended, Beatrice), and I guess that I am the designated heretic.

So this leaves us with the question—What is your role supposed to be, James?

JAMES. A tough question. I have begun to wonder. It would upset the apple cart—or at least upset the balance of prejudice—to have another defender of the faith or another heretic. And Martin is going to help us to think logically—or at least sensibly—on each particular issue we have to address.

But this does leave us with another question, which is one I can try to help with.

BEATRICE. Namely?

JAMES. What are the issues we should focus on? Books on the Authorship Question go into extraordinary detail about quite intricate questions. What was the precise relationship between de Vere and Henry Wriothesley, the Earl of Southampton (the putative "Fair Youth" of the sonnets), for instance. Or what is the most likely scenario for the so-called "Lost Years" (from 1578 to

1592), when we lose the scent in tracking the life story of William Shakspere of Stratford-upon-Avon?

It seems to me that we shall need to choose quite carefully the topics we look into. Some writers who investigate this topic (such as Looney [4]—who preferred that his name be pronounced "Loney"—and the Ogburns [5]) go into great intricacies, comparing details in the plays with details in the lives of the candidate authors. That is all quite fascinating, but that kind of comparison would require more research, I suspect, than we have time for.

Each topic has to be manageable; it must have a reasonable and accessible resource of relevant information; and it must be closely coupled to the overarching Authorship Question. We do not want to spend time chasing topics that are quite decoupled from the prime focus of our project.

So, if you are looking for a role for me (and I sense that you are), I can try to identify topics that are manageable and relevant. Martin can help us structure the topic in such a way that we can hope to address it productively. Beatrice and Claudia can offer their comments and judgments. I can also offer to be the official scorekeeper. I anticipate that we shall be considering a number of different topics and that, for each topic, Beatrice and Claudia will generate some kind of "score," summarizing the extent to which the evidence supports—or does not support—each of our candidates. I can keep track of these scores and—if Martin will show me how—generate a "running score" that somehow combines the results of a sequence of topics.

MARTIN. That sounds good to me, James. Yes, it will be interesting to see if any trend emerges, with more and more evidence supporting one particular candidate, for instance.

But now back to tactics. We have reviewed what is known as Bayes' Theorem. The actual theorem (in Appendix A) takes only a few lines. There are some scientists who think that it is too short and too simple to deserve the impressive name

"Theorem." They suggest it should be demoted to "Bayes' Rule," or something like that. However, the consequences are important enough that I think we should continue to honor it with the title "Theorem."

However, a basic requirement in scientific inference is that one should always work with a complete set of hypotheses. So far, we have mentioned only two hypotheses—that Shake*Speare was Stratford, and that Shake*Speare was Oxford. But those two names do not make a complete set. The author could be somebody else.

BEATRICE. But I do not see how we can possibly consider every candidate. I have heard that more than sixty names have been proposed.

MARTIN. That is indeed a problem, but luckily there is a way around it. We can propose just three hypotheses: that Shake*Speare was Stratford, that Shake*Speare was Oxford, and that Shake*Speare was "Somebody Else." This gives us a complete and mutually exclusive set of hypotheses. Although we do not know who he (or maybe she) is, it is convenient to give him a name. You have met Stratford and Oxford; now meet "Ignotus"! No first name, and no title, either. We know absolutely nothing about him. However, the Bayesian formalism will allow us to express our ignorance mathematically.

CLAUDIA. But how can that possibly be useful? Is it conceivable that our research would show that Ignotus is preferable to both Stratford and Oxford—and, if it did, what could we do about it?

MARTIN. In principle (and possibly in practice—we'll see), it could indeed turn out that way. We can imagine that one set of facts effectively rules out Stratford, but not Oxford or Ignotus. And another set of facts effectively rules out Oxford, but not Stratford or Ignotus. If that were to happen, we would have learned that Shake*Speare was neither Stratford nor Oxford, leaving only Ignotus (somebody else) as our surviving candidate.

How do you think we could proceed if that were to happen?

JAMES. We would have to review our options. The options might then include "Countess X," "Sir Francis Y," et al.

MARTIN. Just so. To bring up names that have been mentioned in the past, we might promote Bacon and Marlowe as our prime suspects. But we would still need to keep our mystery man Ignotus as a third candidate.

CLAUDIA. Maybe we should call him "The Third Man"—except that we might then need a zither.

MARTIN. That is one option—but you must admit that "Ignotus" (Latin!) sounds more scholarly, although Greek would be even more impressive!
My first recommendation is this:

> **In all of our discussions, concerning any fact, purported fact, or other issue, we agree to consider our three candidates—Stratford, Oxford, and Ignotus—on exactly the same footing.**

Note that this procedure is going to avoid an all-too-familiar fallacy: that of proving A by disproving B. One does not establish Stratford as Shake*Speare by arguing that Oxford was not Shake*Speare—or vice versa. We would also need to show that Stratford (or Oxford) is preferable to Ignotus. This requires some form of explicit consideration of the "somebody else" option: The "equal opportunity" rule should apply to all of our discussions. For instance, if we think that knowledge of Latin is a relevant consideration, we shall need to look into that issue for each of our three candidates. For Ignotus, a possible response is simply to say "We have no idea" (in terms of probabilities, of course), but we can discuss this more later. In addition to considering such an issue for the three candidates, we need also to examine the issue in terms of the relevant evidence, which will comprise not only the Shakespeare corpus, but also whatever factual information we have concerning our two explicitly known candidates and the times in which they lived.

I gather that many authors make remarks about Stratford that are based on the assumption that he was the author. This is what is called "circular reasoning," which is an error that we have to avoid at all costs.

James has also told me about his reading of *Shakespeare, the World as Stage* by Bill Bryson [6]. I gather that it is full of remarks such as "appears to have," "doubtless," "according to tradition," and "it is tempting, even logical, to guess . . ." These are what I call "shoehorn arguments," in which one squeezes the facts to fit the theory. This is an absolute no-no in scientific research.

This brings me to my second recommendation:

We should adopt a "compartmentalization" or "interface" procedure.

This will help us avoid circular reasoning and the shoehorn problem. In scientific research, for instance, we may look at a question on the basis of observational (including experimental) evidence, or on the basis of theory. We analyze the relevant evidence, and we analyze the consequences of our various hypotheses. Both analyses are necessary, but it is essential not to get the two mixed up. (If any author of a scientific article were to present both new observational results and a new theory to explain those results, the community would be very skeptical of both claims.)

In our problem, the equivalent of "observation" comprises study of the relevant texts and of relevant factual information. The equivalent of "theory" comprises our inference of what we would expect of each of our three candidates. Hopefully, all this will become clearer when we take one or two simple examples.

My third recommendation is this:

To be fair to all candidates, we need to frame the discussion in as neutral a way as possible.

The way I propose to do this is to specify a question, and then to give a short list of possible answers, presenting them as equally worthy of consideration. The simplest response to any question would be *yes* or *no*, but we shall need to be more flexible than that, and provide for degrees of agreement or disagreement.

I think it would clarify matters if we were to consider a component of the overall problem. Can you help us, James? You have been doing some reading on this subject. Do you have any simple example to suggest?

JAMES. I have been reading the sonnets, and one issue caught my attention. The question is whether or not Shake*Speare was lame. There are two or three references in the sonnets to the author's lameness. I gather that an orthodox scholar, such as Helen Vendler [7], regards this merely as a figure of speech, not as representing the real physical characteristics of the author. On the other hand, those references may imply that Shake*Speare really was lame. I guess that we shall have to decide which interpretation we prefer, and how strongly we prefer it.

However, I understand that we shall need to present our answers in terms of probabilities. Can you give us some basic guidelines?

MARTIN. Here are some basic rules: If you were absolutely sure that he was lame, you would set P = 1 (where we use P for probability). If you were absolutely sure that he was not lame, then you would set P = 0. And if you had no preference either way, you would set P = 0.5. However, this is a good place to make another cautionary remark. It is very unwise to assume that you have so much, and so solid, information that you can set either P = 0 or P = 1. If one were to adopt either of these values, it follows from Bayes' Theorem that you could never change your mind, no matter how much additional information you might receive (Appendix A). That obviously is a situation we should studiously avoid.

So my fourth recommendation is the following:

We should reserve the choices P = 0 and P = 1 for statements that are logically or factually certain.

We are going to organize our thinking by using tables, so we can begin by looking into the question that James just raised, concerning the author's possible lameness.

Here, to start with, is an empty table.

You see that, apart from the header row, which we shall discuss in a minute, there are two rows that contain two statements:

S1: *Shake*Speare was lame at some time in his life,* **and**

S2: *Shake*Speare was never lame at any time of his life.*

Logically, one (and only one) of these statements must be true, so these comprise a "complete and mutually exclusive set."

	Evidence Analysis	Stratford Theory	Oxford Theory	Ignotus Theory
S1: Shake*Speare was lame at some time in his life				
S2: Shake*Speare was never lame at any time of his life				

CLAUDIA. That sounds very impressive. But is it anything more than wordplay?

MARTIN. Only if there were a simpler way of putting it. Apart from spelling out the two statements that we shall be working with, there are four columns. The first column is headed "Evidence Analysis." In this column, we have to evaluate the actual evidence for the two statements. The second, third, and fourth columns are headed "Stratford Theory," "Oxford Theory," and "Ignotus Theory." We have to evaluate these two statements first in terms of the evidence, and then in terms of each of our three theoretical hypotheses (that Shake*Speare was Stratford, or Oxford, or "somebody else"—the mysterious and unknown "Ignotus").

I have drawn a double line between the *Evidence Analysis* column and the *Theory* columns. This is to emphasize that we should clearly separate our evidence analysis from our theoretical analyses.

I should point out that, ideally, we should have one expert (and unbiased) scholar providing the evidence analysis, a different (also unbiased) expert (perhaps someone trained in decision analysis) providing the theoretical analyses. However, we do not live in an ideal world—we shall need to trust Beatrice and Claudia to be as objective as possible in these two different roles.

One way to cancel out bias would be to mix up charts prepared by Beatrice and Claudia. We could, for instance, combine Beatrice's evidence analysis with Claudia's theoretical analyses, and vice a versa. There are probably other games like this that we could play.

Tell us, Claudia, what is your assessment that the poet was lame?

CLAUDIA. Speaking first as an evidence analyst, I note that the poet refers to *lameness* in three of his sonnets.

In Sonnet 37, he writes

So I, made lame by fortune's dearest spite
. . . am not lame, poor, nor despised,
Whilst that this shadow doth such substance give . . .

In Sonnet 66, we find

And strength by limping sway disabled,

And in Sonnet 89, we find

Speak of my lameness, and I straight will halt,
Against thy reasons, making no defense.

If the poet had referred to his lameness only once, I would not necessarily have taken the words literally. But when I find three separate references to lameness in his sonnets, I am inclined to take the statements at face value. I know I am being forced to express my view numerically (which I am not accustomed to doing). It looks to me like a quite strong case for lameness, and I personally would put the odds at 50 to 1.

MARTIN. Thank you, Claudia. What do you say, Beatrice?

BEATRICE. Let me first say that I find these assignments— simple as they seem—quite difficult. As you well know, I have lived for many years with the conviction that the poet and playwright was Stratford. It is difficult to just ignore that conviction, as I am being asked to do. But I will try to overcome this difficulty in this way—I'll imagine that we are discussing the poems of some very minor Elizabethan poet—not the giant we know as "Shakespeare"—and then try to decide what I would make of these lines.

I admit that they do indeed suggest that the poet was lame, but I still have my doubts. The reference to *lameness* could quite conceivably have been a metaphor that was understood as such in Elizabethan times. So I would not set the odds any higher than 5 to 1 that the poet was actually lame.

MARTIN. Fair enough, Beatrice. Now we can move to the other side of what is intended to be an impenetrable barrier, and try to decide the odds on each of the theories that Shake*Speare was Stratford, or Oxford, or Ignotus.

Let us discuss Stratford first. Why don't you go first, this time, Beatrice?

BEATRICE. I guess we know nothing about Stratford's health— except that in his will he writes *In the name of God Amen I William*

Shackspeare of Stratford on Avon in the countrie of Warr' gent in perfect health and memorie god be praysed . . . .[8] This seems, at face value, to imply that Stratford had no health problems, in which case we may assume that he was not lame, but I do wonder whether this may have been a standard formula drafted by the clerk who was preparing the will for Stratford to sign. I notice that he prepared his will only a few weeks before he passed away, but it may also be that the opening remarks were part of an early draft of the will, in which case they would have no bearing on Stratford's state of health when he finally signed the will.

I also note that Stratford was (or is supposed to have been) an actor. An actor needs to be able to move freely and expressively. So—at least while he was an actor, before he retired to Stratford—it would seem pretty safe to assume that he was not lame. All things considered, I put the odds that Stratford was not lame at 10 to 1.

MARTIN. That all seems very reasonable, Beatrice. What do you say, Claudia?

CLAUDIA. My response is short and sweet. I think that Beatrice has argued cogently, and I see no reason to disagree with her. So I go along with 10 to 1 odds that Stratford was not lame.

MARTIN. Excellent. Now we move on to Oxford. What do you say, Claudia?

CLAUDIA. I am struck by the fact that, in his letters written during the 1590s, he several times refers to himself as "lame," as for instance in a letter to Lord Burghley dated March 25, 1595, when he wrote: *Wherefore when Your Lordship shall have [the] best time and leisure if I may know it, I will attend your Lordship as well as any lame man may at your house* [9]. On the basis of this information, it seems to me much more likely than not that Oxford was indeed lame at some stage of his life. I feel quite comfortable at setting the odds that he was lame at 20 to 1.

MARTIN. What do you think, Beatrice?

BEATRICE. I am going to return the compliment to Claudia. Since there were at least two other letters in which Oxford refers to his lameness, I have to admit that odds of 20 to 1 seem reasonably conservative. (In the interest of full disclosure, I again admit that it is very difficult for me to look at these judgments impartially, without subliminally estimating the effect it is going to have on the case for my hero! But I am trying to be an honest witness!)

MARTIN. We are moving along. This leaves us with only Ignotus—the mystery man, or perhaps the mystery woman—to think about. What are your thoughts, Claudia?

CLAUDIA. Since we are really trying to decide what to do when there is a lack of evidence, your advice to Beatrice and me would be very helpful here.

MARTIN. I'll see what I can do. If we had absolutely no information, I would have to recommend assigning even odds to this question—whether Ignotus was lame. However, it is not a complete *tabula rasa*. I would guess that, in England today, there are only 1 or 2 men in 100 who are lame. There were probably more in Elizabethan times. The figure may have been as high as 5 or 10 in 100. Based on this admittedly wild conjecture, I suggest setting the odds at 10 to 1 that our unknown and unknowable citizen, Ignotus, was not lame.

CLAUDIA. Thank you, Martin, I am happy with that recommendation.

BEATRICE. Me, too.

JAMES. I have been keeping score during this discussion, and I see that we now have enough figures to complete the charts on behalf of Beatrice and Claudia. According to my notes, Beatrice's chart looks like this:

Chart 1, Scene 5: Lameness	Evidence Analysis	Stratford Theory	Oxford Theory	Ignotus Theory
Beatrice				
S1: Shake*Speare was lame at some time in his life	5	1	20	1
S2: Shake*Speare was never lame at any time of his life	1	10	1	10

and Claudia's looks like this:

Chart 1, Scene 5: Lameness	Evidence Analysis	Stratford Theory	Oxford Theory	Ignotus Theory
Claudia				
S1: Shake*Speare was lame at some time in his life	50	1	20	1
S2: Shake*Speare was never lame at any time of his life	1	10	1	10

Looking at these charts, I am surprised at how similar they are. But we now need a procedure for converting these estimates into final "scores." How do we do that, Martin?

MARTIN. Here is where I must apologize and seek your indulgence. I like to use what I refer to as the "BASIN" procedure, since it combines "**BA**ye**S**' Theorem" with the idea of an "**IN**terface." It was developed by an obscure scientist, for application to astrophysical problems, back in 1973. It was originally published in the *Astrophysical Journal* [10], but was later republished in the *Journal of Scientific Exploration* [11]. I have prepared a theoretical description (Appendix B) and a short summary of the relevant equations (Appendix C). However, to make life easier for everyone, I have developed a website that will carry out all of the necessary computations. You simply enter what we can refer to as the "weights" in a chart. When we have just one statement and its negative (as in the present chart), the weights simply correspond to the "odds." However, we may use any scale we wish for the numbers—odds of 10 to 1 could appear in a chart as "100 and 10" or as "1.0 and 0.1." If we rescale the weights to sum to unity, the resulting numbers will be probabilities. For instance, weights of 10 and 1 would correspond to probabilities of 0.91 and 0.09. In the present chart we have just two options, but I expect that in later charts we shall have more than two.

If you will allow me, I'll show you the relevant equation:

$$P_n = \frac{W_n}{\sum\limits_{m=1}^{M} W_m}$$

This simply says that you can calculate the probabilities by dividing each weight by the sum of the weights.

Analyzing the evidence for your two different charts, I arrive at what are known technically as the "post probabilities."

For Beatrice,

Chart 1, Scene 5: Lameness	Evidence Analysis	Stratford Theory	Oxford Theory	Ignotus Theory
Beatrice				
S1: Shake*Speare was lame at some time in his life	5	1	20	1
S2: Shake*Speare was never lame at any time of his life	1	10	1	10
Post Probabilities		0.15	0.70	0.15

and for Claudia,

Chart 1, Scene 5: Lameness	Evidence Analysis	Stratford Theory	Oxford Theory	Ignotus Theory
Claudia				
S1: Shake*Speare was lame at some time in his life	50	1	20	1
S2: Shake*Speare was never lame at any time of his life	1	10	1	10
Post Probabilities		0.09	0.82	0.09

So the results of Beatrice's and Claudia's cogitations can be summarized in a few probabilities.

For Beatrice,

P(Stratford) = 0.15

P(Oxford) = 0.70

P(Ignotus) = 0.15

and for Claudia,

P(Stratford) = 0.09

P(Oxford) = 0.82

P(Ignotus) = 0.09

I see that both Beatrice and Claudia give the edge to Oxford, which is not all that surprising, since there is evidence that he was lame at some stage of his life. So even these rudimentary considerations give us a modest pointer in a direction that may make some of us happy and some of us unhappy.

JAMES. I am struck—and rather surprised—by the fact that, although Beatrice and Claudia differed very significantly in their assessment based on the evidence, that did not lead to a big difference in the final results. Although they differ by a factor of 10 in their entries in the "Evidence Analysis" columns, they differ by less than a factor of 2 in their final probabilities for Stratford.

In a way, this is reassuring: It suggests that we may be able to reach a consensus, even if we differ substantially in some of our detailed judgments.

MARTIN. I agree, James. I too find the result somewhat surprising, but also somewhat reassuring.

Of course, the lameness topic was intended simply as a warmup exercise. It does not give anything like a conclusive result, but then it is only one fairly minor issue.

I do have one more suggestion to make. We have already referred to the term "odds." This is related to the concept of probability by

$$Odds = \frac{P}{1 - P}$$

This will obviously be a large number if P is close to unity, and a small number if P is close to zero. As long as we are dealing with probabilities like 0.8 or 0.2, the numbers are simple to write and simple to comprehend. However, we may at a later date be dealing with a very high probability such as 0.9999, or a very small probability such as 0.0001, which corresponds to odds of 10,000 and 0.0001. When we get to such numbers, it is convenient to use a different notation. It is then more convenient to replace probability by the *logarithm* of the odds—which we refer to as *logodds*, which we can denote by *LO* for short. This is defined by

$$LO = \log\left(\frac{P}{1 - P}\right)$$

Even odds leads to *logodds* = 0; P = 0.1 leads to *logodds* = –1, approximately; and P = 0.9 leads to *logodds* = +1, approximately.

The concept of *logodds* becomes most useful when one is dealing with probabilities that are either very small or close to unity. For instance,

P	Odds	Logodds
0.001	0.001	−3
0.01	0.01	−2
0.09	0.1	−1
0.5	1	0
0.91	10	1
0.99	100	2
0.999	1000	3

As you see, a change in *logodds* by one unit corresponds to a change in odds by a factor of 10.

JAMES. Before I became a vintner, I was an engineer. Electrical engineers use a notation that is even more convenient than *logodds*. It is called *decibel*. We still calculate the odds, but we measure the odds in *decibels*, defined this way:

$$Odds \text{ (db)} = 10 \times \log\left(\frac{P}{1-P}\right)$$

An increase in confidence by 10 db corresponds to an increase in odds by a factor of 10. A decrease in confidence by 10 db corresponds to a decrease in odds by a factor of 10.

A big advantage of this procedure is that we normally need not bother with a subdivision of this measure. Going from *logodds* = 3 to *logodds* = 4 is a big jump (a factor of 10), so we would tend to give *logodds* values to at least one decimal place. However, going from 3 db to 4 db is a factor of only 1.3. The odds values that we shall be calculating are not precise enough to warrant quoting odds to better than 1 db.

BEATRICE. May I make another suggestion? I like where we are headed, but I am not happy with the terminology *logodds*. We need something simpler and more appropriate to our project. I suggest we use *Degree of Belief*. We can, if you wish, still use *db* as the unit in which the *Degree of Belief* is measured.

MARTIN. I like that suggestion. Edwin Jaynes, whom I admire greatly, also advocated the use of *logodds* measured in *db* [12]. Using our new terminology, this is a conversion from probability, to odds, to "degree of belief":

P	Odds	Degree of Belief (db)
0.0001	0.0001	−40
0.001	0.001	−30
0.01	0.01	−20
0.1	0.1	−10
0.5	1	0
0.9	10	10
0.99	100	20
0.999	1000	30
0.9999	10,000	40

This is the reverse conversion from *DB* to *odds*, for small values of *DB*:

Degree of Belief (db)	Odds
0	1.0
1	1.3
2	1.6
3	2.0
4	2.5
5	3.2
6	4.0
7	5.0
8	6.3
9	7.9
10	10.0

With these two tables, we can easily interpret any Degree of Belief. Take DB = 23 db, for example. We know that DB = 20 db corresponds to odds of 100, and we know that DB = 3 db corresponds to a factor of 2. It follows that DB = 23 db corresponds to a factor of 200.

These terms *probability, odds, logodds,* and *degrees of belief* are all different ways of expressing our confidence in a statement or hypothesis. To get used to this concept, we can convert our current probability estimates to *degrees of belief.*

We can say that Beatrice's *degrees of belief* for our three candidates are

DB(Stratford) = –8 db

DB(Oxford) = 4 db

DB(Ignotus) = –8 db

and Claudia's degrees of belief are

DB(Stratford) = –10 db

DB(Oxford) = 7 db

DB(Ignotus) = –10 db

Obviously, positive numbers are favorable for your candidate and negative numbers are unfavorable. Claudia draws a somewhat sharper distinction between the three candidates than does Beatrice.

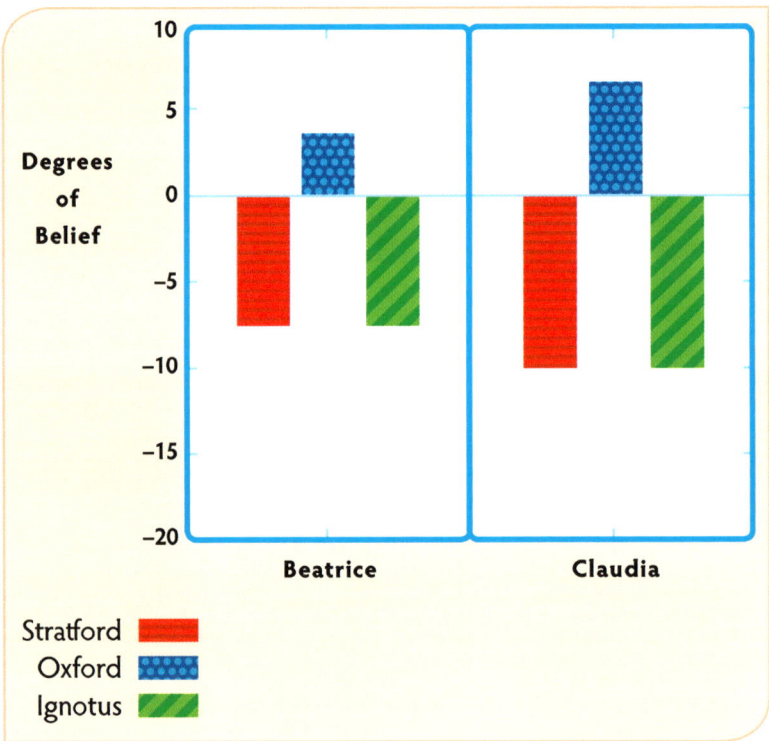

Figure 1. Degrees of Belief for Beatrice and Claudia based on Chart 1.

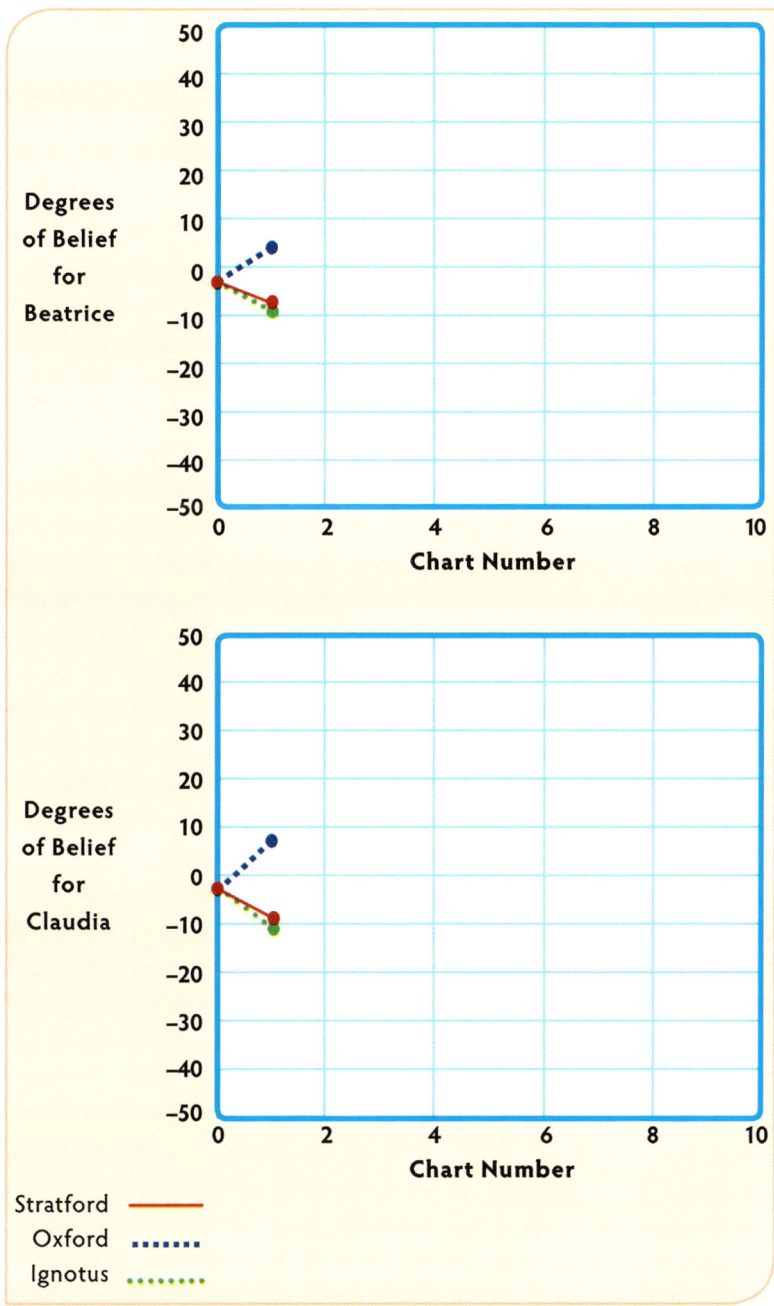

Stratford ———
Oxford ·······
Ignotus ·······

Figure 2. Running Degrees of Belief for Beatrice and Claudia based on Chart 1.

Another big advantage of using *degrees of belief* is that it makes it easier to show the results of an item of evidence in visual form, as in Figure 1, which shows the *DB* values for this one item, as estimated by Beatrice and Claudia. Pictures are always easier to comprehend than numbers! We see that there is not much difference in their evaluations.

It will also prove convenient for showing how the case for each of our candidates is developing. Figure 2 shows the initial entries for a sequence of figures that will show the cumulative effects of subsequent evaluations. (The initial value for each, corresponding to a probability of ⅓ for each hypothesis, is –5 db.) There is not much to see in Figure 2, but it will be very interesting to see how these plots develop as our study proceeds.

This may be a good place to break for the day.

JAMES. But—before we break—Claudia and I have a proposal.

We seem to be on a roll. It seems that we are all enjoying this project, and I sense that we are really making progress. Claudia and I suggest that we continue our meetings up at our vineyard. We call it, humorously, our "Hacienda."

Beatrice—You are just starting your summer break from Marin State—Why not spend part of it at our place? We have plenty of room. You can spend your mornings either preparing next year's lectures, or helping out in our vineyard, as the spirit moves you.

BEATRICE. That is very generous of you both. I am happy to accept. It will do me good to get away from my teaching duties for a while. And I always like to be in touch with the soil.

JAMES. Martin, I know that you have a short break this summer. If you would be willing to join us in the Valley, you could work with your hands (in our vineyard) in the morning, and help us work with our minds (on Shake*Speare) in the afternoon. You can also escape the morning fog you seem to get in Monterey and Carmel in summer. As a final inducement, there are some great tennis courts for you and your sparring partners, just two miles up the road.

MARTIN. This sounds like a great plan to me, too. Thank you both, James and Claudia.

NOTES

1. Jeffreys (1931).
2. Good (1950).
3. Ziman (1968, 1978, 2000).
4. Looney (1920).
5. Ogburn & Ogburn (1958).
6. Bryson (2007).
7. Vendler (1997).
8. Sobran (1997), 227.
9. Sobran (1997), 137.
10. Sturrock (1973).
11. Sturrock (1994).
12. Jaynes (2003), 91.

Reader's Chart

The reader is now invited to enter his or her figures in the following blank chart:

Chart 1, Scene 5: Lameness	Evidence Analysis	Stratford Theory	Oxford Theory	Ignotus Theory
Reader: Date:				
S1: Shake*Speare was lame at some time in his life				
S2: Shake*Speare was never lame at any time of his life				
Probabilities				

Please enter your weights for S1 and S2 in each of the four columns. Our friendly website will calculate the resulting probabilities for you.

The Deck at the *Hacienda*

Some Useful Procedures

A BASIN can have many uses.

JAMES. Well, Martin, it seems to me that we are having a lot of pre-trial hearings—which are fascinating and instructive. Are we ready to move onto the trial itself, do you think?

MARTIN. I think we are getting there—but there are one or two more procedures I think we should discuss before we try to decide the identity of Shake*Speare.

So far we have learned how to analyze an item that involves just two alternative statements, such as "Shake*Speare was lame," or "No, Shake*Speare was not lame." However, we shall need to be a little more flexible; we may need to give three or more options for each question.

Suppose, as an example, that we consider the following question:

*Did Shake*Speare know any Latin?*

We now draw up a list of possible answers, not limiting ourselves to just "yes" or "no." For instance, we might adopt as possible answers:

S1: Shake*Speare knew no Latin.

S2: Shake*Speare had the equivalent of one or two years of Latin.

S3: Shake*Speare had the equivalent of several years of Latin.

S4: Shake*Speare was fluent in Latin.

In principle, we would need to assign a probability to each of these possible answers: once on the basis of the data (the plays, etc.), and once for each of our three candidates. However, we have already decided that it is easier to assign "weights," rather than probabilities. We adopted that procedure in considering just two options (S1 and S2), but it can be applied to any number of statements.

If you feel quite confident that Shake*Speare had learned either the equivalent of one or two years of Latin, or the equivalent of a few years of Latin, but consider it quite unlikely either that Shake*Speare knew no Latin or that he was fluent in Latin, you might set the weights as follows:

S1 Shake*Speare knew no Latin: W = 1.

S2. Shake*Speare had the equivalent of one or two years of Latin: W = 10.

S3. Shake*Speare had the equivalent of a few years of Latin: W = 10.

S4. Shake*Speare was fluent in Latin: W = 1.

If you feel *very* sure of your self, you might be using W = 100 in place of W = 10.

Remember that it is a simple matter to turn weights into probabilities: One simply divides each weight by the sum of the weights. However, it is not necessary for us to do that, because our website will do it for us.

BEATRICE. It was difficult enough to reach agreement when we had only two options for a question. Now we may have three or four or more options! Isn't it going to be very difficult to reach agreement?

MARTIN. It probably would be difficult to reach agreement on any question. But that is not essential. In fact, it is not even our goal. If we agree to subdivide the Authorship Question into a manageable number of specific questions, and if we agree to give our answers in the form of probabilities, and if we agree to separate our evaluations of the available information from evaluations of just three hypotheses—then I think we have made great progress, right there.

CLAUDIA. I am concerned about a basic aspect of our project. We are dealing with probabilities, which is a lot more flexible than being required to give a yes/no answer to any question. But still, a probability—or a weight—is a number. I feel that giving numbers to my assessments is setting them in stone. I am uncomfortable about appearing to be definite about a question when I am really very indefinite about it.

MARTIN. There is another option. Since we are trying to draw on procedures of science to help us sort through a complex problem, we could draw on another standard scientific technique. We could—if we really want to—employ what are known as "error bars," which gives an air of respectability to one's uncertainty.

Any experimenter or observer is always expected to put "error bars" on his measurements. Rather than say that he has measured the diameter of a star to be exactly so many millions of cubits (or furlongs, or whatever his favorite measurement unit is), he is expected to say something like "100 plus or minus 10 millions of kilometers." That would mean that there is a good chance that the actual figure is between 90 and 110; a fair chance that it is between 80 and 90 or 110 and 120; not too unlikely that it is between 70 and 80 or 120 and 130, and so on.

We could, if we wish, do the same. Rather than give a definite value to a "weight," we could give a range of values.

CLAUDIA. Do we have to start thinking about "probabilities of probabilities"? If so, I may have to throw in the towel!

MARTIN. I really do not think that will be necessary. If we were dealing with only one question, and only one assessment, I might well be recommending that we work with error bars. But for any question, we are going to have only a few proposed answers. Each item involves several questions. And the entire project is going to involve a good many items. So even if one of you were really undecided about a question, and even if one considered a wide range of answers, it probably would not matter in the long run.

Even in the "lameness" exercise, we saw that a change of 10 to 1 in the answer to one question had only a slight influence on the final result. The Reverend Bayes is a very forgiving minister.

JAMES. I am relieved to hear that no one of us is going to determine the final answer to the big question. Now are there any other basic issues we should discuss?

MARTIN. Yes, there are two. One concerns " bias," and the other concerns "priors." To take the first point first: Suppose we introduce some bias in our calculations (to strengthen the case for Oxford, or to try to save Stratford from oblivion, or vice versa of course), it may not have much effect on a single item. However, if our bias runs through 5 or 10 or more calculations, even a small amount of bias could have a big effect on the final answer.

Not only is it important to avoid bias in analyzing each item— it is equally important to avoid bias in selecting and framing our items. Here is where we are going to rely on James to be an honest broker. To put it another way—We have to watch out for what is called "cherry-picking" of the evidence. We shall be relying on James to identify issues that hopefully everyone agrees to be significant, and we must then try to frame the relevant questions in as unbiased a way as possible. These are some of the challenges ahead of us.

JAMES. I think we now understand your concern about "bias," and obviously I shall need to very careful about identifying items for us to work on. Now what about your other concern—to do with "priors," I believe.

MARTIN. Yes, we do need to discuss this before we get to work.

You may remember that, when we first met Bayes' Theorem, I referred to $P(H)$ (the probability before one considers a new fact N) as the "prior probability." This is the probability you assign to a hypothesis before you consider any new evidence. If we were to have just one stage in our deliberations, with the goal of identifying Shake*Speare in one fell swoop (or perhaps one friendly swoop), each of us could start off with a probability that represents our previous study—or perhaps our indoctrination. One of us might start off leaning to the view that Stratford was Shake*Speare. Then he or she might start off with three prior probabilities that we can conveniently express in term of "weights" (and with convenient abbreviations for Stratford, Oxford, and Ignotus), such as

$$W(ST) = 10; \; W(OX) = 1; \; W(IG) = 1,$$

which converts to probabilities

$$P(ST) = 0.84; \; P(OX) = 0.08; \; P(IG) = 0.08.$$

For a single process, such as one application of Bayes' Theorem, this would be the standard procedure. However, our plan is to divide up one big journey into a number of smaller steps. What would happen if we were to apply this procedure to, say ten separate steps? This brings us to a question we shall face before long: How do we combine our assessments of two or more topics? The answer is quite simple.

Suppose that item A gives us the following probabilities for ST, OX, and IG:

$$P(ST,A), P(OX,A), \text{ and } P(IG,A).$$

And suppose that item B gives us these probabilities for ST, OX, and IG:

$$P(ST,B), P(OX,B), \text{ and } P(IG,B).$$

We first combine them by multiplying them in pairs:

$$P(ST,A) \times P(ST,B), P(OX,A) \times P(OX,B),$$
$$\text{and } P(IG,A) \times P(IG,B).$$

However, the probabilities must add up to one, so we find the sum

$$SUM = P(ST,A) \times P(ST,B)$$
$$+ P(OX,A) \times P(OX,B) + P(IG,A) \times P(IG,B),$$

and then divide each of the products by this sum.

Now suppose that we were to use the above prior probabilities ten times over. The end result would be the same as applying the following prior probability in one big step:

$$W(ST) = 10^{10}, W(OX) = 1, W(IG) = 1,$$

which converts to probabilities

$$P(ST) = 1 - 2 \times 10^{-10}, P(OX) = 10^{-10}, P(IG) = 10^{-10}.$$

Obviously, that would be completely unreasonable, so we cannot use the same prior probability over and over again.

Incidentally, this is where *degrees of belief* prove useful. The corresponding values are

$$DB(ST) = 97 \text{ db}; \ DB(OX) = -100 \text{ db}; \ DB(IG) = -100 \text{ db}.$$

JAMES. Very interesting! If I am not mistaken, you are describing in mathematical terms an error that is made (in non-mathematical terms) in much of the Authorship debate. A pro-Stratford writer might mention one problem, and then point out that the evidence posed by that one problem is nowhere near strong enough to topple Stratford from his position on top of the sand pile. He or she may then go on to consider the next problem, and make exactly the same argument, and so on. It is as if the writer were using his or her prior probability over and over again!

BEATRICE. This reminds me of David Hume's argument against miracles [1]. For any one piece of evidence, it is more likely that the evidence is fraudulent than that a miracle actually happened, from which Hume concluded that there can be no credible evidence in favor of miracles.

JAMES. If this were a valid argument, we could close up almost every optical observatory. Nowadays, a telescope feeds light into a detector (typically a CCD array—we have them in our electronic cameras). A CCD has many "pixels," and each pixel actually counts photons. For an astronomical telescope, any one photon could be due to the night-sky brightness, or the Milky Way, or something other than the star we are trying to observe. In fact, astronomers often study very faint stars, which are even fainter than the night sky. If we were to follow David Hume's train of thought, we would look at each photon in turn, decide that it is possibly or probably due to the night sky, and throw it away. That obviously is not a very smart thing to do in astronomy—and it would not be a very smart thing to do in analyzing the Authorship Question, either.

On the other hand, we all begin this journey with baggage. How do we cope with the fact that your baggage (which is heavy and a gross impediment) is not the same as my baggage (which is light and unrestrictive, of course). What do you suggest, Martin?

MARTIN. In principle, we could ask Beatrice and Claudia—and any other person who looks into this matter—to consider their initial beliefs about the Authorship Question, and then represent their initial beliefs in terms of probabilities. But that would greatly complicate our scorekeeping and I think it would prove counterproductive. I would like to see us agree to open-mindedly and cooperatively focus on the evidence and follow wherever it may lead. Let us do our best to ignore whatever views we had before we began working together. Let us be perfect jurors who promise to consider only the evidence set before us in this our court.

If we can agree on this, we shall all have precisely the same prior probabilities for this project, namely, a probability of one third for each of our three candidates.

BEATRICE. A challenging goal—but a noble one.

CLAUDIA. An easy goal for me—my initial state of mind was one of confusion.

JAMES. Thank you, Martin—we now seem to have disposed of these preparatory items. However, it has taken a while, so I suggest we take a short break.

NOTE

1. Hume (1777), Section 10.

The Deck at the *Hacienda*

An Unwelcome Complication

May there have been a conspiracy?

JAMES. Now we are re-assembled, we can return to our project. But I am curious to get your feedback, Beatrice and Claudia— Are we making any progress, do you think?

CLAUDIA. Absolutely! Just learning that it is possible to organize the problem in such a way as to avoid circular reasoning is a big step forward.

BEATRICE. I am also impressed by the prospect that we can carve up a huge problem into smaller parts, each of which is hopefully manageable, and then integrate our analyses of those parts to—hey presto!—finally learn whether the Shakespeare scholars have been right all along (as I think they have been), or wrong all along (as Claudia suspects). It would not take much of a case—none at all, in fact—to persuade my colleagues at Marin State that they have been right all along. But it is going to take a pretty impressive case—maybe an impossibly impressive case—to persuade them that they have been wrong all along. I can just see the headline in the college newspaper: "Marin State professor declares that English departments have been misleading their students for four hundred years!" [Not that we have actually had

English departments for that long.] If we end up with 95 items, do you think I should nail them on the Department Chairman's door?

CLAUDIA. Don't get too concerned too early, Beatrice. If you are lucky, we shall end up supporting the Warwickshire yeoman, so that you can toe the party line with a clear conscience. And even if you are unlucky, you may eventually be canonized like Joan of Arc.

BEATRICE. After being burned at the stake?

CLAUDIA. Anyway, I think that all of these concerns are highly premature. There is one more issue, which I find quite troubling, that I would like to talk over.

JAMES. And that is?

CLAUDIA. The conspiracy issue. You cannot read much about the Authorship Question before you realize that we are not facing a simple "Who was the best student in the class?" kind of issue. If we are to consider de Vere at all, we have to face up to the complication that the suppression of his claim to authorship must have involved some kind of conspiracy. None of the other writers, who must have known what was going on, gave any hint (at least, no hint that has come down to us over the ages) that "Shakespeare" or "Shake-Speare," or whatever, was simply the pen-name of the Earl of Oxford, and that William Shakspere of Stratford-upon-Avon was willing to go along with the deception (presumably for a small regular emolument). Nor do any of Oxford's fellow noblemen give the game away.

It strikes me as significant that the First Folio—which is thought to provide the strongest evidence that Shake*Speare was the gentleman from Warwickshire—was dedicated to two noblemen: Philip Herbert, Earl of Montgomery, and William Herbert, Earl of Pembroke, and that Philip was married to Oxford's daughter, Susan. The First Folio (36 plays and several poems, which took over a year to set up for printing) was an expensive undertaking for the syndicate (W. Jaggard, Ed. Blount, I. Smithweeke, and W. Aspley). I understand that some scholars suggest that it may have been bankrolled (presumably clandestinely) by the Herbert brothers [1].

JAMES. I have to blow a whistle and throw in a red card at this point. Our goal is to plan and carry out an even-handed evaluation of the relevant evidence, and here we are already arguing about whether or not there was a conspiracy!

BEATRICE. I agree with James. I think you have really jumped the gun, Claudia.

MARTIN. I agree that Claudia should not now be making the case for a conspiracy, and suggesting who the conspirators may have been. On the other hand, it would be inappropriate to base our investigations on either hypothesis: that there was a conspiracy, or that there was no conspiracy. Claudia thinks that a conspiracy was likely or at least possible, and it seems that both Beatrice and James are inclined to think that a conspiracy was unlikely.

BEATRICE. I see that you are trying to be open-minded and all-seeing, etc., but in my view we should not be giving too much credence to the conspiracy idea. I see headlines on tabloids at the supermarket checkout desk that suggest all kinds of conspiracies. On the other hand, the mainstream newspapers (that publish all the news that is fit to print—or so they would lead us to believe) tend to refer to "European Conspiracy-Mongering." I am basically a simple American country girl (or at least, I was until I came to the San Francisco Bay Area), so it is my inclination to assume there is no conspiracy unless and until I see strong evidence to the contrary. So, for me, your suggestion that we should be open-minded about the conspiracy possibility goes against the grain.

MARTIN. I hear you, Beatrice. But, before we go any further, we have to think about our terminology. I pointed out early on that we should always try to adopt language that is—as far as possible—neutral. The term "conspiracy" is hardly neutral. It reminds us of the Brutus–Cassius plot to assassinate Caesar! It connotes activities that are at best shady, and at worst wicked. Surely there may have been comparatively innocent reasons why the name of the author was hidden. Indeed, it may not have been actually hidden: The identity of Shake*Speare may have been an open secret.

As an analogy, suppose that a young assistant professor in a physics department marries a lady who has—or thinks she has—psychic abilities, and suppose the young man therefore takes an interest in parapsychology. From what I have seen, it is my guess that all of his colleagues would tactfully refrain from mentioning his unusual interests. Rightly or wrongly, they would consider that they are doing the young man a favor in keeping it a secret—albeit an open secret. I doubt if anyone would refer to this agreement as a "conspiracy."

JAMES. A good point, Martin. I agree that the term *conspiracy* is prejudicial, and that we should find some way to avoid it. So the question is, what term should we use in its place?

Does the Professor of English Literature have a suggestion?

BEATRICE. "Agreement" sounds too vague. "Complot" is possible, but sounds a little archaic. I suggest we use "Compact." That connotes something between a loose agreement and a firm commitment. As far as I know, this word has no moral implications for good or for evil.

CLAUDIA. That is fine with me. For "conspiracy," we now read "compact."

MARTIN. That seems a good solution. It is necessary that we try not to be biased either way, and this terminology will help us to achieve that. If we end up convinced that Stratford was

Shake*Speare, then the compact question becomes moot. (Except that we might then have to consider a quite different compact problem—Why was Stratford not honored and celebrated as the great playwright and poet during his lifetime, or on the occasion of his death? Was there a compact to suppress the true role of Stratford in producing the works we attribute to "Shake*Speare"?)

In principle, we should revise our list of hypotheses, and consider separately the possibility that Oxford was Shake*Speare and there was no conspiracy—I mean *compact*—and the possibility that Oxford was Shake*Speare and there was a compact. However, this would make all of our charts and all of our discussions much more complicated. May I suggest a compromise?

BEATRICE. What is that?

MARTIN. My guess is that we are not concerned about the necessity of the compact option in our discussion of Stratford, but it will be necessary to introduce that assumption for Oxford and Ignotus.

BEATRICE. Yes, I agree with that.

CLAUDIA. I agree, too.

MARTIN. Since Ignotus is a mystery man—or woman—it seems to me that it would take a compact (good or bad) to hide his or her identity. Putting these thoughts together, I suggest that we could probably agree to limit our attention to the following three hypotheses:

Stratford—No-Compact (Shake*Speare was Stratford, and there was no compact);

Oxford—Compact (Shake*Speare was Oxford, and there was a compact); and

Ignotus—Compact (Shake*Speare was Ignotus, and there was a compact).

To keep these thoughts in mind, I suggest that we use these terms explicitly in the headings of charts (and implicitly in other references to our three candidates).

Of course, if we were to find that none of the above hypotheses seems to be compatible with the facts, we would have to inspect the other three hypotheses (which would be Stratford—Compact, Oxford—No-Compact, and Ignotus—No-Compact). However, I very much doubt that is going to be necessary.

JAMES. It seems that, with your ingenuity, Martin, and with your flexibility, Beatrice and Claudia, we have sailed safely between Scylla and Charybdis! I think we have earned a little refreshment.

MARTIN. Not so fast. This is an important step we are taking, and every constituent is entitled to his or her vote. From a theoretical point of view, it may be necessary to consider the compact possibility in discussing the Oxford theory and the Ignotus theory. However, we still need to bear in mind that it is more difficult to maintain a conspiracy (or whatever we are calling it) than not to have a conspiracy to start with. So the compact issue will have an impact on our assessments of our three hypotheses. I suggest that Beatrice and Claudia express their opinions in this chart.

Chart 2, Scene 7: Compact	Empirical Opinion	Stratford No-Compact Theory	Oxford Compact Theory	Ignotus Compact Theory
S1: There was a compact		0	1	1
S2: There was no compact		1	0	0
Post Probabilities				

JAMES. You have a good point, Martin. What are your opinions on this question, Claudia?

CLAUDIA. We tend to think, nowadays, that compacts and such like are difficult to organize and maintain. (But of course, that may simply indicate how naïve we are.) Be that as it may, the monarchy and nobility had such control over the population in Elizabethan times that compacts may have been routine. Anyone giving away a state secret, or information that was embarrassing for the nobility, would have had a short career. So, ignoring the hypotheses, and thinking only of what was possible and not possible in those times, I would guess that the odds would have been no better than 10 to 1 that there was no compact.

Chart 2, Scene 7: Compact	Empirical Opinion	Stratford No-Compact Theory	Oxford Compact Theory	Ignotus Compact Theory
Claudia				
S1: There was a compact	1	0	1	1
S2: There was no compact	10	1	0	0
Post Probabilities		0.90	0.05	0.05

JAMES. I guess it is not surprising that this consideration favors Stratford, since that is the only option compatible with the absence of a compact.

What are your thoughts, Beatrice?

BEATRICE. I am not so easily persuaded that a compact or conspiracy would have been feasible. I would lay odds of 100 to 1 that there were no such shenanigans. Here are my entries:

Chart 2, Scene 7: Compact	Empirical Opinion	Stratford No-Compact Theory	Oxford Compact Theory	Ignotus Compact Theory
Beatrice				
S1: There was a compact	1	0	1	1
S2: There was no compact	100	1	0	0
Post Probabilities		0.99	0.005	0.005

JAMES. The probabilities in Beatrice's and Claudia's charts convert to these Degrees of Belief:

Degrees of Belief, based on Chart 2, for Beatrice:

DB(Stratford) = 20 db

DB(Oxford) = –23 db

DB(Ignotus) = –23 db

Degrees of Belief, based on Chart 2, for Claudia:

DB(Stratford) = 10 db

DB(Oxford) = –13 db

DB(Ignotus) = –13 db

These are shown in Figure 3.

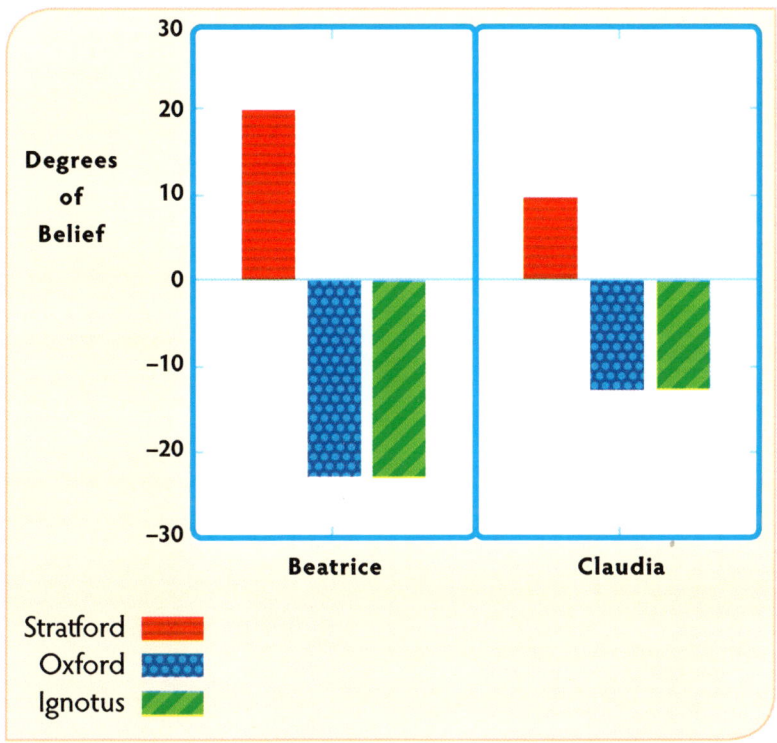

Figure 3. Degrees of Belief for Beatrice and Claudia, based on Chart 2.

I now need to combine these new estimates with the results of our previous chart concerning lameness. What we might call our *Running Probabilities* are:

Running Probabilities, based on Charts 1 and 2, for Beatrice:

RP(Stratford) = 0.97

RP(Oxford) = 0.02

RP(Ignotus) = 0.005

and for Claudia,

$$RP(\text{Stratford}) = 0.64$$

$$RP(\text{Oxford}) = 0.32$$

$$RP(\text{Ignotus}) = 0.04$$

Expressed in terms of Degrees of Belief, these become:

Running Degrees of Belief, based on Charts 1 and 2, for Beatrice:

$$RDB(\text{Stratford}) = 15 \text{ db}$$

$$RDB(\text{Oxford}) = -16 \text{ db}$$

$$RDB(\text{Ignotus}) = -23 \text{ db}$$

and for Claudia:

$$RDB(\text{Stratford}) = 3 \text{ db}$$

$$RDB(\text{Oxford}) = -3 \text{ db}$$

$$RDB(\text{Ignotus}) = -14 \text{ db}$$

The trends of the Running Degrees of Belief are shown in Figure 4.

Refreshments are waiting, but there is one more thing: I understand that Martin is in the finals of the Monterey County Tennis Tournament tomorrow. We all wish you good luck—and sympathetic linesmen, who will never be so unkind as to call you for a foot fault!

MARTIN. Thank you. I am going to need all the support that I can get.

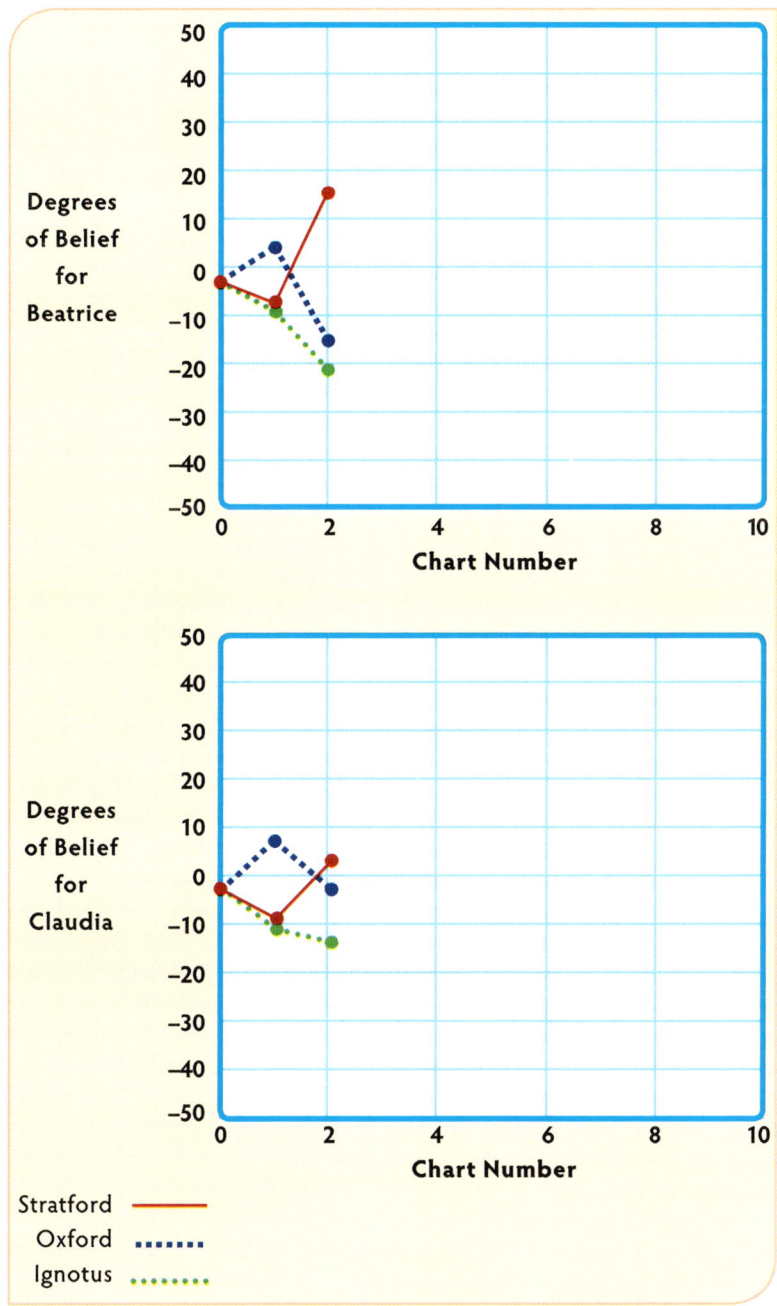

Figure 4. Running Degrees of Belief for Beatrice and Claudia, based on Charts 1 and 2.

NOTE

1. Chiljan (2011), p. 155 et seq.

Reader's Chart

The reader is now invited to enter his or her figures in the following blank chart:

Chart 2, Scene 7: Compact	Empirical Opinion	Stratford No-Compact Theory	Oxford Compact Theory	Ignotus Compact Theory
Reader: Date:				
S1: There was a compact		0	1	1
S2: There was no compact		1	0	0
Post Probabilities				

Please enter your weights for S1 and S2 in the first column. Our friendly website will calculate the resulting probabilities for you.

The Deck at the *Hacienda*

Comparing *Stratford* with Known Writers of His Time

A paper chase.

JAMES. Well, Martin, we all wish to congratulate you on your success on Saturday. We hear that you fought off a tough challenge from one of your up-and-coming colleagues in the County.

MARTIN. Thank you. It sounds as if I am now "down and going!" Maybe I am, but I shall hold off as long as I can.

JAMES. I have been thinking over my assignment to identify topics for us to investigate. I understand that most of our work will involve personal judgments, and that we must expect that we will not all agree in those judgments.

However, Claudia has drawn my attention to a book that impressed her: *Shakespeare's Unorthodox Biography* by Diana Price [1]. I have looked into that book. What caught my eye is what Price calls a "Chart of Literary Paper Trails," in which she compares what we know about Stratford with what we know about 24 known writers (other than Shake*Speare) who lived at the same time as Stratford. It occurred to me that this chart may be susceptible to statistical analysis. I have discussed it with Martin, and he has kindly agreed to look into it. I have brought along copies of this "Chart."

The comparison authors are Ben Jonson (of course), Thomas Nashe, Philip Massinger, Gabriel Harvey, Edmund Spenser, Samuel Daniel, George Peele, Michael Drayton, George Chapman, William Drummond, Anthony Mundy, John Marston, Thomas Middleton, John Lyly, Thomas Heywood, Thomas Lodge, Robert Greene, Thomas Dekker, Thomas Watson, Christopher Marlowe, Francis Beaumont, John Fletcher, Thomas Kyd, and John Webster. [I am not quite sure what determined their order. It is certainly not alphabetical.]

MARTIN. For each writer, Price searched for *literary* and *personal* records (Price's italics) that were left by the writers in their lifetimes, selecting those that were personal, contemporaneous, unambiguous, and relating to literary activity or interest. The process of collapsing all possible categories into something manageable led to the following 10 categories:

1. Evidence of education.

2. Record of correspondence, especially concerning literary matters.

3. Evidence of having been paid to write.

4. Evidence of a direct relationship with a patron.

5. Extant original manuscript.

6. Handwritten inscriptions, receipts, letters, etc., touching on literary matters.

7. Commendatory verses, epistles, or epigrams contributed or received.

8. Miscellaneous records (e.g., referred to personally as a writer).

9. Evidence of books owned, written in, borrowed, or given.

10. Notice of death as a writer.

[Category 10 includes evidence dating up to twelve months following death, to allow for eulogies or reports of death.]

Let us look at the first item in this list: *Evidence of Education.* Price finds that we have evidence of education for 17 of the 24 comparison writers. However, we have no evidence of education for Mr. Stratford. What are we to make of this?

It turns out that there is a well-known rule in statistics that is called the "rule of succession" [2]. It was first formulated by Laplace, whom we met a few meetings ago. The "rule of succession" may be stated very simply: If we examine a well-defined question (that admits of only a *Yes* or *No* answer) N times, and we get a "yes" answer n times, the probability that we shall get a "yes" answer the next (N + 1'th) time is

$$P = \frac{n + 1}{N + 2}$$

It is a reasonable formula. For instance, if n = 0,

$$P = \frac{1}{N + 2} \quad ,$$

making it rather unlikely, but not impossible. Or if n = N,

$$P = \frac{N + 1}{N + 2} \quad ,$$

making it likely (but not certain). And if N is an even number and n = N/2, P = 1/2; even odds, which makes sense. But—bear this in mind—we must accept or assume that we have no evidence other than this sequence of yes–no answers. For example, it would not make sense to say "I have been up at dawn for the last 20 days, and the Sun has risen every time, so there is a probability of 21/22 that it will rise tomorrow! We know a lot more about the Sun and its rising than what has happened the last 20 mornings.

For the "education" item, N = 24 and n = 17, so the rule of succession tells us that the probability that the next trial gives a positive result is

$$\frac{17+1}{24+2}.$$

Or, since there were 17 positive counts, and 7 negative ones, we can adopt 18 and 8 as the "weights" in our calculation.

To apply this rule to the Price Chart of Literary Paper Trails, we now suppose that we are examining a sequence of authors. The first N (24) are those we have just listed. The N +1'th is Stratford. This means that if Stratford belongs to the same "family" as the listed writers, the odds that Stratford would present us with evidence of an education are 18 to 8. So these are the weights we should use for the "Shake*Speare is Stratford" column.

Chart 3/1, Scene 8: Education Are there any records of Stratford's education?	Evidence Analysis	Stratford No-Compact Theory	Oxford Compact Theory	Ignotus Compact Theory
S1: Evidence of education	0	18		
S2: No evidence of education	1	8		
Post Probabilities				

It will be up to you, Beatrice and Claudia, to enter weights for the Oxford and Ignotus hypotheses. You will then be able to use the website to compute the resulting probabilities. What would you say, Claudia?

CLAUDIA. Am I right, Martin, that for this and the rest of the charts dealing with the Literary Paper Trails, the significance of the Oxford and Ignotus hypotheses is that they mean "Not Stratford," so that I should be entering weights in the Oxford and Ignotus columns by thinking about Stratford, not by thinking about about Oxford and Ignotus?

MARTIN. Good for you, Claudia. You are quite right.

CLAUDIA. Thank you, Martin. Then if either Oxford or Ignotus were Shake*Speare, we would have little reason to believe that Stratford was a writer. It is still a non-zero probability, since some citizens who were not authors had an education. Let us say that, to be generous, 10% of the citizens were educated. Here are my entries:

Chart 3/1, Scene 8: Education Are there any records of Stratford's education?	Evidence Analysis	Stratford No-Compact Theory	Oxford Compact Theory	Ignotus Compact Theory
Claudia				
S1: Evidence of education	0	18	1	1
S2: No evidence of education	1	8	9	9
Post Probabilities		0.14	0.43	0.43

JAMES. What would your entries be, Beatrice?

BEATRICE. Not very different from Claudia's, but I might allow a little higher chance—say 1 in 5, reflected in my figures in the Oxford and Ignotus columns—that Stratford had an education, even if he was not the great writer Shake*Speare:

Chart 3/1, Scene 8: Education Are there any records of Stratford's education?	Evidence Analysis	Stratford No-Compact Theory	Oxford Compact Theory	Ignotus Compact Theory
Beatrice				
S1: Evidence of education	0	18	1	1
S2: No evidence of education	1	8	4	4
Post Probabilities		0.16	0.42	0.42

I see that my being more generous to Stratford does not make much difference for the end probabilities.

JAMES. Now that we have dealt with the first item, how do we deal with the other nine?

MARTIN. The other nine items are closely tied to the writing profession. For instance, let us look at item #2, *Record of correspondence, especially concerning literary matters*. If Stratford were Shake*Speare, we should expect that the evidence on this point would be similar to (or, more likely, stronger than) the evidence for the other 24 writers. That means that the odds would be (14 + 1) to (10 + 1) that Stratford would have left behind such a "record of correspondence."

On the other hand, if either Oxford or Ignotus were Shake*Speare, then we would have little reason to expect that Stratford would have left us such a record. What would you say, Beatrice?

BEATRICE. I agree that it would be highly unlikely. I'll say just one chance in one hundred:

Chart 3/2, Scene 8: Correspondence Are there any records of Stratford's correspondence?	Evidence Analysis	Stratford No-Compact Theory	Oxford Compact Theory	Ignotus Compact Theory
Beatrice				
S1: Record of correspondence	0	15	1	1
S2: No record of correspondence	1	11	100	100
Post Probabilities		0.18	0.41	0.41

JAMES. And what would you say, Claudia?

CLAUDIA. I am tempted to say that there would be zero chance that Stratford would have left correspondence (especially correspondence related to literary matters) if he were not an author. But I'll go along with Beatrice's weights of 1 chance in 100.

Chart 3/2, Scene 8: Correspondence Are there any records of Stratford's correspondence?	Evidence Analysis	Stratford No-Compact Theory	Oxford Compact Theory	Ignotus Compact Theory
Claudia				
S1: Record of correspondence	0	15	1	1
S2: No record of correspondence	1	11	100	100
Post Probabilities		0.18	0.41	0.41

MARTIN. Actually, Claudia, it would have made little difference in the final results if you had entered weights of 0 and 1 rather than 1 and 100.

JAMES. If that is the case, maybe it is not really necessary to get separate estimates from Beatrice and Claudia. If you are both willing to adopt the same one-in-one-hundred chance for Oxford and Ignotus for the other items in the list, we can rapidly complete our analyses. Since you are both agreeable, would you fill in the remaining charts, Martin?

MARTIN. The third item is *Evidence of having being paid to write*. There is no evidence of Stratford being paid to write, but we have such evidence for 14 of the 24 comparison writers:

Chart 3/3, Scene 8: Paid to Write Is there any evidence that Stratford was paid to write?	Evidence Analysis	Stratford No-Compact Theory	Oxford Compact Theory	Ignotus Compact Theory
Beatrice and Claudia				
S1: Evidence of being paid to write	0	15	1	1
S2: No evidence of being paid to write	1	11	100	100
Post Probabilities		0.18	0.41	0.41

MARTIN. The fourth item is *Evidence of a direct relationship with a patron*. There is no such evidence for Stratford, but we have such evidence for 16 of the 24 comparison writers:

Chart 3/4, Scene 8: Patron Is there any evidence that Stratford had a patron?	Evidence Analysis	Stratford No-Compact Theory	Oxford Compact Theory	Ignotus Compact Theory
Beatrice and Claudia				
S1: Evidence of a direct relationship with a patron	0	17	1	1
S2: No evidence of a direct relationship with a patron	1	9	100	100
Post Probabilities		0.16	0.42	0.42

The fifth item is *Extant original manuscript*. There is none for Stratford, but there are for 10 of the 24 comparison authors:

Chart 3/5, Scene 8: Manuscript Are there records of any Stratford manuscripts?	Evidence Analysis	Stratford No-Compact Theory	Oxford Compact Theory	Ignotus Compact Theory
Beatrice and Claudia				
S1: Extant original manuscript	0	11	1	1
S2: No extant original manuscript	1	15	100	100
Post Probabilities		0.22	0.39	0.39

The sixth item is *Handwritten inscriptions, receipts, letters, etc., touching on literary matters*. We have none for Stratford, but we do for 15 of the 24 comparison authors:

Chart 3/6, Scene 8: Inscriptions, etc. Are there records of any inscriptions, etc., related to Stratford?	Evidence Analysis	Stratford No-Compact Theory	Oxford Compact Theory	Ignotus Compact Theory
Beatrice and Claudia				
S1: Handwritten inscriptions, etc.	0	16	1	1
S2: No handwritten inscriptions, etc.	1	10	100	100
Post Probabilities		0.16	0.42	0.42

The seventh item is *Commendatory verses, epistles, or epigrams contributed or received*. We have none for Stratford, but we do for 21 of the comparison writers:

Chart 3/7, Scene 8: Commendatory Verses Are there any commendatory verses, etc., related to Stratford?	Evidence Analysis	Stratford No-Compact Theory	Oxford Compact Theory	Ignotus Compact Theory
Beatrice and Claudia				
S1: Commendatory verses, etc.	0	22	1	1
S2: No commendatory verses, etc.	1	4	100	100
Post Probabilities		0.08	0.46	0.46

The eighth item is *Miscellaneous records (e.g., referred to personally as a writer)*. We have none for Stratford, but we do have such records for every one of the comparison writers:

Chart 3/8, Scene 8: Records Are there any records concerning Stratford as a writer?	Evidence Analysis	Stratford No-Compact Theory	Oxford Compact Theory	Ignotus Compact Theory
Beatrice and Claudia				
S1: Miscellaneous records about writing	0	25	1	1
S2: No miscellaneous records about writing	1	1	100	100
Post Probabilities		0.02	0.49	0.49

The ninth item is *Evidence of books owned, written in, borrowed, or given*. We have no such evidence for Stratford, but we do for 9 of the comparison authors:

Chart 3/9, Scene 8: Books Is there any evidence that Stratford possessed any books?	Evidence Analysis	Stratford No-Compact Theory	Oxford Compact Theory	Ignotus Compact Theory
Beatrice and Claudia				
S1: Books	0	10	1	1
S2: No books	1	16	100	100
Post Probabilities		0.24	0.38	0.38

The tenth item is *Notice of death as a writer.* There is no such evidence for Stratford, but there is for 9 of the comparison authors:

Chart 3/10, Scene 8: Notices at Death Were there any notices of Stratford's death?	Evidence Analysis	Stratford No-Compact Theory	Oxford Compact Theory	Ignotus Compact Theory
Beatrice and Claudia				
S1: Notices on his death	0	10	1	1
S2: No notices on his death	1	16	100	100
Post Probabilities		0.24	0.38	0.38

JAMES. When I combine the results for these ten items, I arrive at the following probabilities obtained from our analysis of the *Literary Paper Trail*:

Probabilities, based on Chart 3,

for Beatrice,

$P(\text{Stratford}) = 9\ 10^{-6}$

$P(\text{Oxford}) = 0.5$

$P(\text{Ignotus}) = 0.5$

and for Claudia,

$P(\text{Stratford}) = 7\ 10^{-6}$

P(Oxford) = 0.5

P(Ignotus) = 0.5

These convert to the following Degrees of Belief

for Beatrice

DB(Stratford) = –50 db

DB(Oxford) = 1 db

DB(Ignotus) = 1db

and for Claudia

DB(Stratford) = –52 db

DB(Oxford) = 1 db

DB(Ignotus) = 1db

These are shown in Figure 5.

I now need to combine these new estimates with the results of our previous charts concerning lameness and Compact. What we might call our *Running Probabilities* are:

Running Probabilities, based on Charts 1, 2, and 3,

for Beatrice,

RP(Stratford) = 3 10^{-6}

RP(Oxford) = 0.82

RP(Ignotus) = 0.18

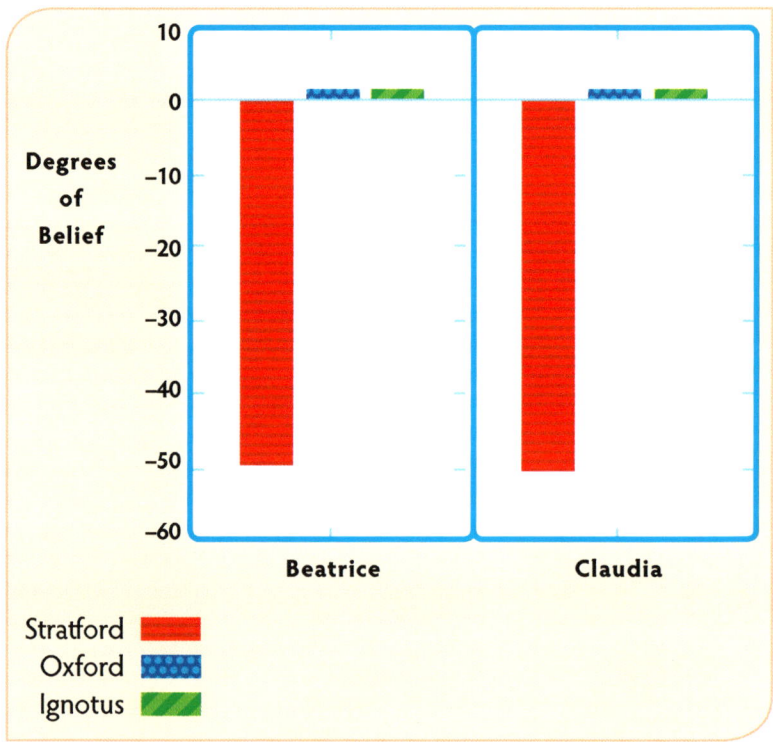

Figure 5. Degrees of Belief for Beatrice and Claudia, based on Chart 3. (Degrees of Belief for Oxford and Ignotus are zero.)

and for Claudia,

$$RP(\text{Stratford}) = 1.4 \; 10^{-6}$$

$$RP(\text{Oxford}) = 0.90$$

$$RP(\text{Ignotus}) = 0.10$$

Expressed in terms of *Degrees of Belief*, these become:

Running Degrees of Belief, based on Charts 1, 2, and 3,

for Beatrice,

> RDB(Stratford) = -55 db
>
> RDB(Oxford) = 7 db
>
> RDB(Ignotus) = -7 db

and for Claudia,

> RDB(Stratford) = -59 db
>
> RDB(Oxford) = 10 db
>
> RDB(Ignotus) = -10 db

The trends of the Running Degrees of Belief are shown in Figure 6.

There is not much difference so far. That is because most of our judgments have been derived from Price's Evidence, using the rule of succession. The only additional judgment that Beatrice and Claudia had to make was along the lines—*What if Stratford were not Shake*Speare? What would then be the probability that Stratford had had an education?* Etc. Since Beatrice and Claudia gave similar or identical answers to these questions, they end up with similar results for Oxford and Ignotus.

However, I expect that much of our remaining evidence will not be so straightforward, and is likely to involve more subjective judgments. It will be interesting to see if our two analysts maintain this closeness in their judgments. If so, I shall conclude that women are more rational than they have been made out to be.

CLAUDIA. I suspect that we are no more rational than the gentleman who thought he could make money out of a vineyard!

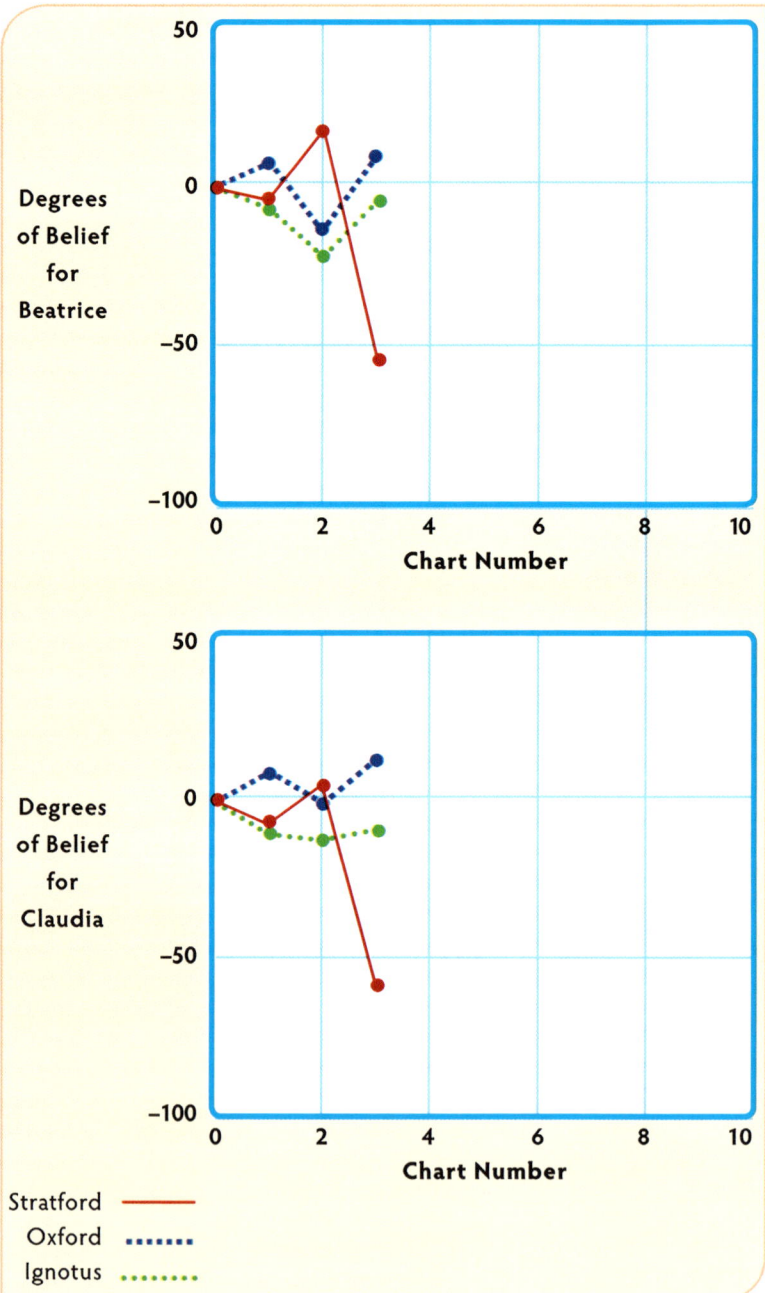

Figure 6. Running Degrees of Belief for Beatrice and Claudia, based on Charts 1, 2, and 3.

JAMES. Touché. This seems an excellent time to adjourn.

NOTES

1. Price (2001), 301.
2. Howson & Urbach (1989), 42.

Reader's Charts

The reader is invited to enter his or her own estimates of the weights in the following charts:

Chart 3/1, Scene 8: Education Are there any records of Stratford's education?	Evidence Analysis	Stratford No-Compact Theory	Oxford Compact Theory	Ignotus Compact Theory
Reader: Date:				
S1: Evidence of education	0	18		
S2: No evidence of education	1	8		
Post Probabilities				

Chart 3/2, Scene 8: Correspondence Are there any records of Stratford's correspondence?	Evidence Analysis	Stratford No-Compact Theory	Oxford Compact Theory	Ignotus Compact Theory
Reader: Date:				
S1: Record of correspondence	0	15		
S2: No record of correspondence	1	11		
Post Probabilities				

Chart 3/3, Scene 8: Paid to Write Is there any evidence that Stratford was paid to write?	Evidence Analysis	Stratford No-Compact Theory	Oxford Compact Theory	Ignotus Compact Theory
Reader: Date:				
S1: Evidence of being paid to write	0	15		
S2: No evidence of being paid to write	1	11		
Post Probabilities				

Chart 3/4, Scene 8: Patron Is there any evidence that Stratford had a patron?	Evidence Analysis	Stratford No-Compact Theory	Oxford Compact Theory	Ignotus Compact Theory
Reader: Date:				
S1: Evidence of a direct relationship with a patron	0	17		
S2: No evidence of a direct relationship with a patron	1	9		
Post Probabilities				

Chart 3/5, Scene 8: Manuscript Are there records of any Stratford manuscripts?	Evidence Analysis	Stratford No-Compact Theory	Oxford Compact Theory	Ignotus Compact Theory
Reader: Date:				
S1: Extant original manuscript	0	11		
S2: No extant original manuscript	1	15		
Post Probabilities				

Chart 3/6, Scene 8: Inscriptions, etc. Are there records of any inscriptions, etc., related to Stratford?	Evidence Analysis	Stratford No-Compact Theory	Oxford Compact Theory	Ignotus Compact Theory
Reader: Date:				
S1: Handwritten inscriptions, etc.	0	16		
S2: No handwritten inscriptions, etc.	1	10		
Post Probabilities				

Chart 3/7, Scene 8: Commendatory Verses Are there any commendatory verses, etc., related to Stratford?	Evidence Analysis	Stratford No-Compact Theory	Oxford Compact Theory	Ignotus Compact Theory
Reader: Date:				
S1: Commendatory verses, etc.	0	22		
S2: No commendatory verses, etc.	1	4		
Post Probabilities				

Chart 3/8, Scene 8: Records **Are there any records concerning Stratford as a writer?**	Evidence Analysis	Stratford No-Compact Theory	Oxford Compact Theory	Ignotus Compact Theory
Reader: Date:				
S1: Miscellaneous records about writing	0	25		
S2: No miscellaneous records about writing	1	1		
Post Probabilities				

Chart 3/9, Scene 8: Books **Is there evidence that Stratford possessed any books?**	Evidence Analysis	Stratford No-Compact Theory	Oxford Compact Theory	Ignotus Compact Theory
Reader: Date:				
S1: Books	0	10		
S2: No books	1	16		
Post Probabilities				

Chart 3/10, Scene 8: Notices at Death Were there notices of Stratford's death?	Evidence Analysis	Stratford No-Compact Theory	Oxford Compact Theory	Ignotus Compact Theory
Reader: Date:				
S1: Notices on his death	0	10		
S2: No notices on his death	1	16		
Post Probabilities				

The Deck at the *Hacienda*

Reviewing
Shake*Speare's Education

Does a genius really need to go to school?

MARTIN. Now that you have seen the BASIN procedure in operation, I guess we can move ahead. James—do you have a topic for us to work on today?

JAMES. When I read some of the books on the Authorship Question, I get lost in a maze of topics—including the conspiracy issue, of course. My view is that we need to start out with some very basic questions—one concerning education, another concerning travel, for instance. We may have to get into some more controversial topics, but I recommend that we leave those for later. So my proposal is that we begin by considering the education required of Shake*Speare, and what we know of the education of Stratford and Oxford.

MARTIN. That is fine with me, and it seems to be acceptable to Beatrice and Claudia.

Let's take the education issue. How would you like to frame the questions, James?

JAMES. It is a matter of how finely we wish to frame the options. To simply say "Shake*Speare was educated," and "Shake*Speare was not educated," is obviously too coarse a breakdown. We need to have a wide enough range of options that it could if necessary accommodate a country lad with no education (at one extreme) and a nobleman with an extraordinary education (at the other extreme), with some other options in between.

So here is my proposed list of options:

S1: Shake*Speare had no education.

S2: Shake*Speare had a few years of schooling.

S3: Shake*Speare had several years of schooling.

S4: Shake*Speare had several years at a good school plus a year or more at a university.

S5: Shake*Speare had private tutors and may have gone to a university.

MARTIN. That seems a pretty good list. It covers the two extremes, with three options in between.

BEATRICE. If anything, I would have preferred a shorter list, but I see no harm in adopting your suggestions.

CLAUDIA. I see no problem with your list. One could add other options, such as time studying law, but that would make the job more complicated, probably for little gain.

MARTIN. OK. I suggest we have Claudia go first, for a change, then Beatrice. Then you can update their scorecards, James.

CLAUDIA. Starting with the evidence column, I personally consider it improbable in the extreme that Shake*Speare had either no education or only a little education. I would say that he had several years of schooling, as an absolute minimum, with the options becoming more and more likely as we work down the list. So, based on the evidence of the extraordinary writing, I would list the weights like this:

Weights for S1 to S5, based on the evidence: 0, 0, 1, 10, 20.

Now I need to consider the Stratford candidacy, and—as I recall—I must be careful not to assume that he was or was not Shake*Speare. I have to put the Shakespeare corpus to one side, and then look at whatever we know about Stratford, quite independently of the work we attribute to "Shakespeare."

From what I can read, it seems that we know very little about Stratford. We know that there was a small school in Stratford-upon-Avon, and that, given his father's status in the town, he would have been entitled to send young William there. But we cannot be sure that he did, so I would set the weights, for Stratford, as follows:

Weights for S1 to S5, for the Stratford hypothesis: 1, 2, 1, 0, 0.

Turning now to the Oxford hypothesis, it seems that we know the answer: He had private tutors, plus years at both Oxford and Cambridge universities. This gives us:

Weights for S1 to S5, for the Oxford hypothesis: 0, 0, 0, 0, 1.

Now we come to consider Ignotus—and here I need a little guidance. My instinctive reaction is to say "Ignotus must have been a writer," and to then look at the list of writers compiled by Diana Price, for instance. However, we have agreed that, in considering Stratford or Oxford, we are forbidden from taking into account any inference from the corpus itself.

My question to Martin is this: If that is the correct rule to apply in considering Stratford and Oxford, should we or should we not apply the same rule to Ignotus?

MARTIN. That is a great question, Claudia. If we were to say, "We know absolutely nothing about Ignotus," the appropriate response would be to give equal weights to the five options. But this does not seem completely reasonable. After all, we certainly cannot base our response on the assumption that 20% of the population had no education, 20% had a few years of schooling, etc., etc.

It is obviously more reasonable to have a certain "population" in mind, with the expectation that, if Shake*Speare was neither

Stratford nor Oxford, it would be a good bet that he was to be found in this population.

BEATRICE. That seems all very reasonable, Martin, but it leaves us with the question—What is this population?

MARTIN. As with many questions in science, there are two ways to try to answer it: We can try to answer it theoretically or empirically.

JAMES. That sounds good, Martin. But how do we implement those options?

MARTIN. Implementing the theoretical option would not be easy. We would have to think about what it would take to produce a truly great writer, and then speculate about how many persons in England at that time would meet those requirements. It would not be easy.

CLAUDIA. So how would you implement the empirical option?

MARTIN. In principle, that is easy. We draw on the work that dozens—if not scores—of people have done before us—perhaps with a little extra flexibility. Referring to Google, I find that (apart from Stratford himself and Oxford), the three leading prospects are Bacon, Derby, and Marlowe.

BEATRICE. But Marlowe was killed in a tavern brawl at the age of 29.

CLAUDIA. Maybe yes, maybe no. From what we learn from the proceedings of the inquest, it is not clear that the conventional story is correct. Marlowe had a very strong incentive to disappear. His other option was to surrender himself to the not-so-tender mercies of the Star Chamber the very next day. A likely consequence of surrendering himself would have been time on the rack.

JAMES. I can see the detective at work, Claudia. What is the alternative theory?

CLAUDIA. Marlowe and his drinking buddies—all on the payroll of Francis Walsingham, Director of Elizabeth's Intelligence Agency—hatched up a plot whereby Marlowe would appear to have been murdered, but actually slipped down to the Thames to board a ship bound for the continent.

JAMES. So even the so-called "empirical" approach is going to be tainted by theory! Isn't that a problem, Martin?

MARTIN. Yes, I guess you are correct. We could choose just how deeply to go into this question—after all, Marlowe is only one writer on Diana Price's list of twenty-four writers. However, my recommendation is that we regard Ignotus as a complete unknown—rather than say "He could have been A, B, C, or D." We could instead ask ourselves how many citizens may have had a reasonable education (together with the requisite drive and talent, of course) to enable him or her to become the great poet and playwright we are referring to as *Shake*Speare*.

As a guide to this hypothetical list, we could consider a few citizens who might have resembled those on Price's list of known authors, a few members of the upper classes who had the advantages of education and leisure, plus a few noblemen (and noble ladies) who might have taken pleasure in poetry and in playwriting. But inevitably, any attribute we assign to Ignotus is sheer guesswork. Can you work with that, Claudia?

CLAUDIA. Yes, that is very helpful, Martin. Assuming once again that we do not have to be over-precise, here are my weights for the five options James specified, for Mr. or Mrs., or Lord or Lady, Ignotus:

Weights for S1 to S5, for the Ignotus hypothesis: 0, 1, 10, 10, 1.

Where does this lead us?

MARTIN. Entering your figures in a chart, I get the following:

For Claudia:

Chart 4, Scene 9: Education	Evidence Analysis	Stratford No-Compact Theory	Oxford Compact Theory	Ignotus Compact Theory
Claudia				
S1: No education	0	1	0	0
S2: Few years of schooling	0	2	0	1
S3: Several years of schooling	1	1	0	10
S4: Several years plus university	10	0	0	10
S5: Private tutors and maybe university	20	0	1	1
Post Probabilities		0.01	0.62	0.37

Entering your weights into our magic program, we arrived at post probabilities:

Stratford, 0.01; Oxford, 0.62; Ignotus, 0.37.

Oxford comes out a little ahead of Ignotus since Claudia was convinced that Shake*Speare had received an outstanding education, and Oxford was rated more highly than Ignotus on that score.

Now it is your turn, Beatrice.

BEATRICE. Well, while I agree with Claudia that a scholarly education would have been a great asset to Shake*Speare, I do not believe that it was essential. The plays and poems have "genius" written all over them. But how important is a fine education to a great genius? I would say that it is definitely a plus, but I do not agree with Claudia that it is essential.

Based on the evidence of the writing, I would list the weights as follows:

Weights for S1 to S5, based on the evidence: 0, 1, 5, 10, 10.

How good an education did Stratford have? Of course, we do not know. But since his father had property and was respected in his town, I consider it most likely that Stratford had some schooling—either a few years or several years. So I would be a little more generous to Stratford than Claudia. My guess is as follows:

Weights for S1 to S5, for the Stratford hypothesis: 1, 5, 5, 0, 0.

For Oxford, I have to agree with Claudia; we know that he had a superb education. So I agree that, for the Oxford hypothesis, we can adopt:

Weights for S1 to S5, for the Oxford hypothesis: 0, 0, 0, 0, 1.

Concerning Ignotus, my instinctive tendency is to differ somewhat from Claudia. I would tend to say that an unknown writer might have had either little education or a fine education, but more likely a middling education or a good education. Something along the following lines:

Weights for S1 to S5, for the Ignotus hypothesis: 0, 1, 10, 10, 1.

MARTIN. So, for Beatrice, I find:

Chart 4, Scene 9: Education	Evidence Analysis	Stratford No-Compact Theory	Oxford Compact Theory	Ignotus Compact Theory
Beatrice				
S1: No education	0	1	0	0
S2: Few years of schooling	1	5	0	1
S3: Several years of schooling	5	5	0	10
S4; Several years plus university	10	0	0	10
S5: Private tutors and maybe university	10	0	1	1
Post Probabilities		0.13	0.37	0.50

As you see, our magic program gives us post probabilities:

Stratford, 0.13; Oxford, 0.37; Ignotus, 0.50.

Beatrice's and Claudia's probabilities convert to the following Degrees of Belief:

for Beatrice,

DB(Stratford) = –8 db

DB(Oxford) = –2 db

DB(Ignotus) = 0 db

and for Claudia,

DB(Stratford) = -20 db

DB(Oxford) = 2 db

DB(Ignotus) = -2 db

These are shown in Figure 7.

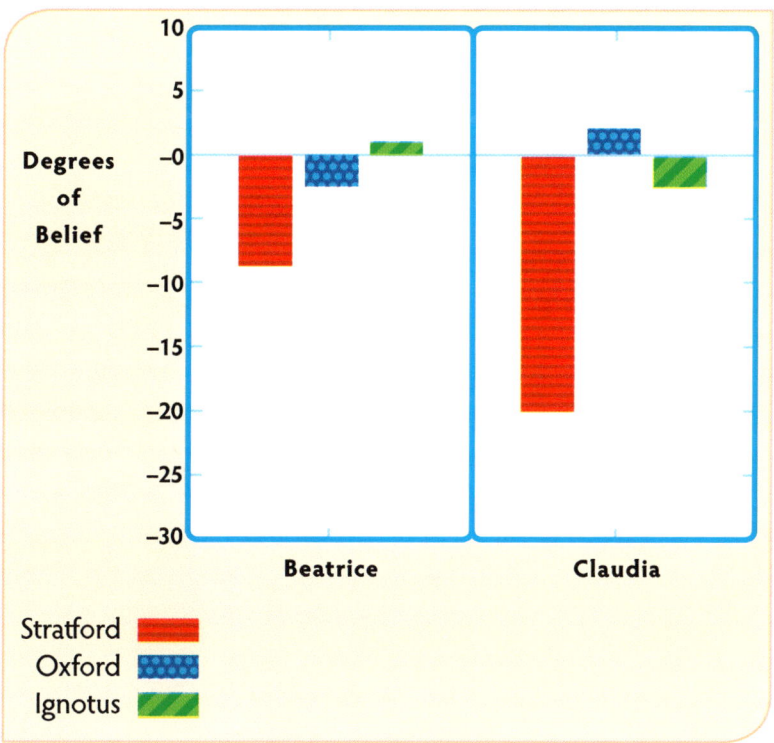

Figure 7. Degrees of Belief for Beatrice and Claudia, based on Chart 4.

It is interesting that you end up favoring Ignotus over Oxford. The reason, I guess, is that you are willing to consider that Shake*Speare had a less than stellar education, which matches more closely with Ignotus than with Oxford. Even so, you are giving them both the edge over Stratford.

What is your impression of this little exercise, James?

JAMES. I am impressed that both Beatrice and Claudia—neither of whom is a mathematician or a statistician—can nevertheless verbalize their thoughts about the decisions they have to make, and then propose numerical estimates that seem to match those thoughts in a way that I find eminently reasonable. So I offer kudos to you both!

Of course, this one item does not lead to any firm conclusion—nowhere near it—but I remember that you showed us, Martin, that five or ten or more unimpressive estimates can lead to a pretty impressive overall result.

Combining our new results for our discussion of education with the previous results that were based on our discussion of lameness and of the "Literary Paper Trail," I arrive at our current running probabilities:

Running Probabilities, based on Charts 1 to 4,

for Beatrice,

$$RP(Stratford) = 10^{-6}$$

$$RP(Oxford) = 0.78$$

$$RP(Ignotus) = 0.22$$

and for Claudia,

$$RP(Stratford) = 2 \; 10^{-8}$$

$$RP(Oxford) = 0.94$$

$$RP(Ignotus) = 0.06$$

Expressed in terms of Degrees of Belief, these become:

Running Degrees of Belief, based on Charts 1 to 4,

for Beatrice,

RDB(Stratford) = −60 db

RDB(Oxford) = 5 db

RDB(Ignotus) = −5 db

and for Claudia,

RDB(Stratford) = −70 db

RDB(Oxford) = 12 db

RDB(Ignotus) = −12 db

The trends of the Running Degrees of Belief are shown in Figure 8.

This seems a good point at which to adjourn for the day. Same time tomorrow?

MARTIN. Yes, but I have a suggestion. I feel we are taking unfair advantage of your hospitality, Claudia and James. I have a pleasant cabin down in Big Sur. It has just enough room to hold us all, and I am willing to barbeque at dinnertime. I would like to invite you all to spend a day or two at what I call my "chalet." Not that it is in the mountains. But it is on the side of a hill with a magnificent view.

BEATRICE. That sounds wonderful. I have not been down to Big Sur for years.

JAMES. It sounds wonderful to Claudia and me, too, Martin. We look forward to it.

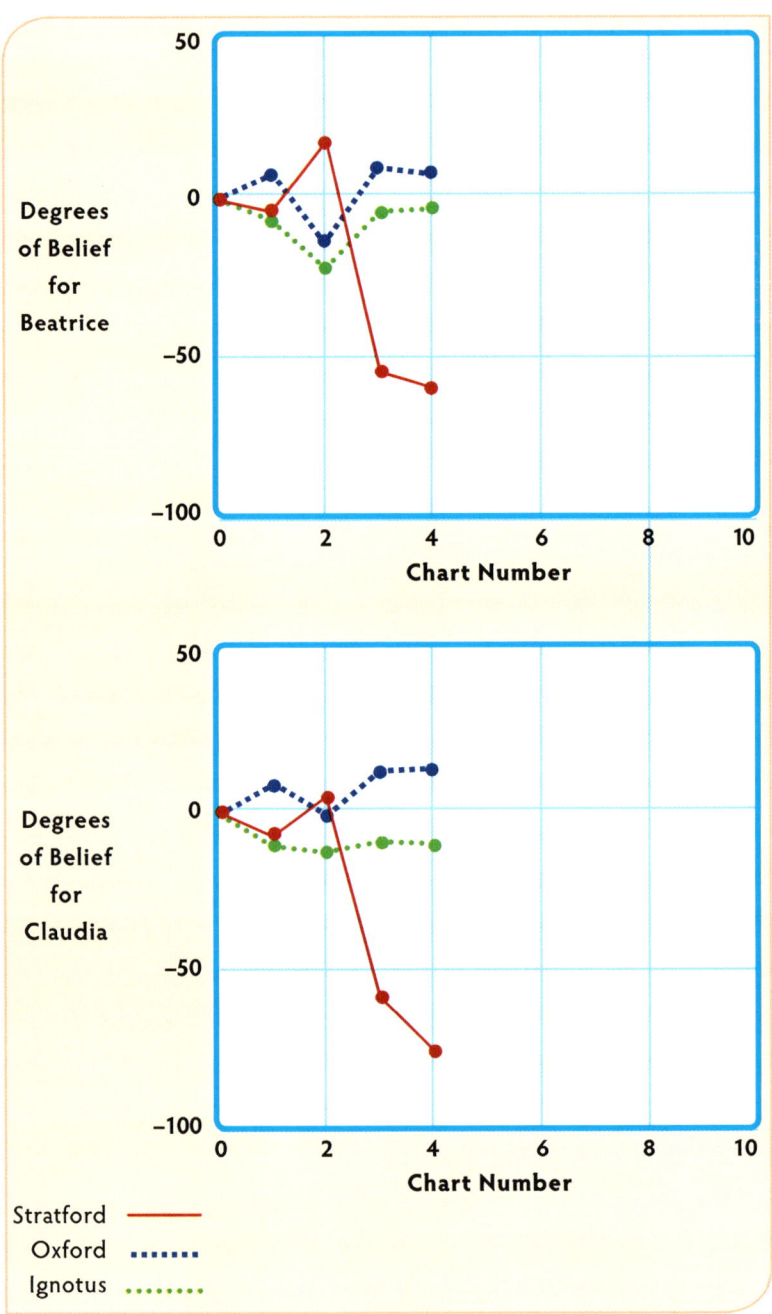

Stratford ———
Oxford ▪▪▪▪▪▪▪
Ignotus ▪▪▪▪▪▪▪▪

Figure 8. Running Degrees of Belief for Beatrice and Claudia, based on Charts 1 through 4.

Reader's Chart

The reader is invited to enter his or her own estimates of the weights in the following chart:

Chart 4, Scene 9: Education	Evidence Analysis	Stratford No-Compact Theory	Oxford Compact Theory	Ignotus Compact Theory
Reader: Date:				
S1: No education				
S2: Few years of schooling				
S3: Several years of schooling				
S4: Several years plus university				
S5: Private tutors and maybe university				
Post Probabilities				

The Patio of Martin's *Chalet* at Big Sur

Geographical Interests and Knowledge

Does a genius need to travel in order to know the world?

JAMES. Thank you, Martin, for this delightful change of scenery. Much as we love Carmel Valley, it is refreshing to get away from time to time. I find the air different down here at Big Sur—ocean air, but clear—not as foggy as it might be on the beach at Carmel.

BEATRICE. Whether or not this ambiance is going to help us focus on the Authorship Question is something I guess we shall soon find out. Remind us, James, what is our assignment for today?

JAMES. Travel. I understand that this is a topic that is almost always raised in Authorship discussions.

CLAUDIA. Especially travel in and around Italy. Of Shake*Speare's 38 plays, 11 are set in Italy. Almost as many as the 12 in England.

BEATRICE. But Ben Jonson set *Volponi* in Italy—in Venice, to be exact. And of Marlowe's four major plays, one was set in Germany (*Doctor Faustus*) and two in what we now call the Middle East (*Tamburlaine* and *The Jew of Malta*). Only one in

England (*Edward The Second*). So I do not see it as so surprising that, of Shake*Speare's 38 plays, 11 were set in Italy and 5 in other parts of Europe.

CLAUDIA. Well, I see a difference, Beatrice. When you read *Doctor Faustus*, you have to remind yourself that it is taking place in Germany. When you read *The Merchant of Venice*, you do not need any reminding about Venice—you are there!

BEATRICE. So what else is new? We all know that Shakespeare—oops, I mean Shake*Speare (!)—was the better playwright of the two.

MARTIN. We could go on with this debate. But our goal is to somehow short-circuit these discussions, and reduce the argument to a few crisp, well-defined, questions. James—have you prepared our agenda for today?

JAMES. My original intention was that we should focus on whether or not Shake*Speare was familiar with Europe. But I think it makes sense to be more precise than that. As Claudia has just pointed out, a striking characteristic of the "Shakespeare" plays is the number of plays that are set in Italy. I am also struck by the fact that they cluster in the Veneto region—Mantua, Padua, Verona, and of course Venice. Since this is a striking fact about Shake*Speare's plays, I think it makes sense to use that fact in assessing our candidates.

So here is my proposed list of statements for today:

S1. Shake*Speare had no interest in or knowledge of Italy.

S2. Shake*Speare had some interest in and knowledge of Italy.

S3. Shake*Speare had substantial interest in and knowledge of Italy, especially Northern Italy.

S4. Shake*Speare had extensive interest in and knowledge of Italy, especially the Veneto region.

Beatrice—Why are you holding up your finger like that?

BEATRICE. I am just checking to see which way the wind is blowing, and I think it is blowing away from Warwickshire. But seriously, I am wondering whether this kind of breakdown of the options is compatible with one of our ground rules—that we should articulate the options in as neutral a way as possible.

MARTIN. That is a great question, Beatrice. I guess we need to be a little more precise about what we mean by "neutral." We obviously cannot require that any set of options be posed in such a way that the end result will be even odds for all three candidates. On the other hand, it would certainly be inappropriate for us to deliberately phrase the questions in a way that uses "inside knowledge" to somehow favor one of our three candidates.

So—to sum up my thoughts—it is OK to draw upon the available evidence in articulating our options, for any item, but it is not OK to use information about a particular candidate for that purpose.

Does this seem reasonable?

BEATRICE. That helps but, I'm sorry, I still have a problem with this set of options. When we were talking about education, there was a clear separation between the five options. If Shake*Speare had only two or three years of schooling, we knew that we could rule out the "no-schooling" option, and the other options, too. However, the chart you are proposing for this topic is not so clear-cut. I can see that S1, if true, rules out S2, S3, and S4. I can also see that S2 rules out S1, and presumably also rules out S3 and S4, if we read "some interest" to mean "a limited interest only." However, the line between S3 and S4 seems quite fuzzy to me. Doesn't someone who has "extensive interest, especially in the Veneto," also have "substantial interest, especially in the north"?

MARTIN. You are on the mark again, Beatrice. I wish that all the students in my classes at the Institute were as sharp as you. Yes, the BASIN procedure does require that the options, for evidence or for hypotheses, should be "complete and mutually exclusive." I have to agree with you that, strictly speaking (and we are aiming at being strict), James's proposed list of "statements" does not satisfy that requirement.

How about the following:

S1. Shake*Speare had no interest in and no experience of Italy.

S2. Shake*Speare had some interest in but no experience of Italy.

S3. Shake*Speare had experience of Italy that was not focused on the Veneto.

S4. Shake*Speare had experience of Italy that was focused on the Veneto.

BEATRICE. That seems unexceptionable. It seems to me that if we adopt any one of the four statements, we are necessarily rejecting the other three. And it also seems clear that one of the four statements must be correct. Putting two and two together, I conclude that we now have what you call a "complete and mutually exclusive" set of options. So, *Avanti!*

JAMES. My apologies to you all. And thank you, Beatrice, for catching my error. I shall try to be more careful in the future in planning our charts. If you are ready, Claudia, would you like to start off and give us your assessments of this revised set of options?

CLAUDIA. Yes, I'll try. Thinking first of the evidence (mainly the plays), it certainly appears that Shake*Speare had an interest in Italy, and it is also clear that this interest focused on Venice and some of the other cities in that area. Roe has recently compiled extensive evidence that Shake*Speare had remarkably detailed knowledge of Italy [1]. So I give maximum weight to S4, less weight to S3, a little to S2, and none to S1. My weights for S1, S2, S3, and S4 are 0, 1, 10, and 100, respectively.

Concerning Stratford, there is nothing in his biography to indicate that he had much interest in any part of the world other than Stratford-upon-Avon and London. And when he retired, he left London for Stratford. However, of course we cannot be absolutely sure he had no interest in Italy, so I allow for a 10% chance that he may have been interested in Italy, but effectively no chance of S3 or S4. So for Stratford, I have to give full weight to S1, a small weight to S2, but no weight to S3 or S4. My weights for S1, S2, S3, and S4 come out to be 10, 1, 0, and 0, respectively.

Concerning Oxford, we know that he spent many months in Italy, especially in Venice and that area. He was sufficiently smitten with Italy that he brought a lot of Italian goods, and some Italian customs, back to England. For instance, he brought a gift of scented gloves to Queen Elizabeth, which she loved. And he often dressed in the Italian style—so much so that he was termed the "Italianate" nobleman. So I give full weight to S4, and zero to S1, S2, and S3.

Now I need to think about Ignotus. A writer has to be broad-minded and curious about the world. It is possible that Ignotus was a nobleman—or noble-lady—who would quite likely have traveled to Europe. However, there is no reason to expect that Ignotus would have preferred Italy to France or Germany or Spain, so I would give most weight to S2, some to S3, and slight weights to S1 and S4, since we cannot rule them out. Specifically, my weights for S1, S2, S3, and S4 come out to be 1, 10, 3, and 1, respectively.

Chart 5, Scene 10: Travel	Evidence Analysis	Stratford No-Compact Theory	Oxford Compact Theory	Ignotus Compact Theory
Claudia				
S1: No interest in and no experience of Italy	0	10	0	1
S2: Interest in but no experience of Italy	1	1	0	10
S3: Experience of Italy—not focused on the Veneto	10	0	0	3
S4: Experience of Italy—focused on the Veneto	100	0	1	1
Post Probabilities		0.001	0.85	0.15

MARTIN. The post-probabilities are, approximately, Stratford, 0.001; Oxford, 0.85; and Ignotus, 0.15. Good for the Earl, not bad for Ignotus, but not so good for the actor.

JAMES. Yes, Beatrice, I'm afraid that Stratford is not faring too well, so far. What are your thoughts about this chart?

BEATRICE. Concerning the evidence provided by the plays, I agree with Claudia that most weight should go to S4, and a lesser weight to S3. However, I would not completely rule out S2. In principle, the playwright could have learned a lot from those of his colleagues who had visited Italy. So I give a somewhat bigger weight to S2. My weights for S1, S2, S3, and S4 are 0, 5, 10, and 20, respectively.

Concerning Stratford, we are really in the dark. It seems pretty certain that he never left England, but beyond that, all options should be on the table. So I give equal weights to S1 and S2. My weights for S1, S2, S3, and S4 are 1, 1, 0, and 0, respectively.

Concerning Oxford, we know that he did visit Italy, so S1 and S2 can be ruled out. Beyond that, I would plead ignorance, and give equal weights to S3 and S4. My weights for S1, S2, S3, and S4 are 0, 0, 1, and 1, respectively.

For Ignotus, I would say it is more likely than not that an unknown writer had not visited Italy. I would also say that "interest" was more likely than "no interest," and that unfocused interest was more likely than interest focused on the Veneto. So my weights for S1, S2, S3, and S4 are 2, 5, 2, and 1, respectively.

Chart 5, Scene 10: Travel	Evidence Analysis	Stratford No-Compact Theory	Oxford Compact Theory	Ignotus Compact Theory
Beatrice				
S1: No interest in and no experience of Italy	0	1	0	2
S2: Interest in but no experience of Italy	5	1	0	4
S3: Experience of Italy—not focused on the Veneto	10	0	1	2
S4: Experience of Italy—focused on the Veneto	50	0	1	1
Post Probabilities		0.04	0.74	0.22

MARTIN. Beatrice's and Claudia's probabilities convert to the following Degrees of Belief:

for Beatrice,

DB(Stratford) = –14 db

DB(Oxford) = 5 db

DB(Ignotus) = –5 db

and for Claudia,

DB(Stratford) = –30 db

DB(Oxford) = 8 db

DB(Ignotus) = –8 db

These are shown in Figure 9.

JAMES. I believe that I am supposed to be keeping track of the cumulative effect of our judgments. Here are the running probabilities so far:

Running Probabilities, based on Charts 1 to 5,

for Beatrice,

RP(Stratford) = $7 \ 10^{-8}$

RP(Oxford) = 0.92

RP(Ignotus) = 0.08

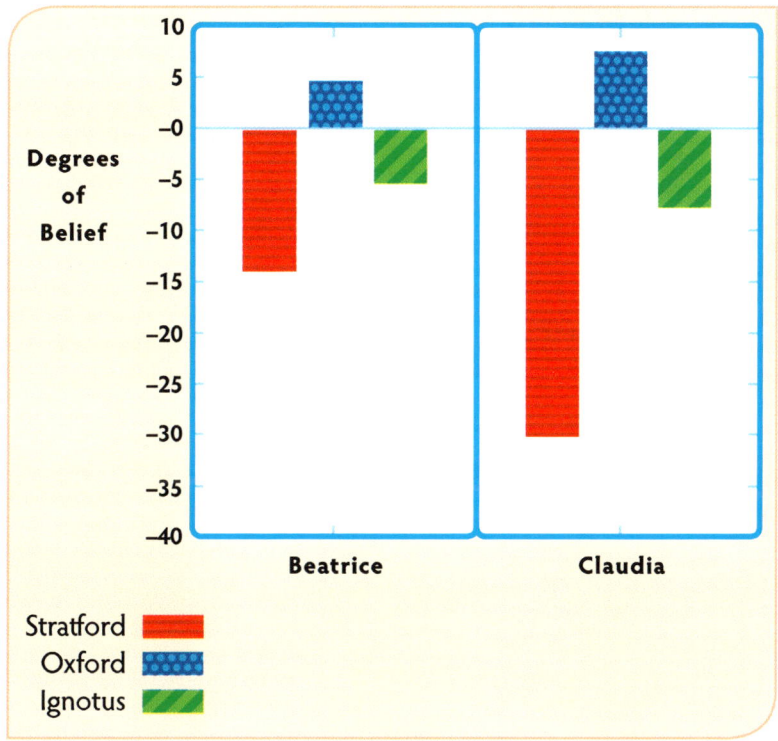

Figure 9. Degrees of Belief for Beatrice and Claudia, based on Chart 5.

and for Claudia,

$$RP(\text{Stratford}) = 3 \ 10^{-11}$$

$$RP(\text{Oxford}) = 0.99$$

$$RP(\text{Ignotus}) = 0.01$$

Expressed in terms of Degrees of Belief, these become:

Running Degrees of Belief, based on Charts 1 to 5, for Beatrice,

$$RDB(Stratford) = -72 \ db$$

$$RDB(Oxford) = 11 \ db$$

$$RDB(Ignotus) = -11 \ db$$

and for Claudia,

$$RDB(Stratford) = -105 \ db$$

$$RDB(Oxford) = 19 \ db$$

$$RDB \ (Ignotus) = -19 \ db$$

The trends of the Running Degrees of Belief are shown in Figure 10.

MARTIN. We do see that Stratford is slipping significantly in the rankings, based on either Beatrice's or Claudia's input. However, there is still not much to choose from between Oxford and Ignotus.

JAMES. I think we are making good progress, but we are still in the early stages of our project.

I would suggest to Beatrice that she start to think about issues that might help the case for Stratford—when analyzed purely objectively, of course.

MARTIN. Now, if you will excuse me, I have more important business to attend to. I have to pound the abalone that I caught this morning, and start the barbeque. It will take a while. I still prefer to use slow-burning coal for fish—but of course I use mesquite for steak.

JAMES. I have agreed to be Martin's sous-chef this evening. I have been deputized to help prepare the abalone. Incidentally, I have taught Claudia to enjoy single-malt scotch, and I have brought down a bottle of our favorite brand. Try a little, Beatrice and Martin. You may like it—and if you do, you may never drink blended again.

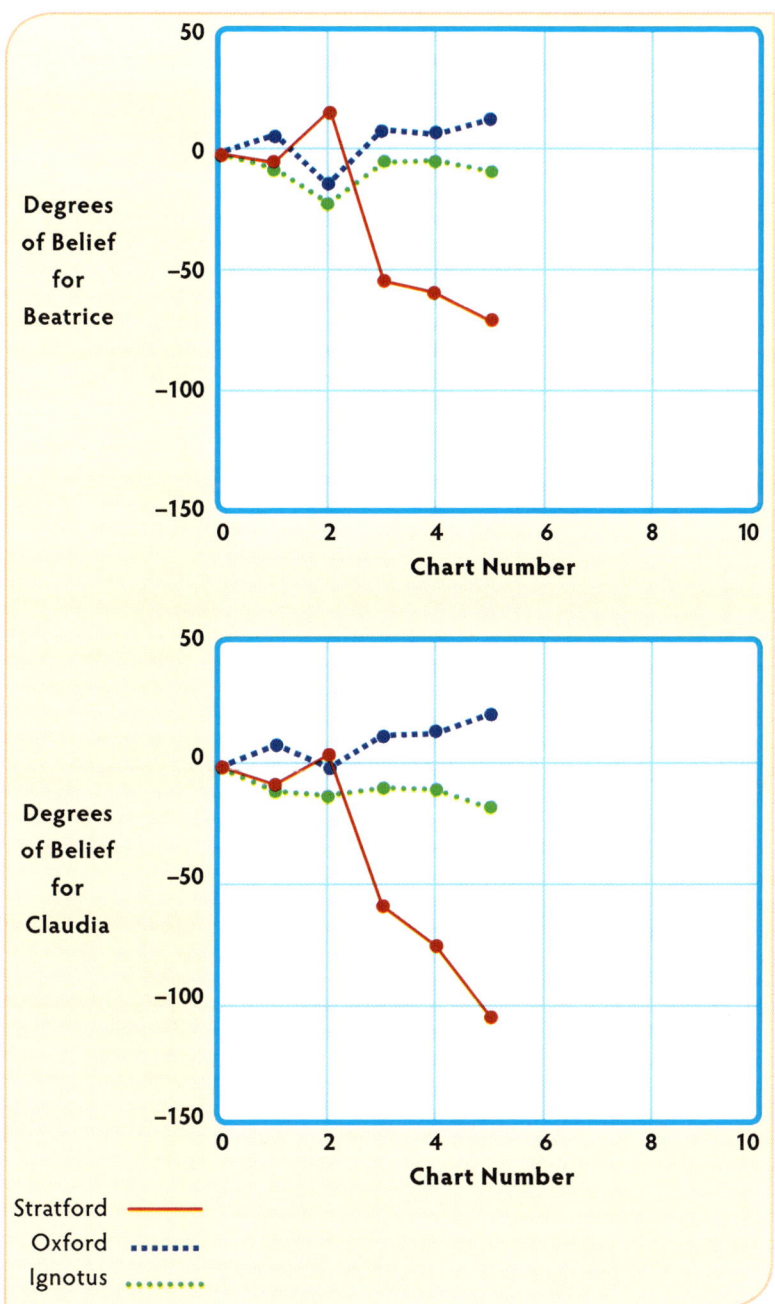

Figure 10. Running Degrees of Belief for Beatrice and Claudia, based on Charts 1 through 5.

NOTE

1. Roe (2011).

Reader's Chart

The reader is invited to enter his or her own estimates of the weights in the following chart:

Chart 5, Scene 10: Travel	Evidence Analysis	Stratford No-Compact Theory	Oxford Compact Theory	Ignotus Compact Theory
Reader: Date:				
S1: No interest in and no experience of Italy				
S2: Interest in but no experience of Italy				
S3: Experience of Italy—not focused on the Veneto				
S4: Experience of Italy—focused on the Veneto				
Post Probabilities				

The Patio of Martin's *Chalet* at Big Sur

Shake*Speare's Social Status

A participant in court life, or just an astute observer?

JAMES. I have been thinking about our agenda for today, and I think the time has come to tackle what is, I think, a crucial issue.

BEATRICE. Namely?

JAMES. Social status. You must admit that this is going to be a tricky topic to address. We know the social status of Oxford. We know a little of the status of Stratford. We obviously know little or nothing about the status of Ignotus. This leaves us with the crucial question: What was the social status of Shake*Speare? We obviously do not know. Our only possibility is to try to infer it from his legacy.

Here again, the initial question is how finely to divide up the possibilities. To just say "upper class" or "lower class" is much too simplistic. As far as I can make out, Elizabethan England was far more finely stratified than England or the United States today. And the divisions depended not only on wealth, but also (perhaps primarily) on hierarchical status: There was an enormous range, from the monarch at one end, to the clodhopper at the other end.

It is no use trying to divide up the options too finely, but it obviously should not be too coarse a subdivision, either. I am suggesting, as a compromise, just four options:

S1: The nobility

S2: High class

S3: Middle class

S4: Low class

CLAUDIA. Let me try to understand you: By "nobility," I assume we mean someone who has a title, or belongs to a titled family; someone who could possibly appear at court and be received by the Queen.

A member of the "low class" would, I assume, be a field-hand or a butcher or a baker, or perhaps a member of the constabulary—if they had constabularies in those days.

But I am not so sure about the "high class" or the "middle class." What is the distinction between the two?

JAMES. I am necessarily—and purposely—vague on these matters. But someone who is merely a knight—such as Sir Toby Belch, or Sir John Falstaff—would not belong to the nobility. So I would class him as a member of the "high class."

BEATRICE. And the middle class?

JAMES. Parsons, doctors, justices, etc. Reputable professional people.

MARTIN. So the lower classes are disreputable, and unprofessional?

JAMES. Not necessarily. They could be honest tradesmen. But of course, they could be dishonest cozeners, too! As you will see, I am being unavoidably vague. You can reflect this vagueness when you fill in the blanks in our charts.

BEATRICE. Even if you could be more precise, I am not sure it would help us a lot. We may be better off that you are being vague—that will allow us to be vague, too.

MARTIN. Well, we now have a chart with lots of empty spaces. Who is willing to fill in some of the blanks?

CLAUDIA. I'll see what I can do. Reflecting on the plays, I have the very strong impression that Shake*Speare was most at home at court. I guess that a member of the high class would have had a window on court life. It seems to me very unlikely that Shake*Speare was a member of either the middle class or the low class, but either of those options is logically conceivable, so I give them non-zero (but very small) weights.

Similarly (but upside-down), I consider that Stratford probably belonged to the low class, but he may have risen to the middle class. I think there is no chance he was a member of the high class.

Oxford himself belonged to the nobility, without a shadow of a doubt. However, I must remember that we are allowing for a "compact." There are reasons to believe that Oxford supported a small stable of young writers, and it is quite possible that some of the "Shakespeare" corpus was written by some of his young colleagues—who may have belonged to the high class, but more likely the middle class.

Ignotus is of course the mystery man. Most other writers (in Diana Price's list, for instance) probably belong to the middle class, but any of the other options is possible.

So, to be specific, I am laying the following odds:

Chart 6, Scene 11: Social Status	Evidence Analysis	Stratford No-Compact Theory	Oxford Compact Theory	Ignotus Compact Theory
Claudia				
S1: Nobility	100	0	100	1
S2: High class	30	0	2	4
S3: Middle class	1	30	5	4
S4: Low class	1	100	0	1
Post Probabilities		0.009	0.69	0.30

JAMES. Martin has come up with their respective probabilities. This is getting to be a familiar result: Oxford first, Ignotus close on his heels, with Stratford bringing up the rear.

Thank you, Claudia. What do you say, Beatrice?

BEATRICE. I am not as convinced as Claudia seems to be that it would take a nobleman, or a quasi-nobleman, to write the plays and poems. They have "genius" written all over them, and I think it is presumptuous to decide what background a genius needs to operate in. A nobleman would certainly have a big advantage in writing about court life (including court intrigues), but a nobleman's upbringing may not have been essential. I am much more open to the possibility that Shake*Speare was a member of the middle class—and may indeed have begun life as a member of the low class.

Concerning our friend William: The evidence suggests to me that he was born into a middle-class family. He became quite prosperous, and he did acquire a coat of arms. However, I have to agree that it is not credible that an actor—or even a shareholder in a theatre—would qualify as "high class."

Concerning Oxford and Ignotus, I am happy to go along with Claudia's suggestions.

Chart 6, Scene 11: Social Status	Evidence Analysis	Stratford No-Compact Theory	Oxford Compact Theory	Ignotus Compact Theory
Beatrice				
S1: Nobility	5	0	100	1
S2: High class	3	0	2	4
S3: Middle class	3	5	5	4
S4: Low class	1	1	0	1
Post Probabilities		0.21	0.40	0.39

MARTIN. Beatrice's and Claudia's probabilities convert to the following Degrees of Belief:

for Beatrice,

$$DB(Stratford) = -6 \text{ db}$$

$$DB(Oxford) = -2 \text{ db}$$

$$DB(Ignotus) = -2 \text{ db}$$

and for Claudia,

$$DB(Stratford) = -20 \text{ db}$$

$$DB(Oxford) = 3 \text{ db}$$

$$DB(Ignotus) = -4 \text{ db}$$

These are shown in Figure 11.

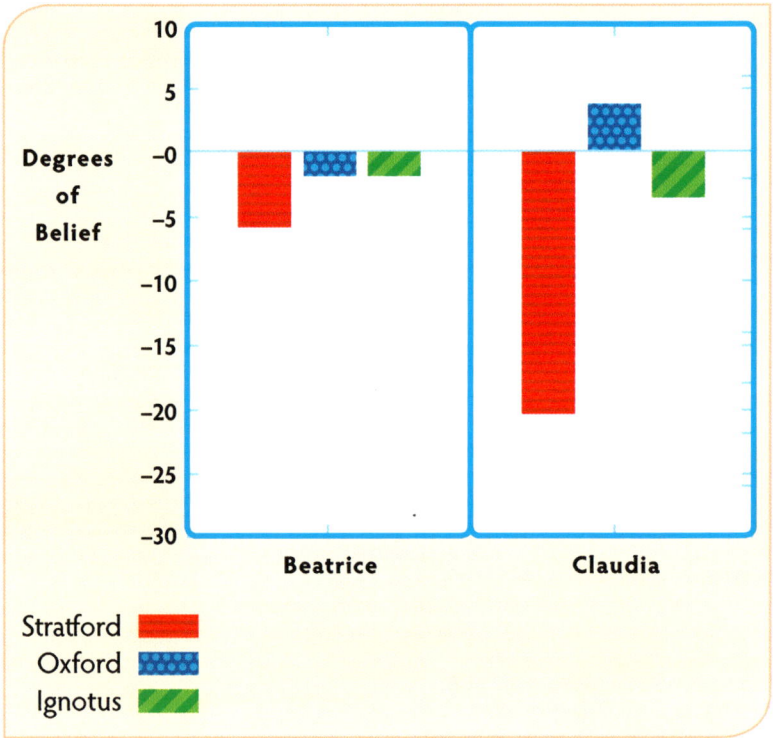

Figure 11. Degrees of Belief for Beatrice and Claudia, based on Chart 6.

JAMES. Since I am keeping track of the cumulative effect of our judgments, here are the running probabilities so far:

Running Probabilities, based on Charts 1 to 6,

for Beatrice,

$$RP(\text{Stratford}) = 4\ 10^{-8};$$

$$RP(\text{Oxford}) = 0.92;$$

$$RP(\text{Ignotus}) = 0.08;$$

and for Claudia,

$$RP(Stratford) = 4 \cdot 10^{-13};$$

$$RP(Oxford) = 0.995;$$

$$RP(Ignotus) = 0.005.$$

Expressed in terms of Degrees of Belief, these become:

Running Degrees of Belief, based on Charts 1 to 6,

for Beatrice,

$$RDB(Stratford) = -75 \text{ db};$$

$$RDB(Oxford) = 11 \text{ db};$$

$$RDB(Ignotus) = -11 \text{ db};$$

and for Claudia,

$$RDB(Stratford) = -124 \text{ db};$$

$$RDB(Oxford) = 23 \text{ db};$$

$$RDB(Ignotus) = -23 \text{ db}.$$

The trend of Running Degrees of Belief are shown in Figure 12.

Ignotus is still in the running—but barely.

We have got through this exercise quite quickly. I suggest we take a short break, and then go on to the next topic.

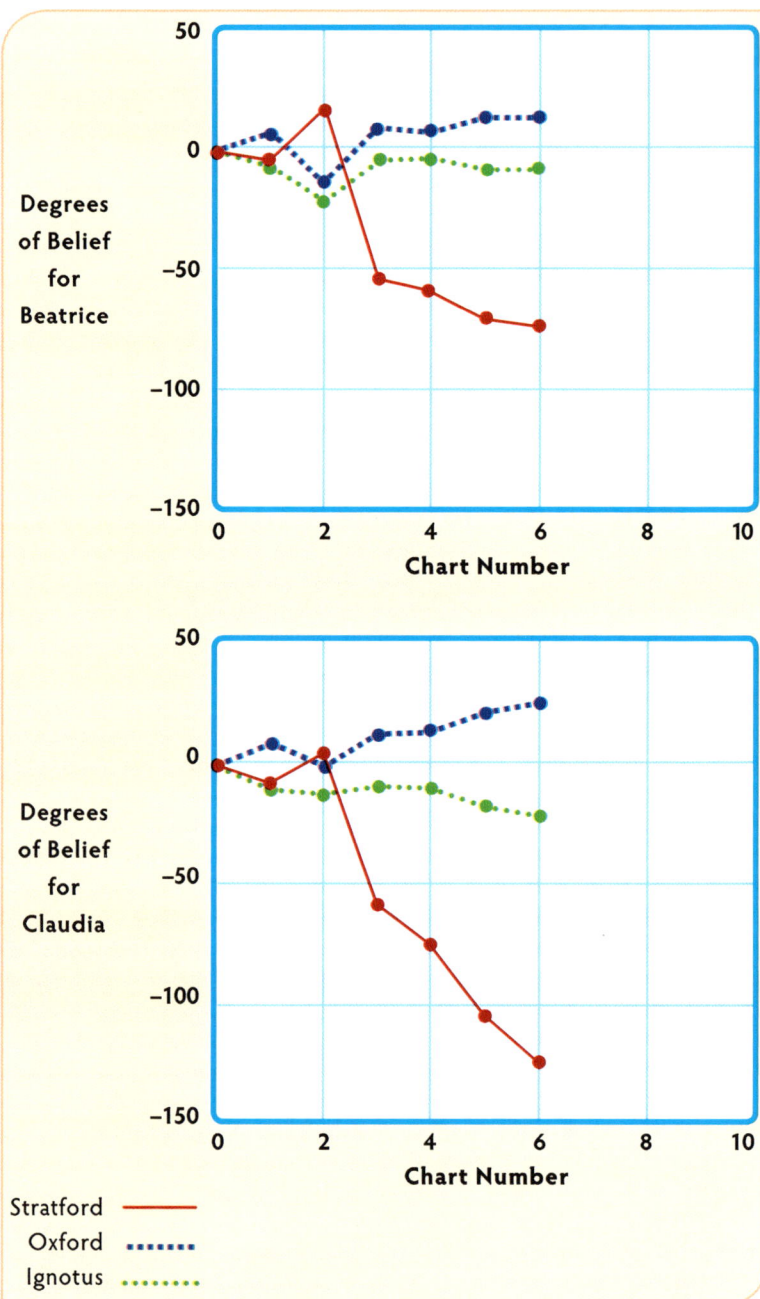

Figure 12. Running Degrees of Belief for Beatrice and Claudia, based on Charts 1 through 6.

Reader's Chart

The reader is invited to enter his or her own estimates of the weights in the following chart:

Chart 6, Scene 11: Social Status	Evidence Analysis	Stratford No-Compact Theory	Oxford Compact Theory	Ignotus Compact Theory
Reader: Date:				
S1: Nobility				
S2: High class				
S3: Middle class				
S4: Low class				
Post Probabilities				

The Patio of Martin's *Chalet* at Big Sur

Stratford's Handwriting

Did Stratford ever suffer from writer's cramp?

JAMES. If we are ready to resume—I wonder whether Martin has any topic he would like to suggest.

MARTIN. I am not nearly as well-informed on this matter as Beatrice and Claudia, so I cannot put my finger on any crucial issue. However, James and Claudia have raised one issue that we might look into.

CLAUDIA. What was that?

MARTIN. Shakespeare's—I mean Stratford's—handwriting. James pointed out that we have just fourteen words in his own hand—his name signed six times and the words "by me" on his will. And I recall that Claudia pointed out how bad the writing was. It occurs to me that this could be a topic for discussion.

JAMES. Do you have a chart for us to focus on?

MARTIN. I have ideas for one. It seems to me that we do not need to consider Oxford's writing (which I would expect to be very good to excellent), or Ignotus's writing (of which we have no information). We can simply compare what we know of

Stratford's writing with what we might expect under our three standard hypotheses.

I am sure there are all kinds of characteristics we could consider, but we can keep it very simple: The writing might have been excellent, good, or fair.

CLAUDIA. Or it might have been nonexistent. The fact that his few signatures differ so much leads some authors to speculate that he may have been illiterate, so that the "signatures" on his will, etc., were not actually Stratford's. They might have been supplied by the clerk who prepared the will. Sir Edwin Durning-Lawrence (a Baconian) was of the opinion that "there is a probability, practically amounting to a certainty, that the Stratford Actor could not so much as manage to scrawl his own name" [1, 2].

MARTIN. In that case, we have four options to consider:

Chart 7, Scene 12: Stratford's Writing	Evidence Analysis	Stratford No-Compact Theory	Oxford Compact Theory	Ignotus Compact Theory
S1: Stratford's handwriting was excellent				
S2: Stratford's handwriting was good				
S3: Stratford's handwriting was fair				
S4: Stratford could not write				
Post Probabilities				

To help us sort through this issue, I have brought along copies of the six signatures attributed to "Shakspere," whom we refer to as Stratford (Plate 5). They are the signature on his

Signature on the Mountjoy Desposition, May 11, 1612

Signatures on the Blackfriars Documents, March 11, 1613

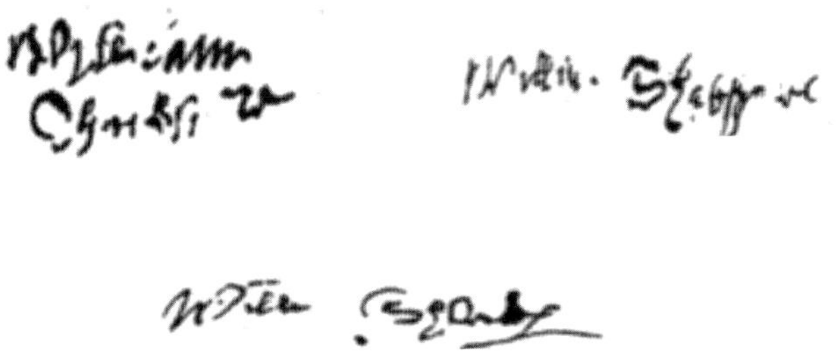

Signatures on the Will, March 25, 1616

The six known signatures of Stratford (William Shakspere)

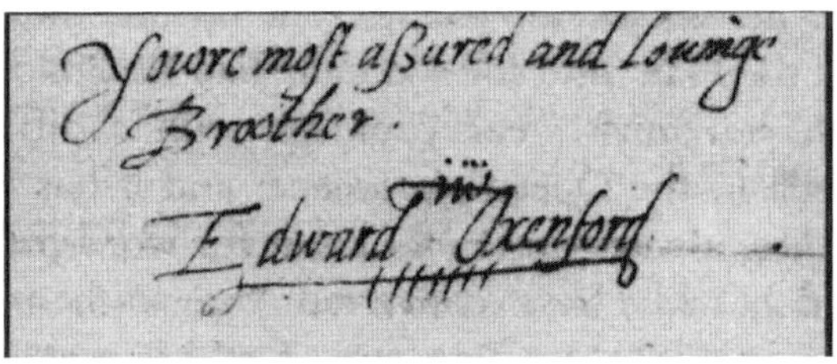

An Oxford signature

Plate 5. Stratford's known signatures, an Oxford signature.

deposition in connection with the Mountjoy case; two signatures on documents related to his purchase of the Blackfriars property; and three signatures on his will.

What are your thoughts, Beatrice?

BEATRICE. Since the date on the will was March 25, 1616 (it was prepared by his lawyer, Francis Collins), and Stratford passed away on April 25 of that year, it seems likely that he had intimations of mortality. Stratford was probably ill, and that may explain either why his handwriting was so bad or why he had a clerk sign his name for him. It seems to me quite conceivable that his normal writing may have been reasonable. It is just that he was in poor physical shape when he came to put his affairs in order. He had waited too long (as many of us do). But I must admit that the evidence points in the direction of S3 or S4.

If Stratford was the Author, then he must have written thousands of lines—tens of thousands of words—so that his *normal* handwriting (as distinguished from the writing on this will) must have been either good or excellent.

If we consider that either Oxford or Ignotus was the Author, then the only reason to consider that Stratford could write would be the assumption that he had attended the Stratford-upon-Avon school, which is likely, but admittedly not certain. So I would expect that his handwriting would have been fair, or possibly good. And, of course, it is possible that Stratford never attended school in Stratford-upon-Avon, in which case his writing may have been nonexistent.

So here are my guesses—which is all that they are—and I see that Martin has figured out the resulting probabilities.

Chart 7, Scene 12: Stratford's Writing	Evidence Analysis	Stratford No-Compact Theory	Oxford Compact Theory	Ignotus Compact Theory
Beatrice				
S1: Stratford's handwriting was excellent	0	5	0	0
S2: Stratford's handwriting was good	5	5	1	1
S3: Stratford's handwriting was fair	10	1	5	5
S4: Stratford could not write	1	0	1	1
Post Probabilities		0.24	0.38	0.38

MARTIN. The result is a bit surprising. The evidence against William is not as bad as one might have expected.

JAMES. What are your thoughts, Claudia?

CLAUDIA. I must take issue with Beatrice on one or two points. Beatrice quite correctly points out that the signatures on the will were written only weeks before his demise. Then why did he begin his will with the statement:

> In the name of god Amen I William Shackspeare, of Stratford upon Avon, in the countrie of Warr., gent., in perfect health and memorie . . .

That does not read like the statement of a man who was at death's door.

The other point I would make is that the Mountjoy deposition was made on May 11, 1612, and the deed for the purchase of the Blackfriars gatehouse was dated March 11, 1613. These signatures were made four years, and three years, respectively, before Stratford passed away, so we cannot blame the bad penmanship in those documents on any terminal illness.

We get an expert opinion from Jane Cox, who was Custodian of the Wills at the Public Records Office in London. She wrote:

> *It is obvious at a glance that these signatures, with the exception of the last two [the Blackfriars signatures] are not the signatures of the same man. Almost every letter is formed in a different way in each. Literate men in the sixteenth and seventeenth centuries developed personalized signatures much as people do today* . . . [3]

To sum up—I do not see that one could possibly imagine that his normal handwriting (if there was such a thing) could be "good." I would say that the evidence shows that his handwriting was either "fair" (I would prefer "poor") or nonexistent. But it is possible that these are the signatures of a clerk. If one focuses on the Blackfriars documents, one might generously concede that his writing may have been good.

On the other hand, if Stratford had been the Author, then he had penned thousands of lines, and I would expect his handwriting to be at least "good," and more likely "excellent."

If the author was either Oxford or Ignotus, there is a slim chance that Stratford had developed a reasonable writing style at school—if he went to school, which I consider problematical—but I consider it more likely that either he was illiterate, or that his handwriting was labored and poor.

Chart 7, Scene 12: Stratford's Writing	Evidence Analysis	Stratford No-Compact Theory	Oxford Compact Theory	Ignotus Compact Theory
Claudia				
S1: Stratford's handwriting was excellent	0	5	0	0
S2: Stratford's handwriting was good	1	1	5	5
S3: Stratford's handwriting was fair	10	0	10	10
S4: Stratford could not write	10	0	10	10
Post Probabilities		0.02	0.49	0.49

MARTIN. Beatrice's and Claudia's probabilities convert to the following Degrees of Belief:

for Beatrice,

DB(Stratford) = –5 db

DB(Oxford) = –2 db

DB(Ignotus) = –2 db

and for Claudia,

DB(Stratford) = –17 db

DB(Oxford) = 0 db

DB(Ignotus) = 0 db

These are shown in Figure 13

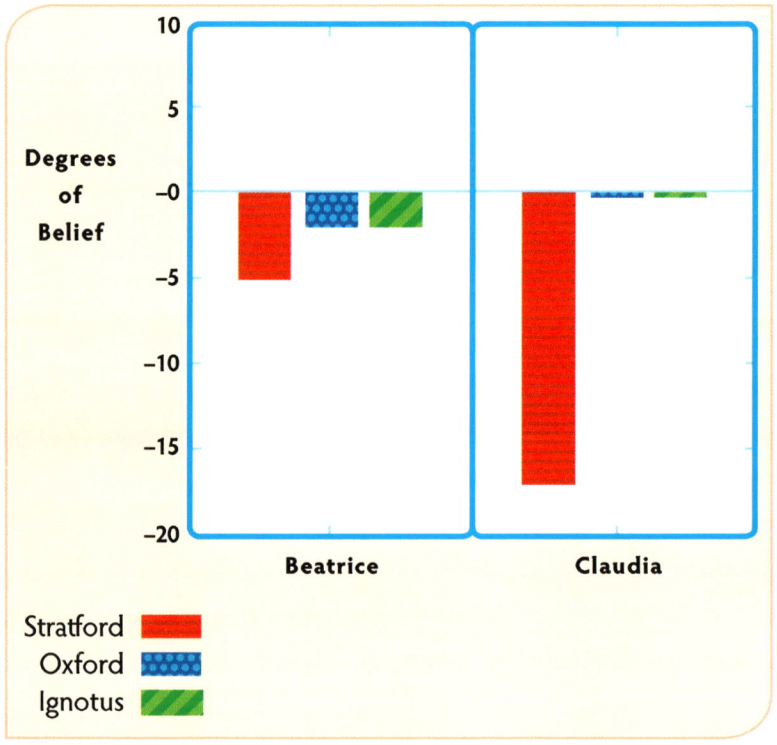

Figure 13. Degrees of Belief for Beatrice and Claudia, based on Chart 7.

JAMES. Here are the running probabilities so far:

Running Probabilities, based on Charts 1 to 7,

for Beatrice,

RP(Stratford) = $2\ 10^{-8}$

RP(Oxford) = 0.92

RP(Ignotus) = 0.08

and for Claudia,

$$RP(\text{Stratford}) = 1.5 \ 10^{-14}$$

$$RP(\text{Oxford}) = 0.995$$

$$RP(\text{Ignotus}) = 0.005$$

Expressed in terms of Degrees of Belief, these become:

Running Degrees of Belief, based on Charts 1 to 6,

for Beatrice,

$$RDB(\text{Stratford}) = -78 \text{ db}$$

$$RDB(\text{Oxford}) = 11 \text{ db}$$

$$RDB(\text{Ignotus}) = -11 \text{ db}$$

and for Claudia,

$$RDB(\text{Stratford}) = -138 \text{ db}$$

$$RDB(\text{Oxford}) = 123 \text{ db}$$

$$RDB(\text{Ignotus}) = -23 \text{ db}$$

The trends of the Running Degrees of Belief are shown in Figure 14.

But right now, I see it is five o-clock—a good time to adjourn. And I gather that Martin is now taking us all to the Cliff-Top Café. Thank you, Martin. It should be a wonderful view.

Tomorrow, back to our *Hacienda!*

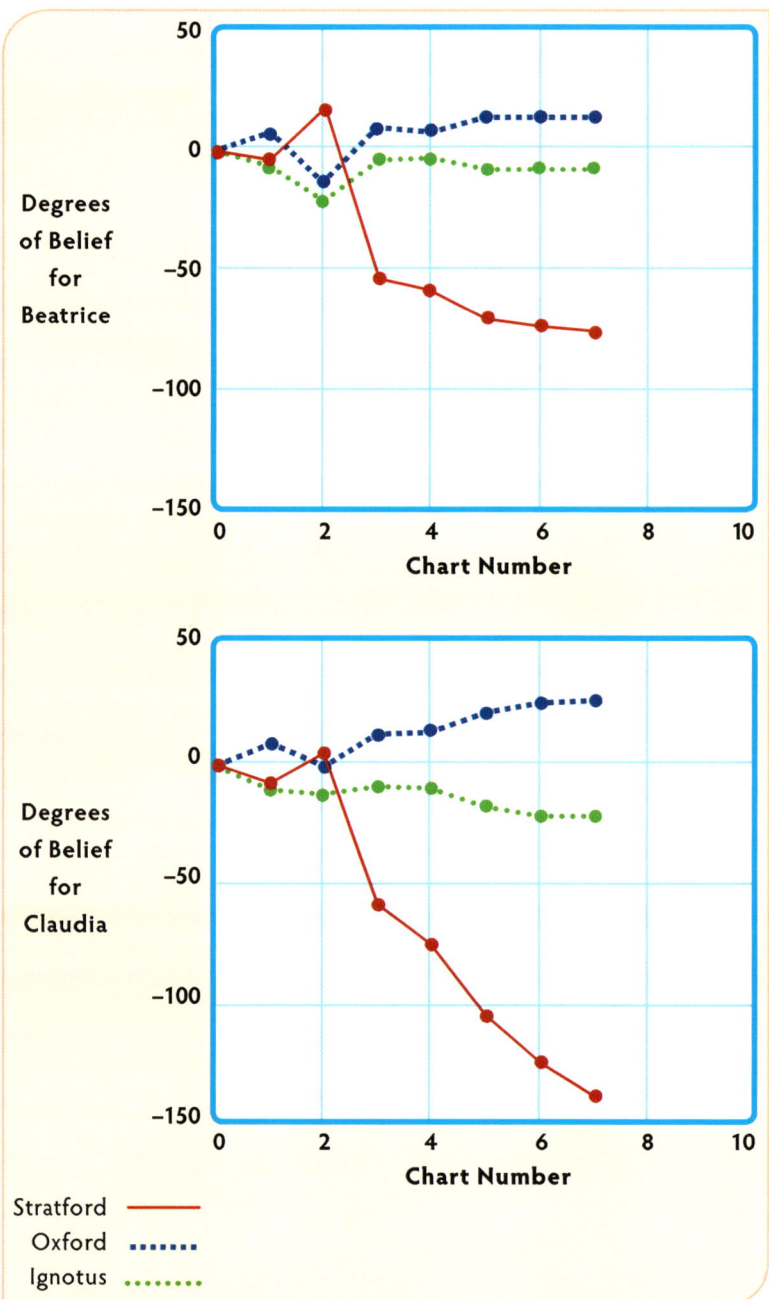

Figure 14. Running Degrees of Belief for Beatrice and Claudia, based on Charts 1 through 7.

NOTES

1. Durning-Lawrence (1910).
2. Michell (1996), p. 99.
3. Michell (1996), p. 100.

Reader's Chart

The reader is invited to enter his or her own estimates of the weights in the following chart:

Chart 7, Scene 12: Stratford's Writing	Evidence Analysis	Stratford No-Compact Theory	Oxford Compact Theory	Ignotus Compact Theory
Reader: Date:				
S1: Stratford's handwriting was excellent				
S2: Stratford's handwriting was good				
S3: Stratford's handwriting was fair				
S4: Stratford could not write				
Post Probabilities				

SCENE 13

The Deck at the *Hacienda*

The Tempest

In a Teapot?

JAMES. With the tide running so strongly against Stratford, I think we have to ask whether we have somehow—quite unwittingly—been unfair to him. Beatrice remarked early on that she has three strong pieces of evidence in his favor, and I think we need to look into those items. However, I remember that when I read Bryson's book, he claimed to be able to demolish Oxford's candidacy, so I suggest that we examine Bryson's claim.

MARTIN. Can you refresh our memory and remind us of his argument?

BEATRICE. As I recall, it had to do with the dating of *The Tempest,* which I gather is usually considered to have been written in 1610 or 1611 [1].

JAMES. Precisely. I'll read Bryson's argument against Oxford:

> . . . *the most troubling weakness of the Oxford argument is that Edward de Vere incontestably died in 1604, when many of Shakespeare's plays had not yet appeared—indeed in some cases could not have been written, since they were influenced by later events. The Tempest, notably, was inspired by an*

account of a shipwreck on Bermuda written by one William
Strachey in 1609. [2]

Beatrice, can you explain these points to us? What makes Bryson think that *The Tempest* was inspired by the Bermuda shipwreck?

BEATRICE. There are two lines of argument. One is that the account of the shipwreck, at the beginning of *The Tempest*, is strongly reminiscent of an account of the wreck of the *Sea Venture* that occurred on the island of Bermuda on July 25th, 1609. William Strachey described that event in a long letter, dated July 15, 1610 (not 1609, as Bryson stated) to an unnamed *Excellent Lady*. His account reads in part as follows: [3]

> *Sir George Summers being upon the watch, had an appari-*
> *tion of a little round light, like a faint Starre, trembling, and*
> *streaming along with a sparkeling blaze, halfe the height*
> *upon the Maine Mast, and shooting sometimes from Shroud*
> *to Shroud, tempting to settle as it were upon any of the foure*
> *Shroudes: and for three or foure houres together, or rather*
> *more, halfe the night it kept with us, running sometimes*
> *along the Maine-yard to the very end, and then returning.*

I find this remarkably similar to the account of the storm that opens *The Tempest*.

CLAUDIA. Although Strachey's letter was written in 1610, I understand that it was not actually published (by Samuel Purchas, who had acquired it from Richard Hakluyt) until 1625, by which time William Shakspere also had passed away (in 1616) [4]. But even if Stratford had somehow secured access to a letter to *an Excellent Lady*, it is not easy to relate that to a play written well before 1625.

Furthermore, this is not the only description of a shipwreck to have been written before Oxford expired in 1604. A book by Richard Hakluyt published in 1600 [5], contains two quite similar accounts:

One reads:

And straightaway we saw upon the shrouds of the Trinity as it were a candle, which of itself shined, and gave a light . . . which appeared on the shrouds.

The other reads:

In the night, there came upon the top of our mainyard and main mast, a certain little light, much like unto the light of a little candle. . . . This light continued aboard our ship about three hours, flying from mast to mast, and from top to top: and sometimes it would be in two or three places at once. [6]

I do not see that we should assume that Shake*Speare had to have read Strachey's letter before writing *The Tempest*. Furthermore, we would need to explain how William knew the contents of a letter that was not published until nine years after he himself passed away.

BEATRICE. But there is another point. I am impressed by a line in the *The Tempest* that refers specifically to Bermuda.

CLAUDIA. Not exactly, Beatrice. If I recall correctly, Ariel—in a little speech to Prospero—says *Thou call'dst me up at midnight to fetch dew from the still-vex'd Bermoothes*. But according to one editor of *The Tempest*, *The Bermudas* (and variations of that spelling) *was also a section of London* (one notorious for harboring thieves and prostitutes) [7]. This suggests that Prospero may simply have instructed Ariel to bring him a little liquid refreshment from a part of London where he knew it to be readily available.

This may be a speculative reading of Ariel's line, but it is not an impossible reading. In the rest of *The Tempest*—as I recall—one is left with the impression that the action takes place somewhere between Naples and North Africa—a few thousand miles from Bermuda.

Anyway, I am reminded of a performance of *The Mikado* a few years ago in San Francisco. The Mikado has the wonderful song "*My object all sublime, . . .*" but this performance included the following verse:

> *The idiot who, in railway carriages,*
> *Scribbles on window-panes,*
> *We only suffer*
> *To ride on a buffer*
> *In Bay Area Rapid Trains.*

It got a good laugh. We laughed much more than we would have done to William Gilbert's original line about "*parliamentary trains.*"

What does this prove? That the lines you read or hear are not necessarily the lines that were originally written by the author!

There is no way of knowing whether the line about "*bringing dew from the Bermoothes*" was written by the original author of *The Tempest* (if there ever was just one author), or whether it was a topical interpolation in the original text by a humorous actor or director.

MARTIN. I am getting the impression that Bryson's argument is not as watertight as he would have us believe. But I have drawn up a chart, so you can both express your opinions on this argument.

BEATRICE. Here are my figures. I still feel that there is sufficient similarity between events described in *The Tempest* and what was probably common knowledge about the wreck of the *Sea Venture* to persuade me that the writer (whoever he was) had heard some details of the event. If the writer was Stratford, he was no doubt fully conversant with news of the day. On the other hand, Oxford died in 1604, so he was in no position to include details of that event in *The Tempest*. Concerning Ignotus, we have no idea. So here are my uneducated guesses on this matter, with thanks to Martin for his prompt calculations:

Chart 8, Scene 13: *The Tempest*	Evidence Analysis	Stratford No-Compact Theory	Oxford Compact Theory	Ignotus Compact Theory
Beatrice				
S1: The Tempest is based upon an event that occurred in Bermuda in 1604	20	20	0	1
S2: The Tempest is not based upon an event that occurred in Bermuda in 1604	1	1	1	1
Post Probabilities		0.63	0.03	0.34

MARTIN. But I have to remind you, Beatrice, that our hypothesis is *Oxford–Compact*.

We have agreed that this hypothesis allows for the possibility of a *compact*, which covers the possibility that he had assistants and colleagues who were occasionally co-authors.

JAMES. Yes, we know that Oxford at one time supported a group of writers. In fact, some Shakespearian scholars detect, in some plays, evidence of co-authors, including John Fletcher, Thomas Middleton, Thomas Nashe, George Peele, and George Wilkins. So our hypothesis allows for the possibility that *The Tempest* was written—completely or partially—by one of Oxford's associates. There is surely some possibility that *The Tempest* was a product of the Oxford school, but not written specifically by Oxford himself.

BEATRICE. Possible, perhaps, but not likely in my opinion. I'll make a slight revision in my chart:

Chart 8, Scene 13: *The Tempest*	Evidence Analysis	Stratford No-Compact Theory	Oxford Compact Theory	Ignotus Compact Theory
Beatrice				
S1: *The Tempest* is based upon an event that occurred in Bermuda in 1604	20	20	1	1
S2: *The Tempest* is not based upon an event that occurred in Bermuda in 1604	1	1	100	1
Post Probabilities		0.62	0.04	0.34

I see that my change makes hardly any difference to the final probabilities. And I see that, in my opinion, the evidence does favor Stratford, but not as strongly as I had expected.

MARTIN. The reason that Stratford does not fare as well as might have been expected is that we are taking Ignotus into account. If we were to take the view that it was just as unlikely for Ignotus as we suspect it was for Oxford—or his consortium—to have written about Bermuda, the probability for Stratford would have bumped up to 0.93, and Oxford and Ignotus would each have been left with a probability of only 0.03. However, that would have run against our rule that we are supremely ignorant concerning Ignotus.

This is a great example of the merit of working with a complete set of hypotheses. Had we incorrectly limited our choice to just Stratford and Oxford, the evidence against Oxford would have translated directly into evidence for Stratford. But since we have prudently agreed to allow for a third (ignorance) possibility, evidence against Oxford translates into evidence that must be shared between Stratford and Ignotus, which means that it is not very strong evidence for either.

But what are your thoughts, Claudia?

CLAUDIA. Personally, I find the evidence linking *The Tempest* to the demise of the *Sea Venture* to be pretty weak. Shipwrecks were not all that uncommon. Oddly enough, a ship owned by Oxford was wrecked in the Bermudas. Also, although *The Tempest* opens with what we expect to be a shipwreck, the wreck does not happen—according to Ariel, the King's ship arrived *"safely in harbor."* Moreover, the scene of the play is the Mediterranean, not the Atlantic. In the opening act, Ariel claimed to have dispersed *"the rest o' the fleet,"* which he last saw *"upon the Mediterranean flote, bound sadly home for Naples."*

However, I would allow a 50–50 chance for such a connection. I would also allow that, had Stratford been Shake*Speare, there may have been a 50–50 chance that he would have heard about the shipwreck, which was probably a topic of conversation in the ale-houses of London, when the news finally arrived there. But remember that William was spending a lot of time—maybe most of his time—in Stratford. For 1604, in particular, we know that he carried out several sales of malt to his fellow citizens in Stratford [8].

I think it reasonable to allow for a small chance that *The Tempest* was written (or at any rate finished) by one of Oxford's associates. This leads me to the following set of figures:

Chart 8, Scene 13: The Tempest	Evidence Analysis	Stratford No-Compact Theory	Oxford Compact Theory	Ignotus Compact Theory
Claudia				
S1: The Tempest is based upon an event that occurred in Bermuda in 1604	1	1	1	1
S2: The Tempest is not based upon an event that occurred in Bermuda in 1604	1	1	10	1
Post Probabilities		0.36	0.28	0.36

Thank you, Martin, for you prompt calculations. This looks pretty inconclusive, to me.

MARTIN. What are your sage thoughts, James?

JAMES. I have done a little reading on this topic, but I find it all very confusing. The view that *The Tempest* was based on Strachey's shipwreck report was apparently first proposed by Edmund Malone, who lived from 1741 to 1812. However, Joseph Hunter, who lived from 1783 to 1861, pointed out similarities between lines in *The Tempest* and lines in a report by Sir Walter Raleigh, written in 1596, concerning an expedition to Guiana. Hunter also finds similarities between *The Tempest* and an epic entitled *Orlando Furioso* by Lodovico Ariosto, first published in 1516 [8].

The trouble is that much of this debate is centered on the assumption that Shake*Speare was Stratford. It is my view that this kind of discussion is of little use if we are trying to decide impartially between Stratford and other possible writers.

MARTIN. So where does all this leave you, James?

JAMES. I agree with Beatrice that the evidence—such as it is— tends to favor Stratford. But I also agree with Claudia in that I find the evidence quite inconclusive.

If this is the best evidence that Bryson has to offer, he finds me a disappointed reader. I am left with the strong opinion that this kind of topic is one that we should try to avoid. It would probably be extremely time-consuming, and it might well end up being extremely inconclusive.

Beatrice's and Claudia's probabilities convert to the following Degrees of Belief:

for Beatrice,

DB(Stratford) = 2 db

DB(Oxford) = –14 db

DB(Ignotus) = –3 db

and for Claudia,

DB(Stratford) = –2 db

DB(Oxford) = –4 db

DB(Ignotus) = –2 db

These are shown in Figure 15.

And here are the running probabilities so far:

Running Probabilities, based on Charts 1 to 8,

for Beatrice,

RP(Stratford) = 2 10^{-7}

RP(Oxford) = 0.58

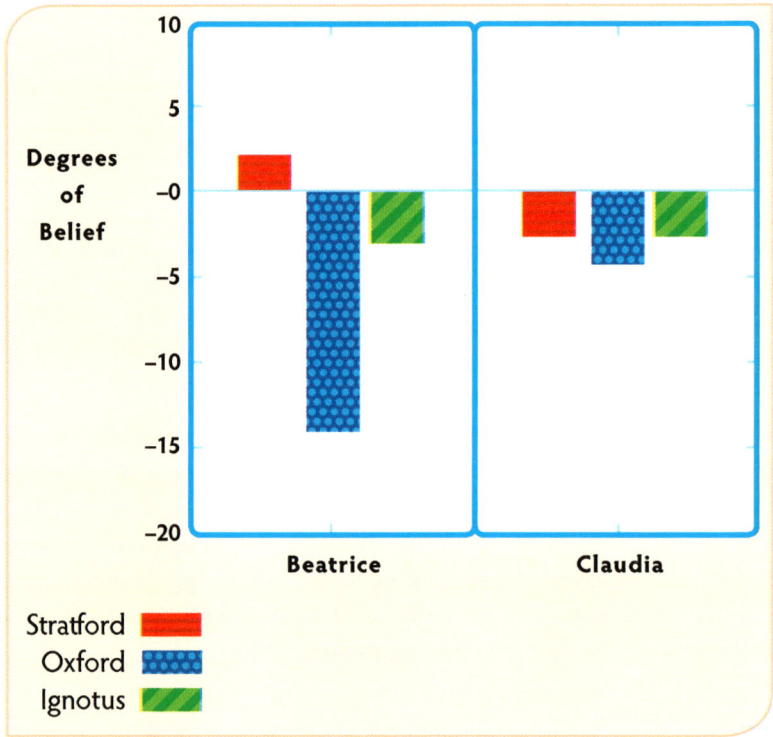

Figure 15. Degrees of Belief for Beatrice and Claudia, based on Chart 8.

$$RP(Ignotus) = 0.42$$

and for Claudia,

$$RP(Stratford) = 2 \cdot 10^{-14}$$

$$RP(Oxford) = 0.99$$

$$RP(Ignotus) = 0.06$$

Expressed in Degrees of Belief, these become:

Running Degrees of Belief, based on Charts 1 to 8,

for Beatrice,

RDB(Stratford) = –67 db

RDB(Oxford) = 1 db

RDB(Ignotus) = –1 db

and for Claudia,

RDB(Stratford) = –137 db

RDB(Oxford) = 22 db

RDB(Ignotus) = –22 db

The trends of the Running Degrees of Belief are shown in Figure 16.

I suggest we adjourn for today. Let us hope that our next project has somewhat more substantial evidentiary impact!

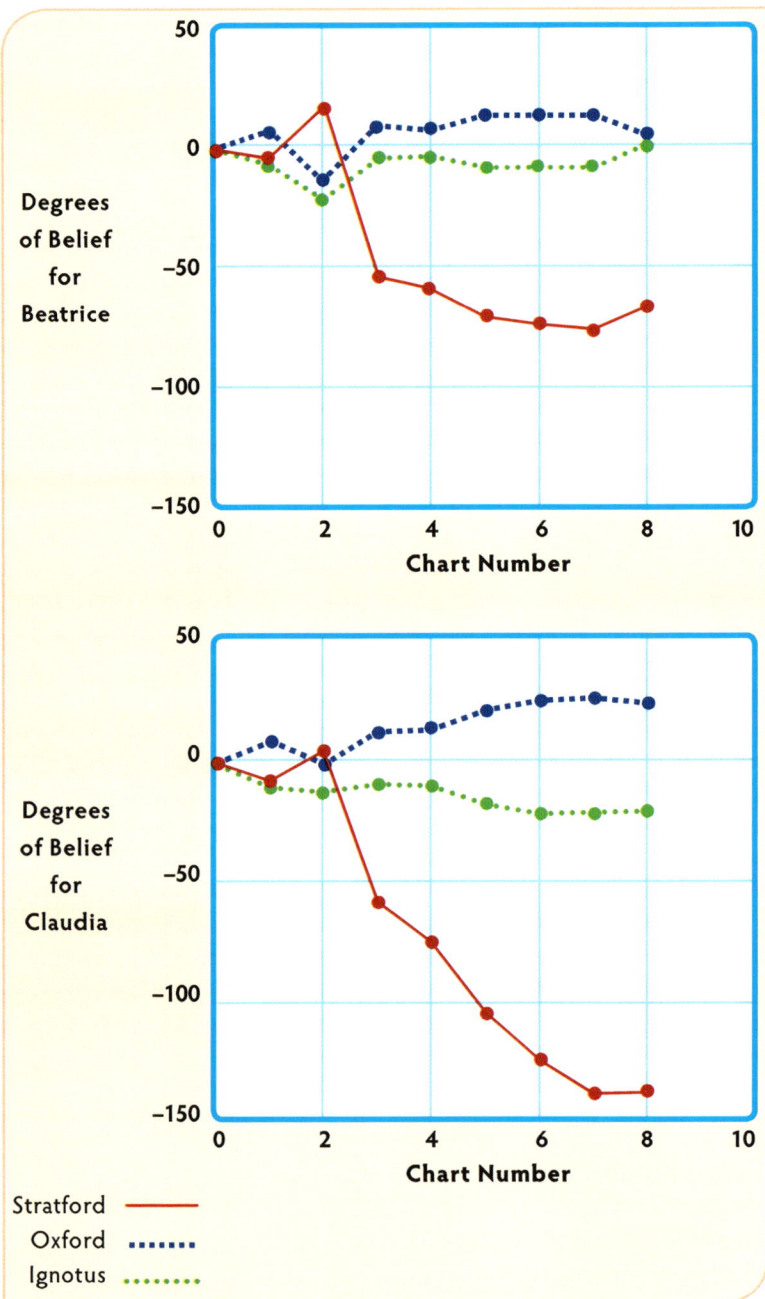

Figure 16. Running Degrees of Belief for Beatrice and Claudia, based on Charts 1 through 8.

NOTES

1. Price (2001), 281.

2. Bryson (2007), 190.

3. Roper (2008), 297.

4. Roper (2008), 298.

5. Hakluyt (1600).

6. Roper (2008), 194.

7. Price (2001), 34.

8. Price (2001), 284.

Reader's Chart

The reader is invited to enter his or her own estimates of the weights in the following chart:

Chart 8, Scene 13: *The Tempest*	Evidence Analysis	Stratford No-Compact Theory	Oxford Compact Theory	Ignotus Compact Theory
Reader: Date:				
S1: *The Tempest* is based upon an event that occurred in Bermuda in 1604				
S2: *The Tempest* is not based upon an event that occurred in Bermuda in 1604				
Post Probabilities				

The Deck at the *Hacienda*

The Monument to Shakspere in the Holy Trinity Church at Stratford-upon-Avon [1]

Who is trying to tell what to whom, and why?

JAMES. As I recall, Beatrice once said that there are three items of evidence that she considers conclusive—or virtually conclusive—evidence that the author was indeed Stratford. As I recall, one of these is the inscription on the monument to Shakespeare in the Church of the Holy Trinity in Stratford-upon-Avon; the second is the dedicatory material in the First Folio; and the third is the title page of "Shake-speares Sonnets." I suggest that we take each of these in turn. If each case proves to be simple, we may get through them in three sessions. However, I believe that we shall be dealing with the tricky question of whether or not each of these documents should be taken at face value. So whether or not we can cope with each item in just one meeting remains to be seen.[1]

Beatrice—Will you introduce us to the Shakespeare Monument?

BEATRICE. "William Shakspere" died on April 23, 1616, according to the "Old Style" of dating (Julian Calendar) in use at that time. According to the "New Style" calendar now in use (Gregorian Calendar), the date was May 3. The Church Register notation of

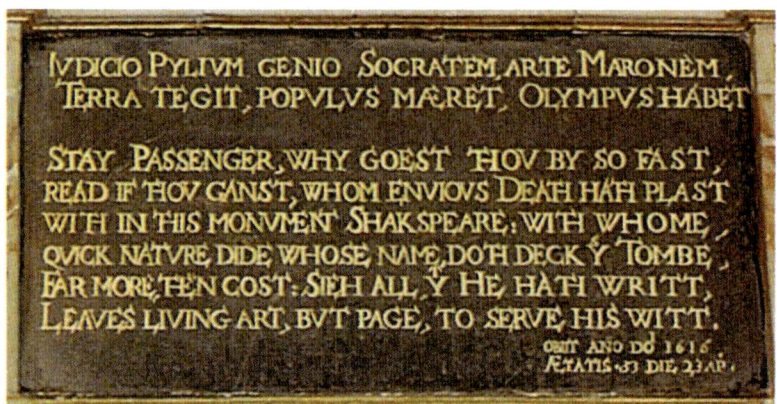

Plate 6. The Inscription on the monument in Holy Trinity Church at Stratford-upon-Avon. [http://en.wikipedia.org/wiki/File:Shakespeare_monument_ plaque.JPG]

the burial reads "April 25 Will. Shakspere gent" [2]. Shakspere is believed to have been buried in the chancel of Holy Trinity Church, but we do not know exactly where, since he was buried in an unmarked grave. The monument of Shakspere is mounted on the wall of the chancel. We do not know when it was put in place, but it was referred to in a collection of "Shakespeare" plays in 1623.

It is the epitaph on the monument that is significant. It is shown in Plate 6.

In modern script, it reads:

JVDICIO PYLIVM. GENIO SOCRATEM, ARTE MARONEM,
TERRA TEGIT, POPULVS MAERET, OLYMPUS HABET.

STAY PASSENGER, WHY GOEST THOV BY SO FAST,
READ IF THOV CANST, WHOM ENVIOVS DEATH HATH PLAST,
WITH IN THIS MONVMENT SHAKSPEARE: WITH WHOME,
QVICK NATVRE DIDE: WHOSE NAME DOTH DECK YS [THIS] TOMBE,
FAR MORE, THEN COST: SIEH ALL, YT [THAT] HE HATH WRITT,
LEAVES LIVING ART, BVT PAGE, TO SERVE HIS WITT.

OBIT ANO DO' 1616
AETATIS 53 DIE 23 AP.

However, note that in the second line, "AE" in "MAERET" appears as the single letter "Æ" [3].

The translation from the Latin of the first two lines is

*"In judgment a Nestor, in intellect a Socrates, in art a Virgil;
the earth encloses, the people mourn, and Olympus holds."*

The last two lines, also in Latin, give the date of death and Shakspere's age at death (53):

Replacing "v" by "u" as necessary, "Ys" by "this," and "Yt" by "that," the English text reads as follows:

Stay passenger, why goest thou by so fast?
Read if thou canst, whom envious death hath plast,
With in this monument Shakspeare: with whome,
Quick nature dide: whose name doth deck this tombe,
Far more, then cost: sieh all, that he hath writt,
Leaves living art, but page, to serve his witt.

(There was no letter "U" in those days.)

In my humble opinion, this inscription unambiguously identifies the person there buried as the author "Shakespeare" (or in our notation "Shake*Speare"), even if the spelling is not quite right. The way a name was spelled was not particularly important in those days. For instance, Christopher Marlowe was baptized as "Marlow," but used the spelling "Marley" in his only surviving signature. Even on the title pages of his plays and poems, we find a variety of spellings: "Marlow," "Marloe," and "Marlo" [4]. So I do not think it is particularly significant that the spelling on this inscription was not the same as that on the Shakespeare poems.

JAMES. I have done a little reading on this topic, in preparation for today's session, and I gather there are a few puzzles concerning the monument. Although the present version shows Shakspere—appropriately enough—with quill in hand, the original version showed him with both hands on a woolsack, which seems more

Plate 7. An engraving of the Stratford monument by Wenceslaus Hollar, based on Dugdale's sketch, which appeared in *Antiquities of Warwickshire* by Sir William Dugdale in 1656. The subject appears to be holding a woolsack, which would be more appropriate for a merchant than a writer.

appropriate for an owner of tithes and dealer in barley than for a famous playwright.

CLAUDIA. There are also some puzzling features of the inscription:

> The word that is spelled "WHOM" in line 2 is spelled "WHOME" in line 3.
>
> "THIS" is written in full in line 3, but abbreviated to "Y^S" in line 4.
>
> Why use the German word "SIEH" in line 5, rather than the English "SEE"?

Why "WRITT," rather than the usual "WRIT"?

It is also a little odd that the name is spelled "SHAKSPEARE," when the poems and plays were always attributed to "SHAKESPEARE." But Beatrice is quite right that spelling was very much a matter of taste in Elizabethan times.

Either the author of this inscription was remarkably careless (but he knew his Latin), or there is more to this inscription than meets the eye—which is of course suggested by the words "READ IF THOV CANST."

BEATRICE. I hope you are not going to start looking for hidden messages, and all of that nonsense. I gather there are hidden messages proving that Shakespeare was Bacon. There are probably other hidden messages proving he was Jonson. I gather it is fashionable today to find hidden messages proving that Shakespeare was the Earl of Oxford!

CLAUDIA. Careful, Beatrice—We are supposed to be reviewing the evidence without prejudice. This inscription may, for you, constitute the simple message that William Shakspere (aka Stratford) was the immortal Shake*Speare, but I find the inscription sufficiently puzzling that I rather suspect there is more to it than meets the eye. I am not sure how we should proceed at this point. We can either evaluate the inscription on the assumption that "What you see is what you get," or we can suspend judgment until we decide whether or not the inscription should be accepted at face value. If we adopt the former, we are prejudging the latter. If we adopt the latter, we are discrediting any information to be obtained by the former.

What do you recommend, Martin?

MARTIN. The safest procedure would be to first determine whether or not there is a hidden message or

Plate 8. The present appearance of the Stratford monument, which was repaired in 1748–1749. The monument went through a metamorphosis: The subject now holds paper and a quill. Since there is no record of any sketch or portrait of William Shakspere made during his lifetime, there is no reason to believe that this depiction bears any relationship to the person it is intended to represent. [Chiljan, 2011, Plate 15]

some other reason to withhold judgment, and then—depending on the outcome—to decide either to review the inscription, taking it at face value, or not to review it. But the very procedure of looking for hidden connotations will—fairly or unfairly—prejudice an unbiased assessment of the inscription, assumed modest and honest.

My recommendation is that we proceed in two steps. First, we evaluate the inscription in a matter-of-fact way (assuming there is no hidden message), trying to decide whether it is a straightforward (although possibly clumsy) composition, and, if it is, what we can learn from it. Second, we carefully inspect the inscription, with any cryptological procedures we may need, to find out whether or not there is a hidden message and, if there is, just what the message may be.

The worst that can happen is that the two procedures yield equal and opposite results that more or less cancel out. But if this were to happen, I would be inclined to say that neither evaluation was worth much, anyway.

JAMES. This may not be a perfect solution, but I think it is a conservative one. It would be hard for anyone to call "foul" if we accept Martin's advice. So unless Claudia has an objection (thank you, Claudia, I see that you do not), I think the ball is back in Beatrice's court. Without any statistical or cryptological analyses, Beatrice, what do you see in the inscription?

BEATRICE. In my naïve opinion, the inscription says quite simply that the monument contains the remains of the great poet and playwright Shake*Speare. It goes on to recommend that the passer-by take time to read and appreciate all that Shake*Speare had written. I admit that the wording is somewhat awkward, and some of the spelling is rather peculiar, but we do not know who composed the inscription. He or she may not have been much of a writer.

JAMES. Thank you, Beatrice—So far, so good. However, if we are to draw any conclusions, and if we are to relate these conclusions to the Authorship Question, we need to concoct a chart with two or more statements. What do you suggest?

BEATRICE. Here is my suggestion:

Chart 9, Scene 14: Monument Inscription	Evidence Analysis	Stratford No-Compact Theory	Oxford Compact Theory	Ignotus Compact Theory
S1: The Inscription identifies Stratford as Shake*Speare				
S2: The Inscription does not identify Stratford as Shake*Speare				
Post Probabilities				

MARTIN. That seems a very reasonable proposal. How would you fill in the blanks?

BEATRICE. Like this

Chart 9, Scene 14: Monument Inscription	Evidence Analysis	Stratford No-Compact Theory	Oxford Compact Theory	Ignotus Compact Theory
Beatrice				
S1: The Inscription identifies Stratford as Shake*Speare	50	1	0	0
S2: The Inscription does not identify Stratford as Shake*Speare	1	0	1	1
Post Probabilities		0.98	0.01	0.01

MARTIN. Now it is your turn, Claudia.

CLAUDIA. I find this quite difficult. I am supposed to take the inscription at face value, on the assumption that there is no hidden message. However, the inscription is so convoluted, that I am left wondering what the author of the inscription was trying to say. The phrase "Read, If Thou Canst," reads to me like a tip-off that we should not take the inscription at face value. And then there are the curious features that I pointed out earlier: "Whom" in line 2, but "Whome" in line 3, etc. The author is NOT saying "Here lies the famous poet and playwright William Shakespeare who was born and died in this town of Stratford-upon-Avon." Nothing so simple and direct. Even in the absence of a hidden message I am led to suspect that the author of the inscription is purposefully planting seeds of doubt in the mind of the reader.

To sum up—I would not place odds of more than two to one that the author of this inscription wishes us to believe that the monument refers to Shake*Speare. Otherwise, I agree with Beatrice.

So here is my chart

Chart 9, Scene 14: Monument Inscription	Evidence Analysis	Stratford No-Compact Theory	Oxford Compact Theory	Ignotus Compact Theory
Claudia				
The Inscription identifies Stratford as Shake*Speare	2	1	0	0
The Inscription does not identify Stratford as Shake*Speare	1	0	1	1
Post Probabilities		0.66	0.17	0.17

A plus for Stratford—but a small one.

JAMES. I find that Beatrice's and Claudia's probabilities convert to the following Degrees of Belief:

for Beatrice,

DB(Stratford) = 17 db

DB(Oxford) = –20 db

DB(Ignotus) = –20 db

and for Claudia,

DB(Stratford) = 3 db

DB(Oxford) = –7 db

DB(Ignotus) = –7 db

These are shown in Figure 17.

And here are the running probabilities so far:

Running Probabilities, based on Charts 1 to 9,

for Beatrice,

RP(Stratford) = $2 \ 10^{-5}$

RP(Oxford) = 0.58

RP(Ignotus) = 0.42

and for Claudia,

RP(Stratford) = $8 \ 10^{-14}$

RP(Oxford) = 0.994

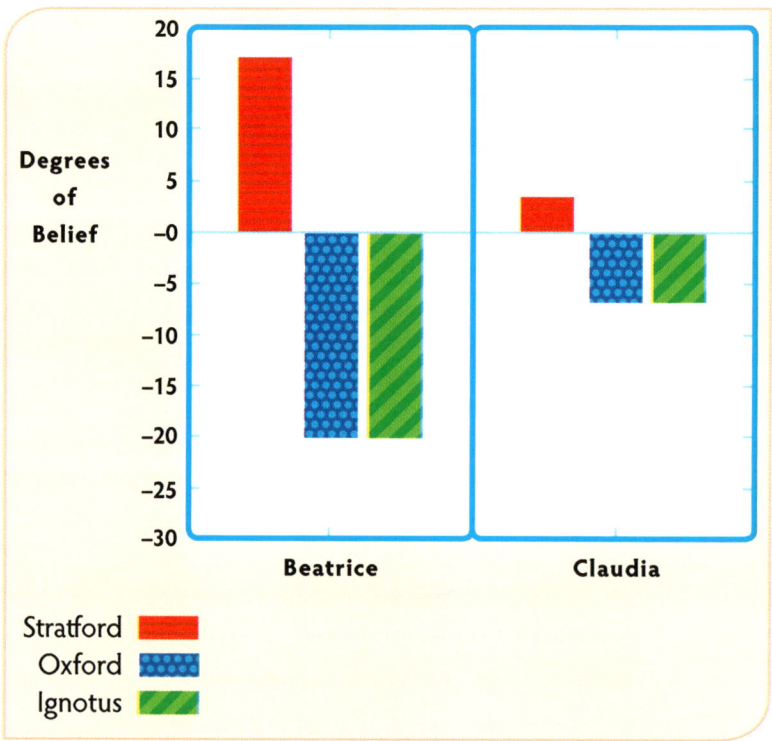

Figure 17. Degrees of Belief for Beatrice and Claudia, based on Chart 9.

$$RP(Ignotus) = 0.006$$

Expressed in terms of Degrees of Belief, these become:

Running Degrees of Belief, based on Charts 1 to 9, for Beatrice,

$$RDB(Stratford) = -47 \text{ db}$$

$$RDB(Oxford) = 1 \text{ db}$$

$$RDB(Ignotus) = -1 \text{ db}$$

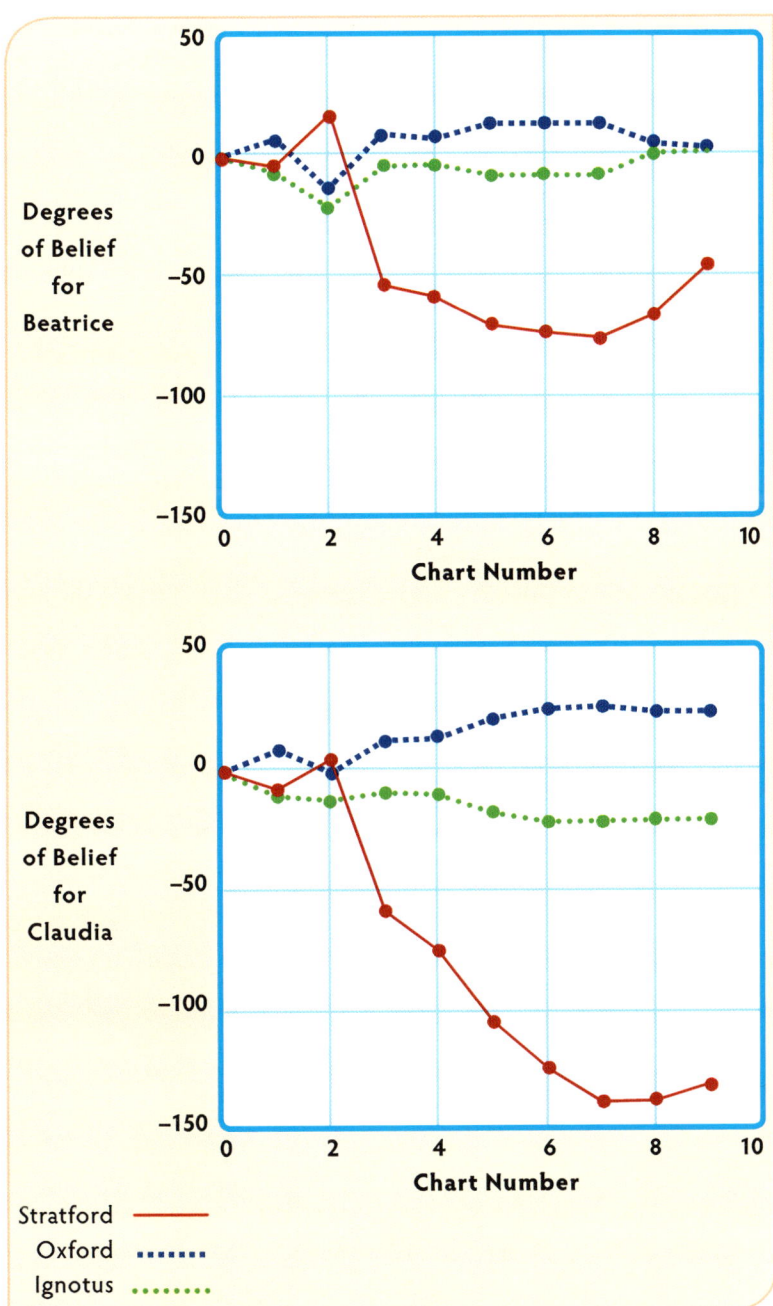

Figure 18. Running Degrees of Belief for Beatrice and Claudia, based on Charts 1 through 9.

and for Claudia,

RDB(Stratford) = –131 db

RDB(Oxford) = 22 db

RDB(Ignotus) = –22 db

The trends of the Running Degrees of Belief are shown in Figure 18.

The next step will be to decide whether or not there is a hidden message in the inscription. What do you advise now, Martin?

MARTIN. I would like a day or two to think over this problem, and prepare for our next session. Hopefully, I can find a fairly simple way for us to arrive at a probability that the inscription contains—or does not contain—a hidden message.

JAMES. That seems fair enough. We can take the weekend off, and be ready for our next challenge on Monday.

BEATRICE. That seems a sensible decision. The French have a word for it—*reculer pour mieux sauter*. We can spend the weekend in retreat—and then see how far we can jump on Monday.

NOTES

1. This discussion of the inscription to the Stratford Monument draws heavily from the work of Roper (2008).

2. Roper (2008), 467.

3. Of the eight lines comprising the inscription, only the second line has been inset, as if to draw attention to that particular line. Bruce Spittle has pointed out that the number of letters in that line is 34, suggesting the appropriate key. By ending the line with *Olympus*, the home of Jupiter, instead of *Parnassus*,

dedicated to Poetry and the home of the Muses, and only by spelling "Maeret" as "Mæret," does the letter count along that inset line comes to exactly 34.

4. http://www2.prestel.co.uk/rey/names.htm

Reader's Chart

Chart 9, Scene 14: Monument Inscription	Evidence Analysis	Stratford No-Compact Theory	Oxford Compact Theory	Ignotus Compact Theory
Reader: Date:				
S1: The Inscription identifies Stratford as Shake*Speare				
S2: The Inscription does not identify Shakspere as Shake*Speare				
Post Probabilities				

James' Study at the *Hacienda*

A Closer Look at the Inscription on the Stratford Monument [1]

An Introduction to Cryptology

JAMES. Since today's meeting may need all of our attention, I thought it would be more convenient to meet around my conference table. Not that I have many conferences these days, since I have unburdened myself of most of my business commitments. I also thought that we should meet in the morning, over coffee, rather than in the afternoon with a glass of wine.

Would you introduce us to our assignment for today, Martin?

MARTIN. You are right, James—today's will not be the simplest of our sessions. We have to discuss whether or not there is a secret message hidden in the inscription on the "Stratford" monument, meaning the inscription on the monument in the Holy Trinity Church in Stratford-upon-Avon, concerning (in our notation) either Stratford or Shake*Speare.

I gather that there have been many claims of encrypted messages in the works of Shake*Speare—not to mention the Bible, the Koran—and probably the Mahabharata, too. I have found that there have been several impressive investigations of this topic in the context of the Authorship debate in recent years—notably by Rollett [2], Roper [3], and Bond [4].

JAMES. I have done a little reading, too. I gather that these investigators have adopted criteria for the significance of a revealed message from a seminal work of the Friedmans.

MARTIN. Yes, William F. and Elizabeth S. Friedman [5] were very highly respected cryptographers. William headed the U.S. Army cryptanalytic bureau that cracked the Japanese Purple Code! According to David Kahn, also a distinguished cryptographer, the Friedmans agreed to accept as valid any cipher that fulfills two conditions: *that its plaintext makes sense, and that this plaintext be unique and unambiguous—that, in other words, it not be one of several possible results* [6].

CLAUDIA. So do you plan to use the Friedmans' criteria in addressing our problem?

MARTIN. I think that would be difficult. Their criteria probably work very well when one is deciphering a long document such as a hidden diplomatic message. However, the inscription on the Shakespeare monument contains only 220 letters. (In later meetings, we shall be dealing with the Dedication to *ShakeSpeare's Sonnettes,* which contains even fewer—only 144—letters.) We can hardly expect an entire, grammatical sentence to be hidden in such a small space. The best we can hope for is a single word, or at most a very few words that may comprise some kind of message.

The other important point is this: It is not enough to know that there is a hidden message. If we find that there is, we shall then need to assess its significance for each of our three candidates.

BEATRICE. So do we throw our hands up, and cede that the evidence is useless, or do you have an alternative procedure that we can use? I suspect the latter.

MARTIN. The BASIN procedure seems to have served us well so far. I suggest that we try to bring it to bear on the *hidden-*

message issue. This has the big advantage that, if it can be applied, the outcome can be combined with the rest of the evidence we have been accumulating.

CLAUDIA. So I guess we shall need to invent an appropriate chart.

JAMES. But before we develop the chart, we shall need to have some idea of the possible techniques that may have been used to secrete a message. Which cryptographic procedure are we to assume would have been used by someone living in Elizabethan times—someone who had a message to give us, and who for some reason wished to give us that message secretly, not overtly? If there is a secret message which is going to identify the author, I guess it must come from either Oxford or Ignotus: If Stratford were Shake*Speare, that would have been something to proclaim from the rooftops, not something to hide. It would not have been information to be shared surreptitiously.

CLAUDIA. A good point, James. We have agreed explicitly to take account of the possibility that either Oxford or Ignotus was involved in a "compact" or "conspiracy." However, according to the ground rules that we have set up, we are assuming that there is no "compact" connected to Stratford. If we do find a hidden message, it may well be compatible with either the Oxford or Ignotus hypothesis, but it would not be compatible with the Stratford hypothesis, as we have posed it.

BEATRICE. But suppose we found a message that reads "I, William Shakspere, have pretended that Edward de Vere has pretended to be me." Would that not be evidence in favor of Stratford?

MARTIN. It would, indeed. However, it would be incompatible with the Stratford hypothesis as we have framed it—one that does not admit the possibility that Stratford himself was involved in a conspiracy. That is why we specify *No-Compact* for the *Stratford* hypothesis.

JAMES. No doubt the BASIN procedure will be useful once we have found something. But how do we go about finding something?

CLAUDIA. I gather that the so-called "Cardano Grill" was used extensively in Elizabethan times.

MARTIN. You are ahead of me, Claudia. Since you have made that suggestion, perhaps you could explain it to James and Beatrice.

CLAUDIA. I'll try. What is called the "Cardano Grill" was invented by Girolamo Cardano in about 1550, and it was certainly widely used in diplomatic circles for hundreds of years after its invention [7]. I have a note of one version of the procedure:

> *Small holes were punched in an irregular pattern in a piece of card, which was used as an overlay on top of a letter. This method allows for reading only single letters at a time, but it can be adapted to use larger holes so that syllables or whole words appear in the window. It is necessary that the sender and the receiver both have copies of the same stencil. The sender constructed what seems like an innocuous message, but arranges that the letters or words revealed by the stencil spells out the important secret message. The receiver could find the secret message by laying his copy of the stencil on the text he has received.*

BEATRICE. So if there is a hidden message in the monument inscription, it can be read only by someone who has been provided with the stencil. That would require the author of the inscription to supply everyone in his target readership with a copy of the grill. That would seem very odd—why not just give them the supposed secret message?

CLAUDIA. An excellent point. Of course, the Secretary of State in France would have sent two messages—by two different couriers—to the French Ambassador at the Court of Queen Elizabeth:

one with the message that needs to be decrypted, and the other with the grill that was necessary for its decryption.

However, someone who was privy to some sensitive information, and who wished to share it with some of his smart fellow writers, might have chosen to make the message available only to readers who were willing to take the trouble to look for it. Then he might use another version of the Cardano Grill.

One such version is what is called the "Equidistant Letter Sequence" or "ELS" procedure. The author of the message would pick a number—say "10" as an example—and then compose an overt message that conceals a covert message. The way to do this is to copy all the letters into a rectangular grid, the width of which is set by the key. So for a key of 10, letters 1 through 10 would run along the top row, then letters 11 through 20 in the second row, and so on. Then the covert message would show up as words read vertically (up or down) in one or more of the columns. I suspect that we shall be dealing with an example of this procedure.

BEATRICE. Let us suppose that, four hundred years ago, we had wandered into the church at Stratford-upon-Avon and come across this inscription. Suppose that, for some reason, we suspected there might be a hidden message. How would we go about testing that idea?

MARTIN. It would be a straightforward procedure. We would begin by arranging the text in many grills of all different sizes and examining each in turn.

JAMES. But Martin, how do you decide what is a sensible range of sizes of these possible grills?

MARTIN. The number of rows should be neither too small nor too large. There are 220 letters in the inscription, so I would tend to consider row widths from, say, 10 up to, say, 44. Since we have 220 letters, this would lead to columns of length 22 down to 5. For fewer than 5 letters, it would be hard to be sure that one is identifying a word or a part of a word. On the other hand, one would not want to have too few columns.

BEATRICE. So we rearrange the text into all these possible grills. Then what exactly do we look for?

MARTIN. Something suspicious. If there is nothing suspicious, we have drawn a blank, and we can move on to the next part of our project. On the other hand, if there is something suspicious, we can draw up what seems like an appropriate chart, and then try to fill in the cells as best we can.

We have agreed to use the BASIN procedure with the goal of arriving at probabilities for our three candidate authors. This has the advantage that we do not need to specify or delimit our search in advance. We shall not be concerned with deciding how likely or unlikely a certain phrase is in absolute terms. We shall simply be comparing the likelihood or unlikelihood of the phrase among our three prospects. Finding that a certain phrase is highly unlikely will be insignificant if the phrase is equally unlikely for all three prospects.

JAMES. I gather that Roper has already been through this exercise. What did he come up with?

MARTIN. Roper found that the grill with a width of 34 letters seems to contain a sensible message. I show in bold letters the text that caught his attention.

If arranged in a certain order, the message reads:

S	T	A	Y	P	A	S	S	E	N	G	E	R	W	H	Y	G	O	E	S	T	T	H	O	V	B	Y	S	O	F	A	S	T	R
E	A	D	I	F	T	H	O	V	C	A	N	S	T	W	H	O	M	E	N	V	I	O	V	S	D	E	A	T	H	H	A	T	H
P	L	A	S	T	W	I	T	H	I	N	T	H	I	S	M	O	N	V	M	E	N	T	S	H	A	K	S	P	E	A	R	E	W
I	T	H	W	H	O	M	E	Q	V	I	C	K	N	A	T	U	R	E	D	I	D	E	W	H	O	S	E	N	A	M	E	D	O
T	H	D	E	C	K	Y	S	T	O	M	B	E	F	A	R	M	O	R	E	T	H	E	N	C	O	S	T	S	I	E	H	A	L
L	Y	T	H	E	H	A	T	H	W	R	I	T	T	L	E	A	V	E	S	L	I	V	I	N	G	A	R	T	B	V	T	P	A
G	E	T	O	S	E	R	V	E	H	I	S	W	I	T	T																		

SO TEST HIM I VOW HE IS EVERE DE AS HE ME I B.

However, combining these words (read vertically) with the word "Shakspeare" (read horizontally), Roper suggests that the message should read as follows:

SO TEST HIM: I VOW HE IS DE VERE AS HE, SHAKSPERE: ME, B.I.

BEATRICE. What on earth are the last four letters supposed to mean?

MARTIN. Roper reads them as the signature of the author of the inscription, whom he identifies as Ben Jonson. There was no letter J at that time, so that Jonson's initials would have been "B.I." If the letters had been entered in the correct order, this would have led to spelling errors in the text of the inscription.

JAMES. I suppose that our next step is to invent some kind of chart for comparing this message with our three hypotheses.

MARTIN. In principle, we could do that. However, it would not be easy to assign probabilities to this sentence on the basis of each of our hypotheses. I suggest that we set ourselves a much more limited task. Instead of considering the likelihood or unlikelihood of finding the complete sentence, I suggest that we focus simply on the sequence EVERE. After all, these are the letters that have special significance for one of our three candidate authors, namely Oxford (Edward de **VERE**). Since we are using such a small part of the total message, any calculation we may make will be very conservative.

CLAUDIA. Do you know where this may lead us?

MARTIN. I have looked into this. To be conservative, I have calculated the probability of finding in one of the grills the 5-letter sequence EVERE. There are three steps to this calculation. We begin by counting the number of times each letter is used in the inscription. With this information, we can calculate the probability of constructing the sequence EVERE from five letters taken at random. This is a very small number. However, we must then calculate how many 5-letter sequences we can find in any of the grills we have constructed. (The details are given in Appendix D.) Taking into account the fact that we may need to read the text upward or downward, we find the probability that the sequence the EVERE occurred by chance is 0.025.

This is not a particularly small number, so this particular exercise is not going to give us any really significant information about the authorship.

JAMES. However, it is going to be instructive for us to complete this calculation.

This may be a good time to take a short break.

NOTES

1. This and the subsequent scenes rely heavily on the work of David Roper [3] and Jonathan Bond [4].

2. Rollett (1999).

3. Roper (2008).

4. Bond (2009).

5. Friedman & Friedman (1957).

6. Roper (2008), 22.

7. Roper (2008), 19.

James' Study at the *Hacienda*

Search for a Hidden Message in the Inscription on the Monument

One man's noise is another man's signal.[1]

JAMES. We have now concluded that the five letters EVERE are unlikely to have turned up by chance in the inscription on the Shakespeare monument. It is not a strong case, but it is worth looking into. It will be interesting to see what impact it has on the case for each of our three candidates.

But I am curious that we need to go further, Martin. Most investigators who look for hidden messages simply computed the probability that the message has appeared by chance. What are the pros and cons of that procedure?

MARTIN. Knowing that a certain message is improbable does not, in itself, tell us what we should conclude. If one is thinking of only one question (Was Shake*Speare Stratford? or Was Shake*Speare Oxford?), one should be able to convert the probability that the message appeared by chance to evidence in favor of, or against, that candidate.

However, we are explicitly considering three different candidates. We need to know the impact of the evidence, from the cryptogram, for each of those possibilities. Luckily, our BASIN procedure gives us a way of doing just that.

JAMES. So I guess that the next step is to draw an appropriate chart. Who would like to volunteer?

CLAUDIA. It seems pretty straightforward. Either those letters were secreted by intent, or they turned up by chance.

Chart 10, Scene 16: Monument—Cryptogram	Evidence Analysis	Stratford No-Compact Theory	Oxford Compact Theory	Ignotus Compact Theory
Claudia				
S1: EVERE was secreted in the inscription	1	0	1	0
S2: EVERE was not secreted in the inscription	0.025	1	25	1
Post Probabilities		0.008	0.98	0.008

I guess that the calculations that Martin carried out give us the entries to the first column. As I recall, there is a probability of only 2.5% that the sequence EVERE turned up by chance.

Now let us think about our candidates. We agreed early on that we are not considering that Stratford was involved in a conspiracy. Anyway, it would make no sense to imagine that the inscription on the monument would inform us, in secret (!), that the author was William Shakspere. So we have to enter a zero for the first option, that EVERE was secreted in the inscription.

It is not so obvious what we should enter for the other two candidates. If Oxford was in fact the Author, but that was supposed to be a secret, it is quite possible that the creator of the inscription would have wished to impart that secret to whomever was sufficiently interested to look for a hidden message. However, there are several ways that he could have used some or all of the name Edward de Vere.

Suppose that there is one chance in five that the author of the inscription wished to indicate that Shake*Speare was Oxford, and suppose there is one chance in five that he would have chosen the particular sequence EVERE. Then there would be one chance in 25 that that sequence would have been secreted in the inscription.

Now suppose that Ignotus was Shake*Speare. In that case, there would seem to be no reason whatever for the creator of the inscription to suggest that Shake*Speare was actually Oxford.

Martin has done the calculations, and we see that the probability for either Stratford or Ignotus is a little less than 1%.

JAMES. Thank you, Claudia. What are your thoughts, Beatrice?

BEATRICE. I would like to allow for the possibility that Stratford entered that sequence of letters in the inscription. However, I have been instructed that that is not allowed. That would imply that Stratford was involved in some kind of conspiracy, and we have ruled that out of order. Even if we had not made that rule, I cannot imagine that Stratford would wish to drop a hint that Shake*Speare was actually Oxford. For both reasons, I have to agree with Claudia concerning the inscription on the Stratford monument.

If I could jump across to the Ignotus column, I cannot imagine why Ignotus—if he were Shake*Speare—would go to the trouble of planting a secret message that pins the glory on Oxford.

However, you really do not know who composed the inscription. Maybe there was a double conspiracy. Maybe Shake*Speare was neither Stratford nor Oxford but some one, or some organization, wishing to mislead anyone who was looking too closely into the secret. So secreting the letters EVERE in a cryptogram that was not too difficult to crack would have been disinformation.

CLAUDIA. Really, Beatrice, I thought that I was the speculative member of our quartet!

BEATRICE. That is the usual situation, but now I am turning the tables on you. However, I must admit that this is a very implausible argument, so I shall assign that possibility only one chance in a million.

JAMES. Now you need to deal only with the Oxford column.

BEATRICE. I follow Claudia's line of thought, but I am not quite as generous. I would guess that there is only one chance in one hundred that the composer of the inscription would secrete the letters EVERE in the text if Oxford were in fact Shake*Speare.

So here are my entries:

Chart 10, Scene 16: Monument—Cryptogram	Evidence Analysis	Stratford No-Compact Theory	Oxford Compact Theory	Ignotus Compact Theory
Beatrice				
S1: EVERE was secreted in the inscription	1	0	1	1
S2: EVERE was not secreted in the inscription	0.025	1	100	10^6
Post Probabilities		0.008	0.98	0.008

JAMES. This is odd, The end result is the same as Claudia's!

MARTIN. Yes, it turns out that the probability for Stratford is pretty insensitive to the entries for Oxford and Ignotus, provided only that there is some possibility of the message being secreted for either the Oxford or Ignotus options.

On the other hand, if we were to enter the same weights in both the Oxford and Ignotus columns, the end result would be unchanged for Stratford, but Oxford and Ignotus would then share the spoils:

Chart 10, Scene 16: Monument— Cryptogram	Evidence Analysis	Stratford No-Compact Theory	Oxford Compact Theory	Ignotus Compact Theory
Martin's Example				
S1: EVERE was secreted in the inscription	1	0	1	1
S2: EVERE was not secreted in the inscription	0.025	1	100	100
Post Probabilities		0.02	0.49	0.49

BEATRICE. Instructive, but not particularly realistic.

MARTIN. I agree. I was simply trying to make a point.

Where does this lead us, in the grand scheme of things, James?

JAMES. I find that Beatrice's and Claudia's probabilities convert to the following Degrees of Belief:

for Beatrice,

DB(Stratford) = –21 db

DB(Oxford) = 17 db

DB(Ignotus) = –21 db

and for Claudia,

$$DB(\text{Stratford}) = -21 \text{ db}$$

$$DB(\text{Oxford}) = 17 \text{ db}$$

$$DB(\text{Ignotus}) = -21 \text{ db}$$

These are shown in Figure 19.

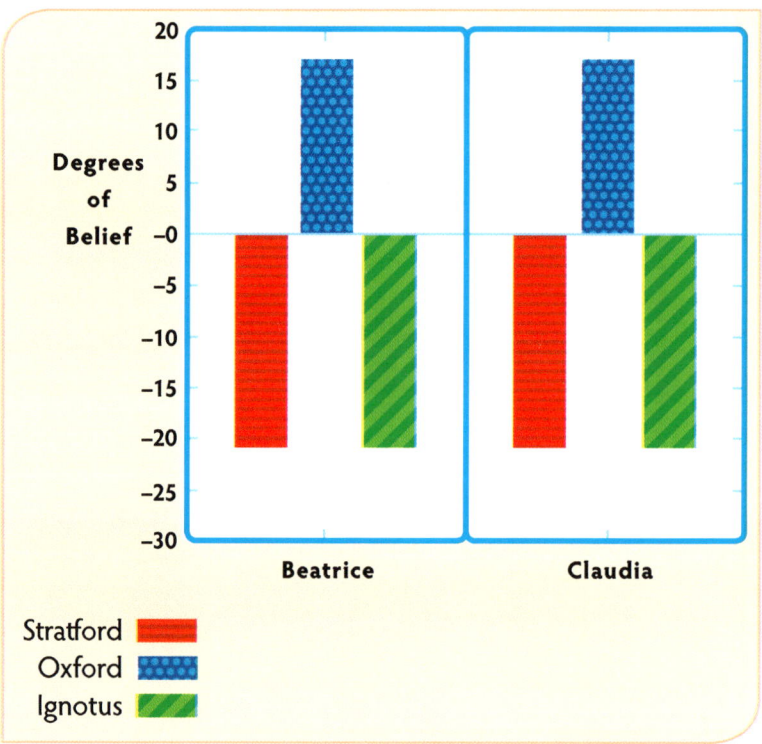

Figure 19. Degrees of Belief for Beatrice and Claudia, based on Chart 10.

And here are the running probabilities so far:

Running Probabilities, based on Charts 1 to 10,

for Beatrice,

$RP(Stratford) = 3 \ 10^{-7}$

$RP(Oxford) = 0.994$

$RP(Ignotus) = 0.006$

and for Claudia,

$RP(Stratford) = 6 \ 10^{-16}$

$RP(Oxford) = 1 - 5 \ 10^{-5}$

$RP(Ignotus) = 5 \ 10^{-5}$

Expressed in terms of Degrees of Belief, these become:

Running Degrees of Belief, based on Charts 1 to 10,

for Beatrice,

$RDB(Stratford) = -65 \ db$

$RDB(Oxford) = 22 \ db$

$RDB(Ignotus) = -22 \ db$

and for Claudia,

$RDB(Stratford) = -152 \ db$

$RDB(Oxford) = 43 \ db$

$RDB(Ignotus) = -43 \ db$

The trends are shown in Figure 20.

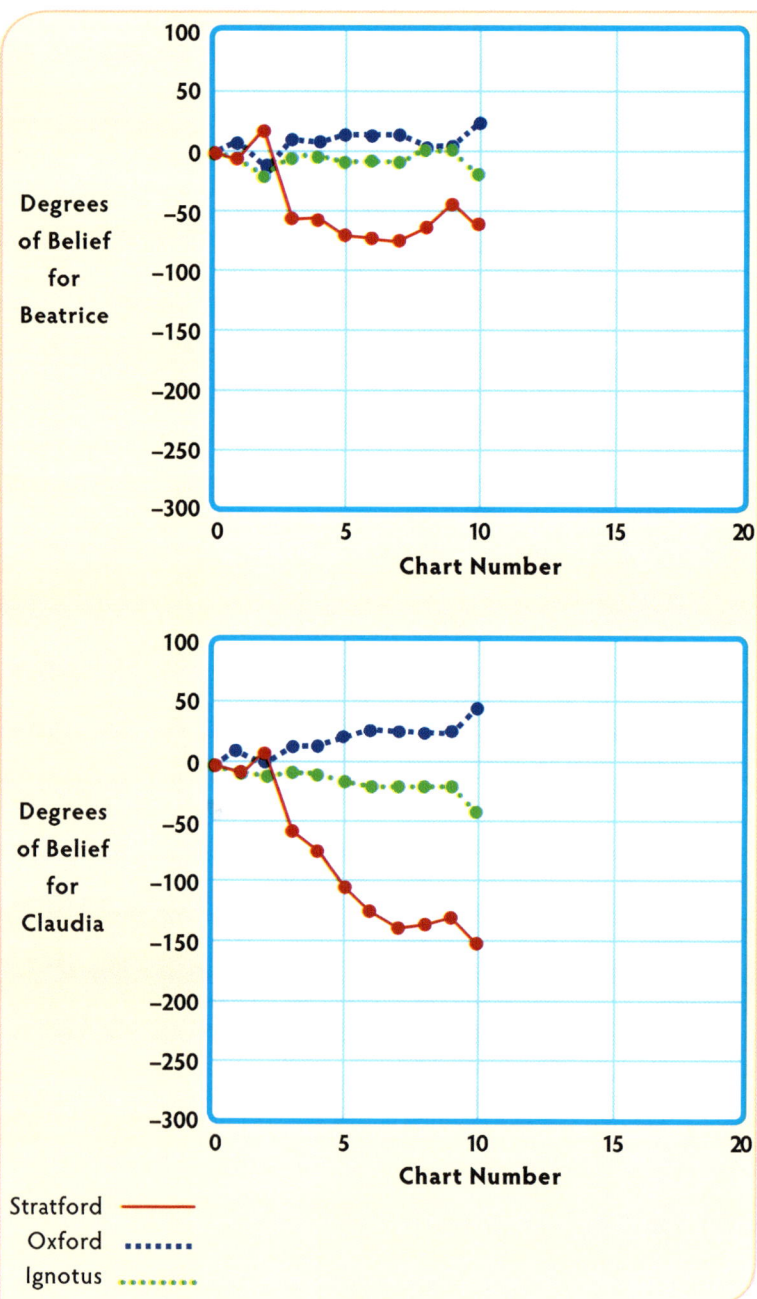

Figure 20. Running Degrees of Belief for Beatrice and Claudia, based on Charts 1 through 10.

When we began our project, I think we were all dubious that the study of a number of quite different topics could lead to a significant result. It is beginning to appear that those doubts were unwarranted.

We have only two more items to consider. They will have to lead to most significant results if they are to save Stratford from extinction.

I suggest that we call it a day, but I have a request. I need to attend a meeting in Napa next week—the annual meeting of the Northern California Vintners' Association—but I do not wish to interrupt our meetings. Would you all be willing to travel up with me? We can stay at the Eldorado Hotel in Rutherford, which is quiet and pleasant.

BEATRICE. That sounds wonderful. Thank you. What secrets do you have to share with your fellow vintners?

JAMES. I do not have a useful secret—but the vintners in central Sicily do. They have a similar climate, a similar terrain, and I think they grow similar grapes. Yet they do it all without irrigation. Think how much money that would save us each year if we could do the same.

MARTIN. That is a great suggestion, James. Thank you. It will be good for me to rest my tennis arm for two or three days.

NOTE

1. Wolfendale (2008).

Reader's Chart

The reader is invited to enter his or her own estimates of the weights in the following chart:

Chart 10, Scene 16: Monument—Cryptogram	Evidence Analysis	Stratford No-Compact Theory	Oxford Compact Theory	Ignotus Compact Theory
Reader: Date:				
S1: EVERE was secreted in the inscription				
S2: EVERE was not secreted in the inscription				
Post Probabilities				

A Patio at the Eldorado Hotel in Rutherford

The Monumental First Folio

Introducing "Mr. William SHAKESPEARE"

JAMES. I hope you all had a pleasant day yesterday, while I was hearing about the trials and tribulations of being a vintner!

CLAUDIA. Yes, we did. But you must have heard some success stories, too.

JAMES. I heard one that surprised me. We all know that Napa produces better Chardonnay than France. (At least, according to the motion-picture industry!) Now there are claims that the Alexander Valley produces a better Montepulciano than Italy!

MARTIN. As assessed by non-California tasters in a blind tasting, I hope!

JAMES. I'm not sure about that. Would you recommend Italian tasters in a non-blind tasting?

But back to business—As I recall, Beatrice would next like us to consider the First Folio—and especially its dedications and testimonials—as providing strong evidence in support of Stratford as Shake*Speare.

Beatrice—would you like to give us a little background information?

BEATRICE. Before 1598, all of the Shakespeare plays that had been published were pirated editions with the author unnamed [1]. Then, in September 1598, a Cambridge graduate named Francis Meres entered in the Stationer's Register a book entitled *Palladis Tamia, Wit's Treasury* [2]. In this book, Meres named "Shakspeare" as the author of twelve plays, all of which had been staged anonymously. Before that time, "Shakespeare" had been known only as the author of two highly successful narrative poems: *Venus and Adonis,* published in 1593, and *The Rape of Lucrece,* published in 1594.

CLAUDIA. I wonder if it is purely coincidental that Lord Burghley, who had been in control of publications as Lord Chamberlain, died in 1597?

BEATRICE. Possibly. *Conspiracy Theorists* tend to think so. However that may be, a few more plays were attributed to "Shakespeare" between 1598 and 1616, when Shakspere passed away.

Then, in 1623, a monumental literary event took place—the publication of what is known as the "First Folio," the term "folio" referring to the size of the printed sheet. It contains thirty-six plays (eighteen of which had not previously been published), which had been written over a timespan of sixteen years (according to the standard Shakespearian chronology). The title was

MR. William SHAKESPEARES Comedies, Histories, & Tragedies, Published according to the True Originall Copies

The next line is

Printed by Isaac Iaggard and Ed. Blount, 1623

which is followed by

TO THE MOST NOBLE AND INCOMPARABLE PAIRE OF BRETHREN.

WILLIAM, Earle of Pembroke, &c. Lord Chamberlaine to the Kings most Excellent Majesty

AND

PHILIP, Earle of Montgomery, &c. Gentleman of his Maiesties [Majesties] Bed-Chamber.

Both Knights of the most Noble Order of the Garter, and our singular good LORDS.

CLAUDIA. I seem to recall that Montgomery's wife was Susan Vere, the youngest daughter of the Earl of Oxford, and that Pembroke was at one time engaged to Bridget, another of Oxford's daughters. This must mean that *The Incomparable Paire* had more than a passing knowledge of and interest in the late Earl of Oxford.

BEATRICE. Your facts are correct, but I am not sure where they lead us. But to continue our discussion of the First Folio: It opens with a dedication to the two *good LORDS* by the editors John Heminge and Henry Condell, who were well-known actors who considered themselves friends and associates of "Shakespeare."

If two contemporaries of the playwright knew his identity, they must have been Heminge and Condell. So I regard their role as editors of the First Folio as practically iron-clad proof that Shake*Speare (as we call him) was indeed William Shakspere of Stratford-upon-Avon.

And if this were not proof enough, we should note that the First Folio includes a dedicatory poem by none other than Ben Jonson, and three further dedications: one by someone with the initials "J.M.," who may have been John Marston [3] or James Mabbe [4]; one by Leonard Digges, an Oxford scholar; and one by Hugh Holland, who was a representative of Cambridge University.

JAMES. This seems a little odd—and somewhat suspicious. William Shakspere had no connection whatever with either Oxford or Cambridge, whereas—you know my follow-up— Edward de Vere had received degrees from both universities.

BEATRICE. Are we still conspiracy-mongering?

MARTIN. I don't know about "conspiracies," but we did agree weeks ago to take account of that possibility. That is why we label the Oxford and Ignotus hypotheses with the term *Compact*.

BEATRICE. Yes—I remember—somewhat to my chagrin. But to return to the First Folio. I have to assume that the representatives of the two universities were honest scholars, and they were writing tributes to someone whom they honestly believed was Shake*Speare. Altogether, there were six presumably honest citizens who were willing to vouch for "William Shakespeare of Stratford-upon-Avon" as the true and legitimate playwright we are referring to as "Shake*Speare."

CLAUDIA. Except that nowhere in those six testimonials does anyone explicitly identify "Shakespeare" as a citizen of Stratford-upon-Avon—we are left to connect a reference to "Avon" in one place, and a reference to "Stratford" in another place! Nor are there any other identifying biographical facts in those six testimonies, which I consider rather odd.

BEATRICE. I sense that we shall be engaged in some nitpicking concerning the First Folio. But before we get to the nits, I would like us to find a way to register our non-conspiratorial opinions concerning the provenance of the First Folio. Can you suggest a suitable procedure for that, Martin?

MARTIN. I'll try. But it is not easy to formulate options that may prove, on later thought, to be invalid. For instance, we should not now express an opinion that is based on the assumption that we can take Ben Jonson at his word, if there is the prospect that we shall subsequently find reason to question his propensity for veraciousness.

JAMES. Are you suggesting that he might have told fibs? What a shocking idea!

CLAUDIA. Actually, I understand that Jonson cherished his reputation for honesty. My guess is that if he had to tell a fib, he would have tried to find a way to let the astute reader know that his verisimilitude was not to be taken at face value.

MARTIN. This can happen. I am reminded of a famous UFO report by Edward U. Condon where he makes all kinds of pronouncements that the unwary accept at face value [5]. However, Condon at one point remarks that "Where secrecy exists, one can never be sure that one knows the truth," and then later on he informs us that some of his investigations had in fact been limited by secrecy. One wonders whether he had made statements that he knew to be untrue, and was then trying to salve his conscience.

BEATRICE. Very interesting, but not particularly relevant. What is our next step, Martin?

MARTIN. How about these three statements:

> "All of the contributors to the dedications and testimonials were of the belief that Stratford was Shake*Speare
>
> "Some but not all were of the belief that Stratford was Shake*Speare"
>
> "None was of the belief that Stratford was Shake*Speare"

This may represent the overall sense one gets from the document, without limiting the prospect of nitpicking—or worse—later on.

BEATRICE. I can live with that as the opening motion of our debate.

CLAUDIA. It will be interesting to see what the consequences turn out to be, in terms of probabilities for our three candidates.

MARTIN. Would you like to lead off, Beatrice?

BEATRICE. My reading of the dedications and letters is that every one of the contributors was of the opinion that Stratford was indeed the revered author Shake*Speare. However, I obviously cannot be absolutely certain, so I am prepared to allow a 10% chance that some of the contributors harbored some doubts, and a 1% chance that they all harbored doubts.

Now for the hypotheses:

If Stratford was indeed Shake*Speare, I would expect all the contributors to be firmly of that opinion. On the other hand, if Oxford were Shake*Speare, then it is most likely that all of the contributors would at least know that Stratford was not Shake*Speare. However, I allow even odds that one or more may not have been in on the secret. Similarly for Ignotus.

So here are my figures, for what they are worth.

Chart 11, Scene 17: First Folio— Beliefs	Evidence Analysis	Stratford No-Compact Theory	Oxford Compact Theory	Ignotus Compact Theory
Beatrice				
S1: All contributors believed that Stratford was Shake*Speare	100	10	0	0
S2: Some but not all contributors believed that Stratford was Shake*Speare	10	0	1	1
S3: No contributor believed that Stratford was Shake*Speare	1	0	1	1
Post Probabilities		0.90	0.05	0.05

JAMES. Congratulations, Beatrice. You have found some significant support for Stratford. Now I am curious to see what Claudia makes of this same evidence.

CLAUDIA. Frankly, I do not read these lines as providing strong support for the proposition that Shake*Speare was indeed Stratford. We have already noticed that neither Jonson nor any other of the contributors provides any biographical data in support of that assumption. I am not impressed by Jonson's use of the term "Sweet Swan of Avon." There are many "River Avons" in England. One is close to property that was once owned by Oxford, and another runs by Wilton House, the home of Lady Mary Herbert and the earls William and Philip Herbert, a place frequented by both Oxford and Ben Jonson [6].

The way that I read the dedicatory statements, I would give most weight to the option that "Some but not all of the contributors believed that Stratford was Shake*Speare." I have in mind, in particular, that Hugh Holland (who lived in Cambridge) and the enigmatic "J.M." (believed to be James Mabbe, who lived in Oxford) probably knew little about the theatrical world of London. So I would give a weight of 100 to the statement that "Some but not all contributors believed that Stratford was Shake*Speare"; maybe a weight of 10 that all were of that opinion, and a weight of 1 that none were of that opinion. Those dedications and testimonials strike me as pretty murky. That is why my judgments are correspondingly murky.

As far as the hypotheses are concerned, I am happy with Beatrice's proposals.

So here is my chart:

Chart 11, Scene 17: First Folio—Beliefs	Evidence Analysis	Stratford No-Compact Theory	Oxford Compact Theory	Ignotus Compact Theory
Claudia				
S1: All contributors believed that Stratford was Shake*Speare	10	1	0	0
S2: Some but not all contributors believed that Stratford was Shake*Speare	100	0	1	1
S3: No contributor believed that Stratford was Shake*Speare	1	0	1	1
Post Probabilities		0.4	0.3	0.3

JAMES. It is interesting that some quite strong assumptions lead to quite wishy-washy results. I find that Beatrice's and Claudia's probabilities convert to the following Degrees of Belief:

for Beatrice,

$$DB(Stratford) = 10 \text{ db}$$

$$DB(Oxford) = -13 \text{ db}$$

$$DB(Ignotus) = -13 \text{ db}$$

and for Claudia,

$$DB(Stratford) = -2 \text{ db}$$

$$DB(Oxford) = -4 \text{ db}$$

$$DB(Ignotus) = -4 \text{ db}$$

These are shown in Figure 21.

And here are the running probabilities so far:

Running Probabilities, based on Charts 1 to 11,

for Beatrice,

$$RP(Stratford) = 5 \ 10^{-6}$$

$$RP(Oxford) = 0.994$$

$$RP(Ignotus) = 0.006$$

and for Claudia,

$$RP(Stratford) = 8 \ 10^{-16}$$

$$RP(Oxford) = 1 - 5 \ 10^{-5}$$

$$RP(Ignotus) = 5 \ 10^{-5}$$

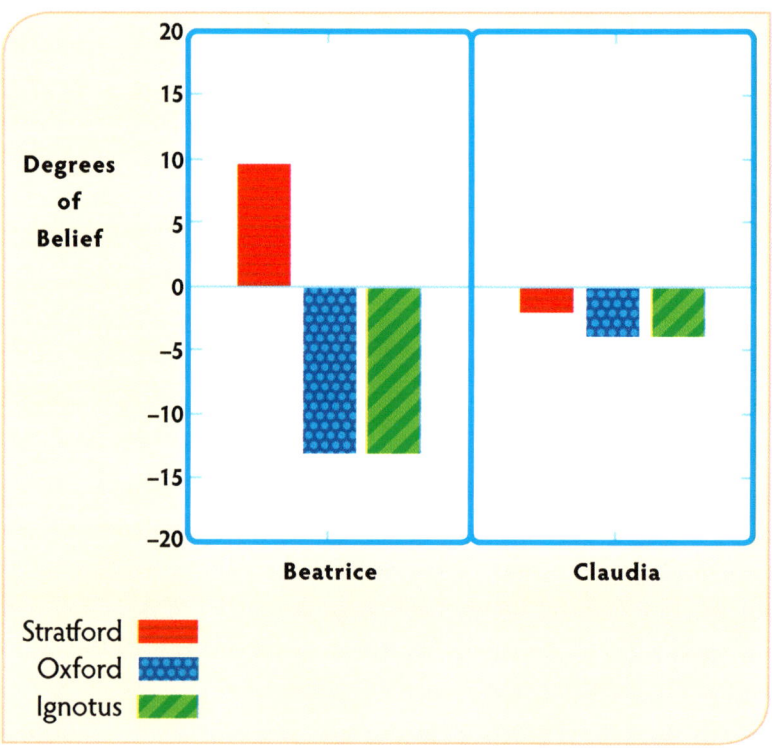

Figure 21. Degrees of Belief for Beatrice and Claudia, based on Chart 11.

Expressed in terms of Degrees of Belief, these become:

Running Degrees of Belief, based on Charts 1 to 11,

for Beatrice,

RDB(Stratford) = −53 db

RDB(Oxford) = 22 db

RDB(Ignotus) = −22 db

and for Claudia,

RDB(Stratford) = −151 db

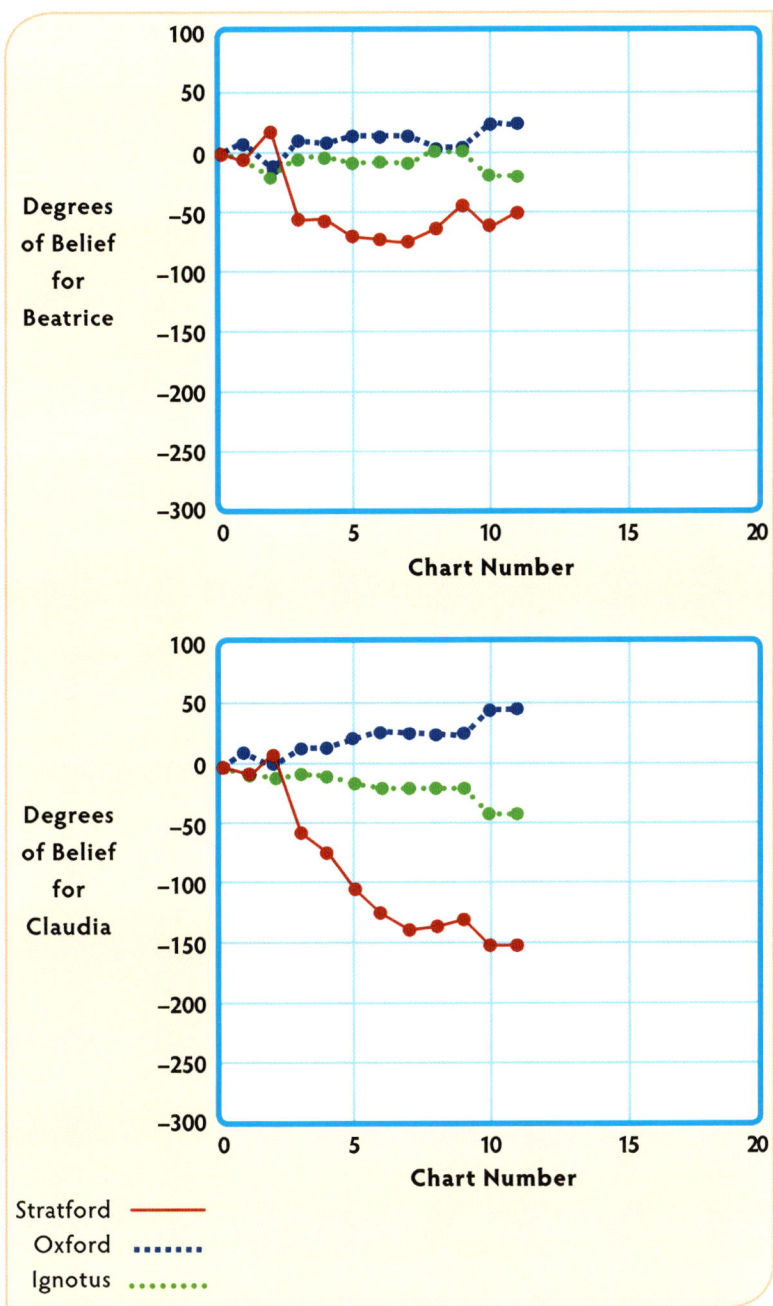

Stratford ——————
Oxford ·······
Ignotus ·······

Figure 22. Running Degrees of Belief for Beatrice and Claudia, based on Charts 1 through 11.

$$RDB(Oxford) = 43 \text{ db}$$

$$RDB(Ignotus) = -43 \text{ db}$$

The trends of the Running Degrees of Belief are shown in Figure 22.

As we would expect, these scores have hardly changed, since Claudia gave approximately equal weights to the three candidates.

We must now allow time for Claudia's nitpicking of the dedications and testimonials. But I propose that we take that up at our next meeting.

NOTES

1. Roper (2008), 392.

2. Roper (2008), 286.

3. Roper (2008), 407.

4. Chiljan (2011), 139.

5. Condon & Gillmor (1969).

6. Roper (2008), 422.

Reader's Chart

The reader is invited to enter his or her own estimates of the weights in the following chart:

Chart 11, Scene 17: First Folio—Beliefs	Evidence Analysis	Stratford No-Compact Theory	Oxford Compact Theory	Ignotus Compact Theory
Reader: Date:				
S1: All contributors believed that Stratford was Shake*Speare				
S2: Some but not all contributors believed that Stratford was Shake*Speare				
S3: No contributor believed that Stratford was Shake*Speare				
Post Probabilities				

A Patio at the Eldorado Hotel in Rutherford

The Provenance of the First Folio

How do Editors go about finding "cur'd and perfect" texts?

JAMES. Now we have taken an overview of the First Folio, I gather that Claudia would like us to examine one or two details. Where should we start, Claudia?

CLAUDIA. There are several features of the dedications and testimonials that might raise an astute eyebrow—but I'll limit myself to two.

The first big question, in my mind, is the source of all of that wonderful material. Heminge and Condell assert that the versions of the plays then in circulation were *diverse stolen, and surreptitious copies, maimed and deformed by the frauds and stealthes of injurious impostors.* By contrast, they were presenting texts *offered to your view cur'd, and perfect in their limbs; and all the rest, absolute in their numbers,* as he conceived them. However, Shakespeare scholars consider these claims to be unfounded: None of the texts in the First Folio was "perfect;" it appears that a number of them were derived from earlier imperfect quartos.

Where did Heminge and Condell find these so-called "perfect" copies? Not from the theaters or other public sources, it would seem, since *King John, All's Well That Ends Well, Coriolanus,* and *Timon of Athens* were unknown before they appeared in the First Folio.

But what are the possibilities? The texts of plays that had not already been published in quarto form must have been obtained either from the home of the author, or from some other safe repository of the author's manuscripts. This leads me to the following chart:

Chart 12, Scene 18: First Folio— Previously Unpublished Texts	Evidence Analysis	Stratford No-Compact Theory	Oxford Compact Theory	Ignotus Compact Theory
Claudia				
S1: Heminge and Condell obtained the texts from theatrical premises				
S2: . . . from the home of or premises associated with Stratford				
S3: . . . from the home of or premises associated with Oxford				
S4: . . . from the home of or premises associated with Ignotus				
Post Probabilities				

Since some of the plays had never been presented on the stage, and since Heminge and Condell claimed that they had obtained versions of the texts "as he had conceived them," that makes theatrical premises highly unlikely. To be cautious, I give that a 1% probability. However, the home of Stratford also seems highly unlikely, since there is no mention of such valuable property in the last will and testament of "William Shakspere." To be generous, I give that a 5% probability. In terms of weights, I suggest 1, 5, 50, and 50 for these four options.

Now we come to the three hypotheses. It seems most likely that the authors would have chosen to keep their manuscripts safely in their homes, but I allow a small (5%) probability that the texts were in fact concealed in some theatrical premises.

Chart 12, Scene 18: First Folio— Previously Unpublished Texts	Evidence Analysis	Stratford No-Compact Theory	Oxford Compact Theory	Ignotus Compact Theory
Claudia				
S1: Heminge and Condell obtained the texts from theatrical premises	1	5	5	5
S2: . . . from the home of or premises associated with Stratford	5	100	0	0
S3: . . . from the home of or premises associated with Oxford	50	0	100	0
S4: . . . from the home of or premises associated with Ignotus	50	0	0	100
Post Probabilities		0.06	0.47	0.47

MARTIN. I see that the results are not favorable for Stratford. What are your thoughts, Beatrice?

BEATRICE. I would give more weight to the possibility that the author had transferred all of the manuscripts to the safekeeping of one of the theaters, and I would not be quite as negative about the possibility that they were hidden somewhere in the Stratford estate.

So here are my figures:

Chart 12, Scene 18: First Folio— Previously Unpublished Texts	Evidence Analysis	Stratford No-Compact Theory	Oxford Compact Theory	Ignotus Compact Theory
Beatrice				
S1: Heminge and Condell obtained the texts from theatrical premises	50	10	10	10
S2: ... from the home of or premises associated with Stratford	10	50	0	0
S3: ... from the home of or premises associated with Oxford	50	0	50	0
S4: ... from the home of or premises associated with Ignotus	50	0	0	50
Post Probabilities		0.16	0.42	0.42

MARTIN. Not quite as negative for Stratford. How are our running scores, James?

JAMES. I find that Beatrice's and Claudia's probabilities convert to the following Degrees of Belief:

for Beatrice,

$$DB(Stratford) = -7db$$

$$DB(Oxford) = -1 \ db$$

$$DB(Ignotus) = -1 \ db$$

and for Claudia,

DB(Stratford) = −12 db

DB(Oxford) = −1 db

DB(Ignotus) = −1 db

These are shown in Figure 23.

And here are the running probabilities so far:

Running Probabilities, based on Charts 1 to 12, for Beatrice,

RP(Stratford) = $2\ 10^{-6}$

RP(Oxford) = 0.994

RP(Ignotus) = 0.006

and for Claudia,

RP(Stratford) = 10^{-16}

RP(Oxford) = $1 - 5\ 10^{-5}$

RP(Ignotus) = $5\ 10^{-5}$

Expressed in terms of Degrees of Belief, these become:

Running Degrees of Belief, based on Charts 1 to 12, for Beatrice,

RDB(Stratford) = −57 db

RDB(Oxford) = 22 db

RDB(Ignotus) = −22 db

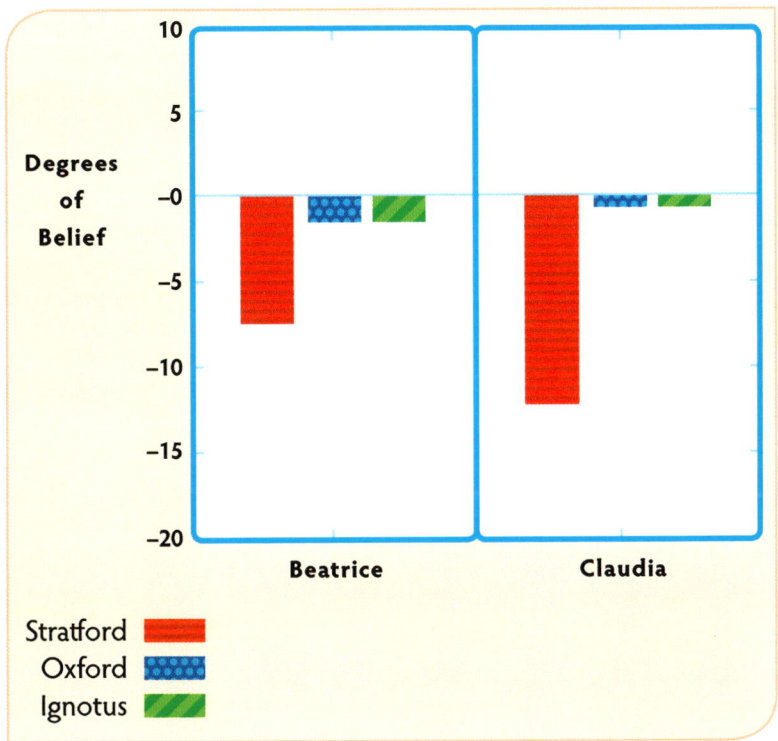

Figure 23. Degrees of Belief for Beatrice and Claudia, based on Chart 12.

and for Claudia,

$$RDB(Stratford) = -160 \text{ db}$$

$$RDB(Oxford) = 43 \text{ db}$$

$$RDB(Ignotus) = -43 \text{ db}$$

The trends of the Running Degrees of Belief are shown in Figure 24.

Time for a little refreshment, I think.

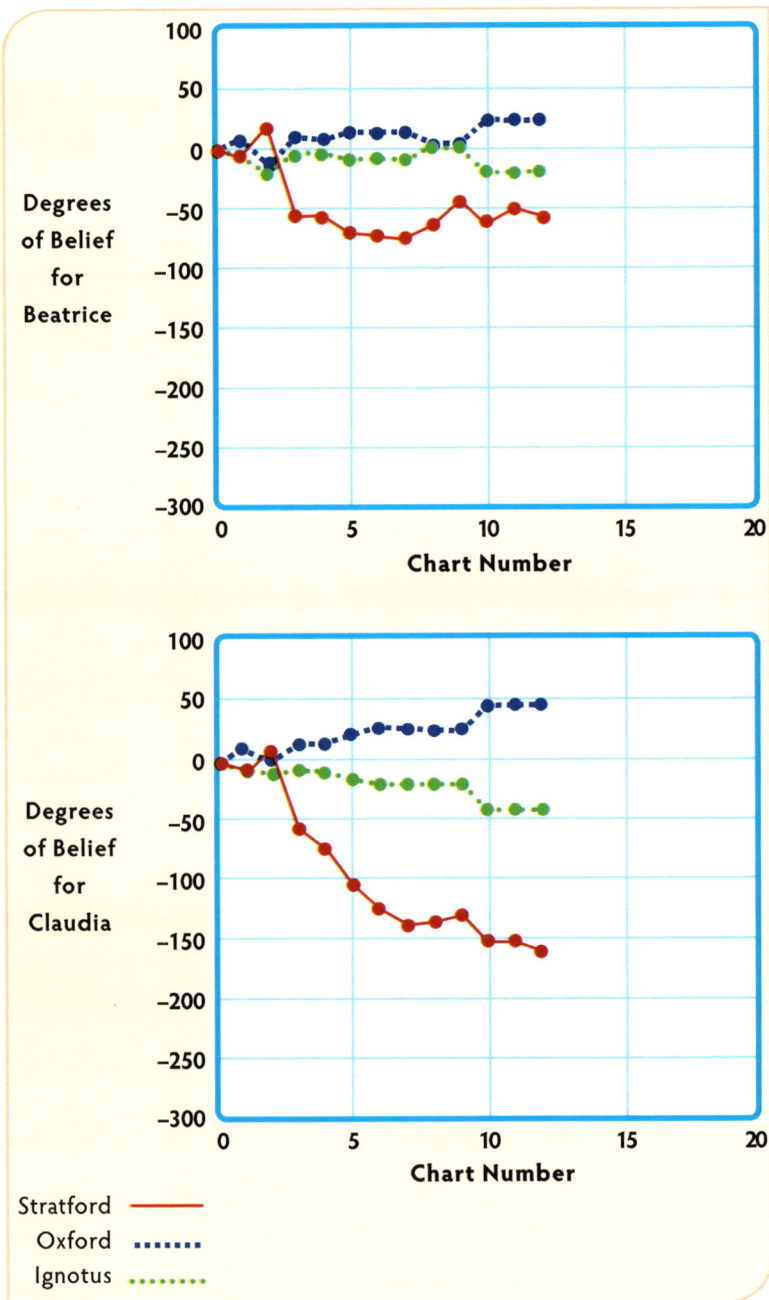

Figure 24. Running Degrees of Belief for Beatrice and Claudia, based on Charts 1 through 12.

Reader's Chart

The reader is invited to enter his or her own estimates of the weights in the following chart:

Chart 12, Scene 18: First Folio—Previously Unpublished Texts	Evidence Analysis	Stratford No-Compact Theory	Oxford Compact Theory	Ignotus Compact Theory
Reader: Date:				
S1: Heminge and Condell obtained the texts from theatrical premises				
S2: ... from the home of or premises associated with Stratford				
S3: ... from the home of or premises associated with Oxford				
S4: ... from the home of or premises associated with Ignotus				
Post Probabilities				

A Patio at the Eldorado Hotel

Jonson's Mixed Messages

The great Shakespeare was never interred in Westminster Abbey. Why not?

JAMES. Well, Claudia, you have drawn attention to one problem you see in the First Folio. Do you have any other concerns?

CLAUDIA. Indeed, I have a number of concerns, but I am going to limit myself to just one.

In his dedicatory poem, Jonson writes:

I will not lodge thee by
Chaucer, or Spenser, or bid Beaumont lye
A little further, to make thee a roome

What is this all about?

Jonson is addressing the question of whether the playwright should be honored with burial in Westminster Abbey, where Geoffrey Chaucer, Edmund Spenser, and Francis Beaumont had been interred.

However, earlier in the poem, Jonson had written

I confesse thy writings to be such,
As neither Man, nor Muse, can praise too much

And, later,

> *Soule of the Age!*
> *The applause! Delight! The wonder of our Stage!*

Given such adulation (and Jonson was not known to be overgenerous with his praise), and given the impressive contents of the First Folio, one would expect Jonson to advocate that whomever he had in mind for the mantle of Shake*Speare was well worthy of being in the company of Chaucer, Spenser, and Beaumont. However, it is clear that Jonson was in fact opposed to having some person so honored.

So the key question is—Whom precisely did Jonson have in mind when he wrote *I will not lodge thee by,* etc.?

Whom exactly did Jonson wish *not* to be honored with a place in Westminster Abbey?

This leads me to suggest the following chart:

Chart 13, Scene 19: First Folio— Texts	Evidence Analysis	Stratford No-Compact Theory	Oxford Compact Theory	Ignotus Compact Theory
S1: Jonson objected to seeing Stratford buried in Westminster Abbey				
S2: Jonson objected to seeing Oxford buried in Westminster Abbey				
S3: Jonson objected to seeing Ignotus buried in Westminster Abbey				
Post Probabilities				

MARTIN. That chart looks pretty good to me. Very clear-cut questions. How do you fill out the blanks, Claudia?

CLAUDIA.
I first consider the *evidence*. Jonson's eulogy (and the entire First Folio) appear to be intended to support the claim of Stratford to be Shake*Speare. However, Jonson's words are not entirely unambiguous, so I allow a small chance that they subliminally hint that Shake*Speare was not Stratford. These thoughts lead me to set the weights in the first column as 10, 1, and 1.

Now for the *hypotheses*. If Shake*Speare had been Stratford, Jonson would surely have been privy to that fact. It is then hard to believe that he would object to seeing Stratford join Chaucer and Spenser and Beaumont in Westminster Abbey. On the other hand, given this assumption that Shake*Speare was Stratford, Jonson would have strongly objected to seeing either Oxford or Ignotus installed in the Abbey. I think I am being quite conservative in setting the corresponding weights as 1, 10, and 10.

Presumably, similar arguments would apply if either Oxford or Ignotus was Shake*Speare. So here are my figures:

Chart 13, Scene 19: First Folio— Texts	Evidence Analysis	Stratford No-Compact Theory	Oxford Compact Theory	Ignotus Compact Theory
Claudia				
S1: Jonson objected to seeing Stratford buried in Westminster Abbey	10	1	10	10
S2: Jonson objected to seeing Oxford buried in Westminster Abbey	1	10	1	10
S3: Jonson objected to seeing Ignotus buried in Westminster Abbey	1	10	10	1
Post Probabilities		0.12	0.44	0.44

I see that my arguments do not make much of a case for any of the three candidates.

MARTIN. What would your figures be, Beatrice?

BEATRICE. It seems clear that Jonson's eulogy and the other contributions to the First Folio were intended to make the case that Shake*Speare was Stratford. So, based on the relevant *evidence,* I have to conclude that Stratford was the intended target of those lines. But there can be a simple explanation. Stratford was living in comfortable retirement in Stratford-upon-Avon. He could be interred in a church in the town where he grew up. Why bring him all the way back to London to be buried?

However, turning now to the *hypotheses,* it is my opinion that if Shake*Speare was indeed Stratford, Jonson would *not* have objected to his being honored with a place in the Abbey. (He would have supported it.) On the other hand, he would then certainly have objected to seeing either of the imposters (Oxford and Ignotus) so honored.

Appropriately modified arguments apply for the Oxford and Ignotus hypotheses. So here are my figures:

Chart 13, Scene 19: First Folio— Texts	Evidence Analysis	Stratford No-Compact Theory	Oxford Compact Theory	Ignotus Compact Theory
Beatrice				
S1: Jonson objected to seeing Stratford buried in Westminster Abbey	100	1	100	100
S2: Jonson objected to seeing Oxford buried in Westminster Abbey	1	100	1	100
S3: Jonson objected to seeing Ignotus buried in Westminster Abbey	1	100	100	1
Post Probabilities		0.02	0.49	0.49

JAMES. This is a most interesting result, Beatrice. Although you have been leaning toward Stratford for the mantle of Shake*Speare, I see that you here end up with a result that is *less* favorable to Stratford than did Claudia! The basic difficulty with this topic is presumably the conflict we noted at the very beginning: Jonson appears to praise his man (whoever he was) to the sky, but he then states that he would not want to see him placed in Westminster Abbey. This surprising conflict apparently leads to surprising conclusions.

MARTIN. Not quite as negative for Statford. How are our scores, James?

JAMES. I find that Beatrice's and Claudia's probabilities convert to the following Degrees of Belief:

for Beatrice,

> DB(Stratford) = –17 db
>
> DB(Oxford) = 0 db
>
> DB(Ignotus) = 0 db

and for Claudia,

> DB(Stratford) = –9 db
>
> DB(Oxford) = –1 db
>
> DB(Ignotus) = –1 db

These are shown in Figure 25.

And here are the running probabilities so far:

> Running Probabilities, based on Charts 1 to 13,

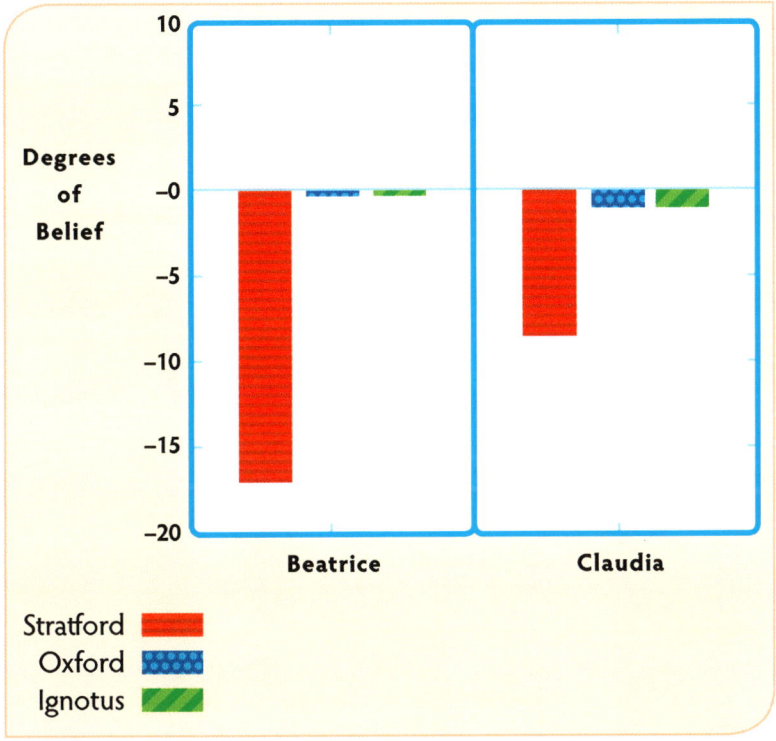

Figure 25. Degrees of Belief for Beatrice and Claudia, based on Chart 13.

for Beatrice

$$RP(Stratford) = 8\ 10^{-8}$$

$$RP(Oxford) = 0.995$$

$$RP(Ignotus) = 0.006$$

and for Claudia,

$$RP(Stratford) = 3\ 10^{-17}$$

$$RP(Oxford) = 1 - 5\ 10^{-5}$$

$$RP(Ignotus) = 5\ 10^{-5}$$

Expressed in terms of Degrees of Belief, these become:

Running Degrees of Belief, based on Charts 1 to 13, for Beatrice,

RDB(Stratford) = –71 db;

RDB(Oxford) = 22 db;

RDB(Ignotus) = –22 db,

and for Claudia,

RDB(Stratford) = –165 db;

RDB(Oxford) = 43 db;

RDB(Ignotus) = –43 db.

The trends of the Running Degrees of Belief are shown in Figure 26.

Now I think we have dealt with the First Folio. What is left?

CLAUDIA. The sonnets, of course. Or, rather, the dedication of the sonnets. It is a very big puzzle, and may be the pièce de résistance.

JAMES. Very good. We'll see if our "resistance" holds out.

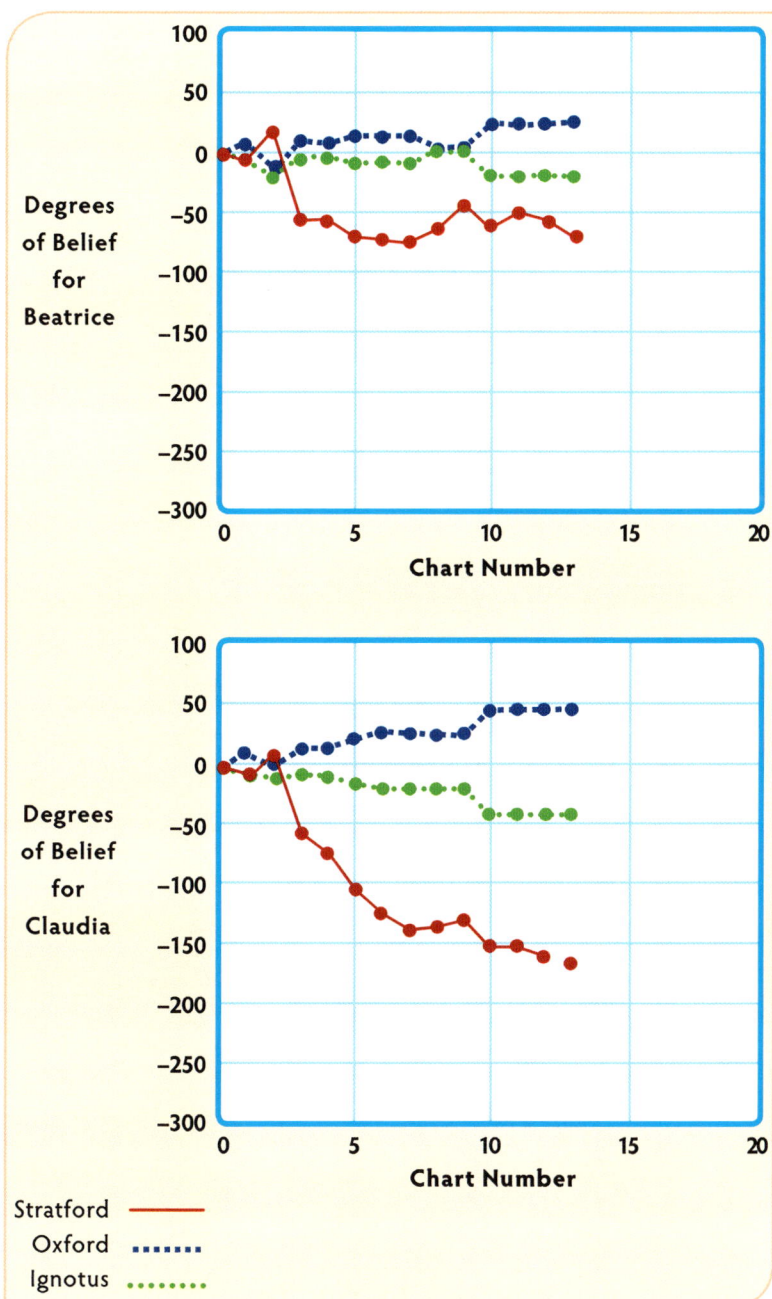

Figure 26. Running Degrees of Belief for Beatrice and Claudia, based on Charts 1 through 13.

Reader's Chart

The reader is invited to enter his or her own estimates of the weights in the following chart:

Chart 13, Scene 19: First Folio—Texts	Evidence Analysis	Stratford No-Compact Theory	Oxford Compact Theory	Ignotus Compact Theory
Reader: Date:				
S1: Jonson objected to seeing Stratford buried in Westminster Abbey				
S2: Jonson objected to seeing Oxford buried in Westminster Abbey				
S3: Jonson objected to seeing Ignotus buried in Westminster Abbey				
Post Probabilities				

James' Study at the *Hacienda*

The Sonnets

Shakespeare's Sonnettes appear—before they disappear.

JAMES. Now we are back to Carmel Valley, and since there will be some material for us to look over, I thought it would be convenient for us to again meet in my study—which I regret I do not make much use of these days.

Beatrice, I think we now come to the third topic you had on our agenda. Would you like to introduce it?

BEATRICE. We have discussed how the name "Shakespeare" came to be identified with the plays associated with that name. However, in addition to the plays, there were a number of poems associated with that name. In fact, "Shakespeare" first burst upon the scene as the author of two long narrative poems: *Venus and Adonis*, published in 1593, and *The Rape of Lucrece*, published in 1594. Both poems were dedicated *TO THE RIGHT HONORABLE HENRY WRIOTHESLEY, Earl of Southampton and Baron of Titchfield*. Those who attribute the Shake*Speare corpus to Stratford interpret the dedications as solicitations for financial and political support, which was the standard usage of dedications. However, I am sorry to say that there is no evidence that Stratford ever received such support. Both poems were a tremendous success, and each was reprinted a number of times.

However, today I wish to focus on his sonnets.

On May 20, 1609, the publisher Thomas Thorpe registered with the Stationer's Company *A Booke called Shake-Speare's Sonnettes.* The title page reads

SHAKE-SPEARES
SONNETS
Never before Imprinted.

AT LONDON
By G. Eld for T.T. and are
To be folde by John Wright, dwelling
At Christ Church gate.
1609.

The book contains 154 sonnets. The dedication, presumably written by Thorpe, since it carries his initials, was set out as follows:

TO.THE.ONLIE.BEGETTER.OF.
THESE.INSVING.SONNETS.
Mr. W.H. ALL.HAPPINESSE.
AND.THAT.ETERNITIE.
PROMISED.
BY.
OVR.EVER-LIVING.POET.
WISHETH.
THE. WELL-WISHING.
ADVENTURER.IN.
SETTING.
FORTH.
T.T.

I admit that this dedication has been a big puzzle for the last four hundred years. No one has been able to assign a convincing identity to "Mr. W.H."

However, the important point is that these poems are entitled *Shake-Speares Sonnets*. With due allowance for the variety in the spelling of his name, this strongly suggests that the poems were the work of William Shakspere (Stratford, in our notation).

In his book *The Case for Shakespeare: The End of the Authorship Question*, Scott McCrea highlights a number of points about the sonnets that support the case for Stratford as Shake*Speare [1]. For instance, he "toils" by day (Sonnets 27, 28); he is "poor" (Sonnet 37); he contrasts himself with "the rich" (Sonnet 52); he is barred from "public honour and proud titles" (Sonnet 25); we can infer from Sonnet 152 that he is married; and—most important of all—he tells us in Sonnet 136 that his name is "Will." McCrea finds that *this account sounds suspiciously like William Shakespeare.*

CLAUDIA. However, as I recall, McCrea himself is concerned about the speaker's age. In Sonnets 62, 63, 73, and 138, the author refers to himself as old. McCrea points out that what are now referred to as Sonnets 138 and 144 were published (by William Jaggard) on or before 1599, when Stratford was only thirty-five years old.

I also think it is a real stretch to suggest that the sonnets depict the author as a poor man. Take Sonnet 91, for instance, which contains the lines:

> *Some glory in their birth, some in their skill,*
> *Some in their wealth, some in their body's force,*
> *Some in their garments though new-fangled ill;*
> *Some in their hawks and hounds, some in their horse;*
> . . . .
> *Thy love is better than high birth to me,*
> *Richer than wealth, prouder than garments' cost,*
> *Of more delight than hawks and horses be;*

Sonnet 125 begins with the lines

Were't aught to me I bore the canopy . . .

Only noblemen carried the canopy over the Queen on state occasions.

BEATRICE. I freely admit that there are contradictions in the sonnets. One can make a case that the author of the sonnets must have been rich, but one can also make a case that he must have been poor.

MARTIN. I guess this is where the Reverend Bayes can come to the rescue. Can you suggest a suitable chart, Beatrice?

BEATRICE. No—but I can suggest two that would cover the points we have been discussing. One on the social status of the author, and the other on the name "Will." Of course, we discussed the author's social status some time ago, but that discussion was based on our reading of the plays. Martin—Is it acceptable to review the same topic, but now on the basis of the sonnets rather than the plays?

MARTIN. I don't see why not. They are two distinct datasets, so it is no different from weighing yourself with two different scales, and looking to see if they agree. If they don't agree, some people might choose the one that assigns him or her the lower weight. But I am sure that none of us would ever think of bending the evidence on account of vanity or prejudice or obstinacy or anything as unscholarly and unscientific as that.

Here is the chart we used before:

Chart 6, Scene 11: Social Status	Evidence Analysis	Stratford No-Compact Theory	Oxford Compact Theory	Ignotus Compact Theory
S1: Nobility				
S2: High class				
S3: Middle class				
S4: Lower class				
Post Probabilities				

Would you like to enter your weights, Beatrice, now in relation to the evidence of the sonnets?

BEATRICE. You will not be surprised to learn that I am going to follow the lead of Scott McCrea. According to his analysis, the author of the sonnets was probably middle class—probably not lower class—and possibly, but not very likely, high class or nobility.

As far as the hypotheses go, I can simply repeat the weights I used previously. I have to remind myself that *Compact* covers the possibility that Oxford had assistants or apprentices who were most likely middle class.

Chart 14, Scene 20: Social Status	Evidence Analysis	Stratford No-Compact Theory	Oxford Compact Theory	Ignotus Compact Theory
Beatrice				
S1: Nobility	1	0	100	1
S2: High class	5	1	2	4
S3: Middle class	20	5	5	4
S4: Lower class	10	1	0	1
Post Probabilities		0.54	0.05	0.41

MARTIN. And what are your thoughts about the sonnets, Claudia?

CLAUDIA. They are very different from Beatrice's. I am more impressed by the references to wealth and court life than I am to McCrea's purported references to poverty and hard labor. Reproducing my earlier weights for the hypotheses, I arrive at the following:

Chart 14, Scene 20: Social Status	Evidence Analysis	Stratford No-Compact Theory	Oxford Compact Theory	Ignotus Compact Theory
Claudia				
S1: Nobility	10	0	100	1
S2: High class	5	0	2	4
S3: Middle class	2	30	5	4
S4: Lower class	1	100	0	1
Post Probabilities		0.09	0.52	0.39

MARTIN. What are the new scores, James?

JAMES. I see Beatrice has been a little more generous to Stratford this time, and allowed for a small chance that he may have made it to the upper classes—not that it will make much difference to the end result, I suspect.

I find that Beatrice's and Claudia's probabilities convert to the following Degrees of Belief:

for Beatrice,

DB(Stratford) = 1 db

DB(Oxford) = –13 db

DB(Ignotus) = –2 db

and for Claudia,

DB(Stratford) = –10 db

DB(Oxford) = 0 db

DB(Ignotus) = –2 db

These are shown in Figure 27.

And here are the running probabilities so far:

Running Probabilities, based on Charts 1 to 13,

for Beatrice,

RP(Stratford) = 9 10^{-7}

RP(Oxford) = 0.953

RP(Ignotus) = 0.047

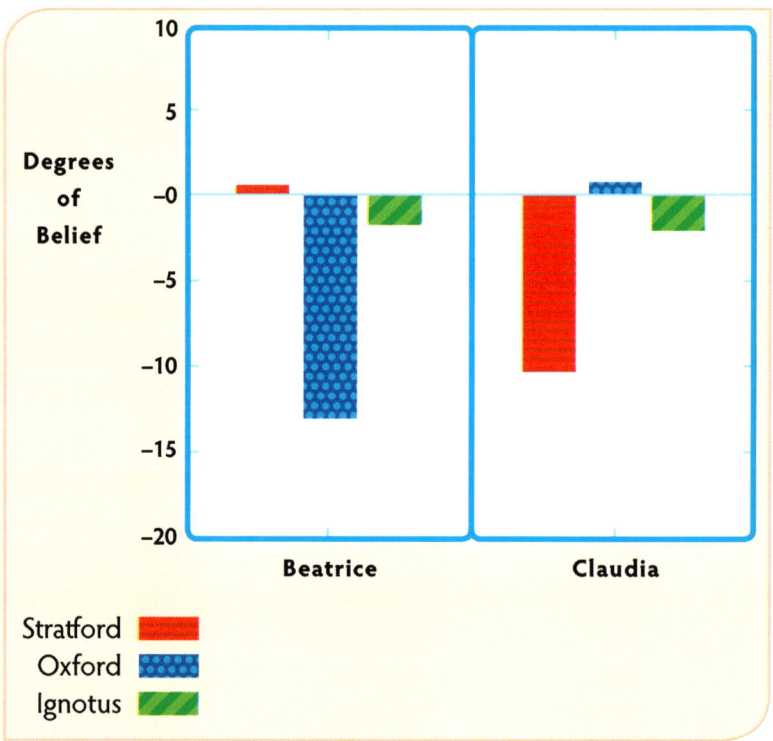

Figure 27. Degrees of Belief for Beatrice and Claudia, based on Chart 14.

and for Claudia,

$$RP(\text{Stratford}) = 5 \ 10^{-18}$$

$$RP(\text{Oxford}) = 1 - 4 \ 10^{-5}$$

$$RP(\text{Ignotus}) = 4 \ 10^{-5}$$

Expressed in terms of Degrees of Belief, these become:

Running Degrees of Belief, based on Charts 1 to 14,

for Beatrice,

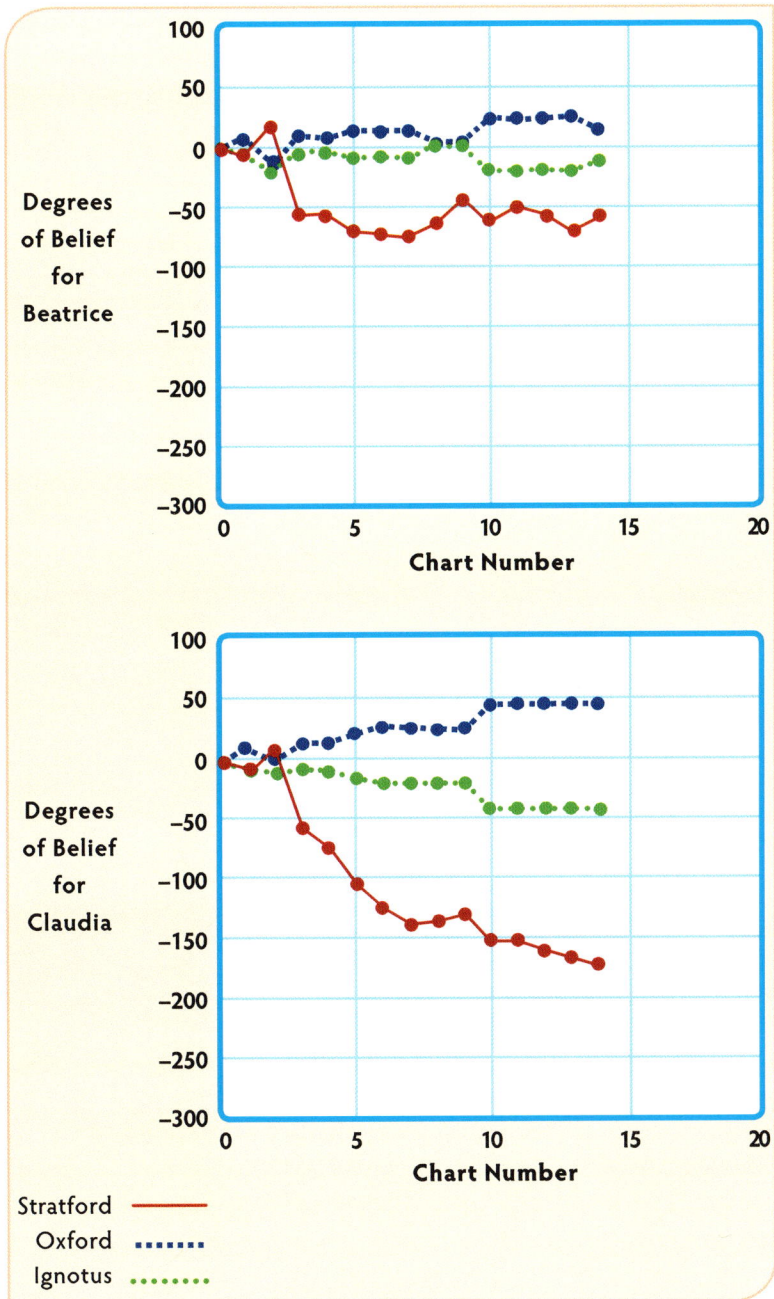

Figure 28. Running Degrees of Belief for Beatrice and Claudia, based on Charts 1 through 14.

RDB(Stratford) = −61 db

RDB(Oxford) = 13 db

RDB(Ignotus) = −13 db

and the Degrees of Belief for Claudia,

RDB(Stratford) = −173 db

RDB(Oxford) = 44 db

RDB(Ignotus) = −44 db

The trends of the Running Degrees of Belief are shown in Figure 28.

Miracles may happen, but it seems highly unlikely that our estimates are going to converge.

Let us take a break, and then see what we make of the occurrence of the name "Will" in the sonnets.

NOTE

1. McCrea (2005), 105.

Reader's Chart

The reader is invited to enter his or her own estimates of the weights in the following chart:

Chart 14, Scene 20: Social Status	Evidence Analysis	Stratford No-Compact Theory	Oxford Compact Theory	Ignotus Compact Theory
Reader: Date:				
S1: Nobility				
S2: High class				
S3: Middle class				
S4: Low class				

James' Study at the *Hacienda*

Wordplay in the Sonnets

Where there's a Will, there may be a way.

JAMES. As I recall, Beatrice, you have another item for us to discuss, related to the word or name "Will"—in Sonnet 136, I believe.

BEATRICE. Indeed. The word *will* is used extensively in Sonnets 135 and 136: twelve times in 135, and seven times in 136. There appear to be several usages of the word "will" in these poems, but the appearance of the word, in the last line of 136, seems unequivocal. It reads:

"And then thou louest me for my name is *Will.*"

The name *Will* is in italics, with uppercase "W," in the original Quarto. As McCrea has pointed out [1], this clearly indicates that the name of the poet was "Will." Remember that the first name of Stratford was "William," but the first name of de Vere was "Edward."

CLAUDIA. True enough, Beatrice. But I have looked over these two sonnets, as they were originally printed in 1609. In Sonnets 135 and 136, the word *will* appears nineteen times. In ten of these appearances, the word is in italics, with the "W" in uppercase. So it is not at all obvious to me that one of these ten appearances denotes a proper name.

BEATRICE. Your numerology is correct, Claudia, but I think that context is significant. The last four words of 136 seem unequivocal to me—"my name is Will."

JAMES. If the poet is using the word *will* twenty-one times in twenty-eight lines, he must have had several possible meanings in mind. I have looked into the edition of the sonnets by Stephen Booth [2], which is highly regarded by Shakespeare scholars, and I find that he lists several possible meanings of the word—of which three have sexual connotations.

CLAUDIA. Booth also points out that, if we regard *Will* as someone's name, that someone may be William Shakspere, but it may also be the name of the poet's friend, or that of the dark lady's husband (or conceivably William Herbert, Willie Hughes, or William Hall, . . .).

BEATRICE. All these possibilities may be true in principle. But I regard them as unlikely.

MARTIN. Then perhaps the time has come to assign weights to our conjectures. Since this is your motion, Beatrice, would you like to start?

BEATRICE. Here is my proposed chart:

Chart 15, Scene 21: Sonnets— "Will"	Evidence Analysis	Stratford No-Compact Theory	Oxford Compact Theory	Ignotus Compact Theory
S1: The poet is named "Will" or uses the name "Will"				
S2: The poet is not named "Will" and does not use the name "Will"				
Post Probabilities				

MARTIN. That seems a good choice, Beatrice. It covers the question we are discussing, and your statements comprise a "complete and mutually exclusive" set. We'll make a mathematician of you, yet!

What weights do you enter into your chart?

BEATRICE. I agree with McCrea that Sonnet 136 contains a pretty clear statement that the poet's name is *Will*. However, I realize that the poet was engaging in wordplay, so I allow a 10% chance that there may have been some other meaning.

As far as the hypotheses go: Anyone named "William" is also known as "Will" from time to time, so I give full weight to S1 in the Stratford column.

Someone named "Edward" is not usually known as "Will," so I give zero weight to that option.

Concerning Ignotus, I would guess that there is about a 5% chance that a man, chosen at random, might have the name "William."

So here are my entries:

Chart 15, Scene 21: Sonnets—"Will"	Evidence Analysis	Stratford No-Compact Theory	Oxford Compact Theory	Ignotus Compact Theory
Beatrice				
S1: The poet is named "Will" or uses the name "Will"	10	1	0	1
S2: The poet is not named "Will" and does not use the name "Will"	1	0	1	20
Post Probabilities		0.86	0.05	0.09

MARTIN. I see you have found some of the not-too-abundant evidence that supports Stratford and discounts Oxford.

What do you have to say, Claudia?

CLAUDIA. You will not be surprised that my assessments are very different from Beatrice's.

To start off with, I do not see much difference between the poet's use of the word "Will" in the final line of Sonnet 136 and in the other eighteen usages in Sonnets 135 and 136. We have noted that even Booth—a dedicated Stratfordian—lists a number of alternative meanings of that word [2]. The fact that it is capitalized is not significant, since nine other occurrences of the word in those two sonnets are also capitalized. To my mind, the probability that the poet intended to give his name away is at best 10%.

Concerning the hypotheses: Beatrice is right, of course, that Stratford could have been known familiarly as "Will." But I allow a 10% chance that he did not use that name.

Concerning Oxford, the situation is a little more complicated. Although we are taking account of the possibility that Oxford may have had some associates in writing his plays, I would never suggest that any of his poems involved teamwork. However, I can imagine that a nobleman, in his interactions with members of the lower classes—such as actors, producers, and stagehands—or in his conversations with the "dark lady" (whom he seemed to regard as something of a "tart") might well have used—or let them use— some name less formal than "My Lord" or even "Edward."

I can give you an example to back that up. My elder brother was named "Malcolm," but that was too fancy a name for his schoolmates to use. They all called him "Bill."

Furthermore, according to the Oxford hypothesis, he was using the nom-de-plume "William Shakespeare," so he may have found it amusing to adopt the nickname "Will" in his less formal encounters—including his sexual ones. So I am going to allow a 10% chance that Oxford may, in certain circles, have been known as "Will."

For Ignotus—I go along with Beatrice's guess that there is a 5% chance that the unknown third man was named William, and could therefore be addressed as "Will."

So here are my entries:

Chart 15, Scene 21: Sonnets— "Will	Evidence Analysis	Stratford No-Compact Theory	Oxford Compact Theory	Ignotus Compact Theory
Claudia				
S1: The poet is named "Will" or uses the name "Will"	1	10	1	1
S2: The poet is not named "Will" and does not use the name "Will"	10	1	10	20
Post Probabilities		0.12	0.43	0.45

MARTIN. Where do these new entries leave us, James?

JAMES. I find that Beatrice's and Claudia's probabilities convert to the following Degrees of Belief:

for Beatrice,

DB(Stratford) = 8 db

DB(Oxford) = –13 db

DB(Ignotus) = –10 db

and for Claudia,

DB(Stratford) = –9 db

DB(Oxford) = –1 db

DB(Ignotus) = –1 db

These are shown in Figure 29.

And here are the running probabilities so far:
Running Probabilities, based on Charts 1 to 13,

for Beatrice,

RP(Stratford) = $1\ 10^{-5}$

RP(Oxford) = 0.92

RP(Ignotus) = 0.08

and for Claudia,

RP(Stratford) = $1\ 10^{-18}$

RP(Oxford) = $1 - 4\ 10^{-5}$

RP(Ignotus) = $4\ 10^{-5}$

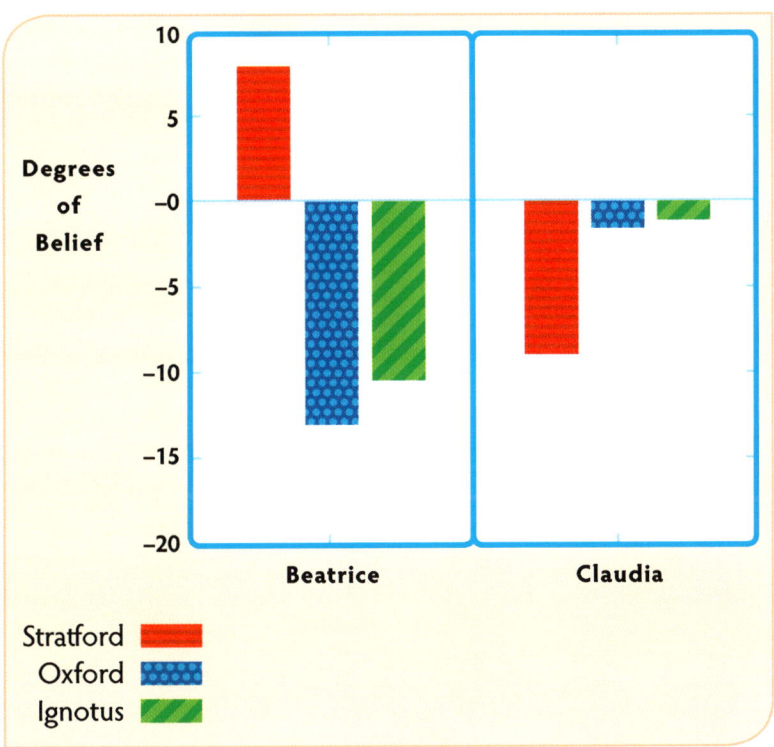

Figure 29. Degrees of Belief for Beatrice and Claudia, based on Chart 15.

Expressed in terms of Degrees of Belief, these become:

Running Degrees of Belief, based on Charts 1 to 14,

for Beatrice,

RDB(Stratford) = –48 db

RDB(Oxford) = 11 db

RDB(Ignotus) = –11 db

and for Claudia,

RDB(Stratford) = −178 db

RDB(Oxford) = 44 db

RDB(Ignotus) = −44 db

The trends of the Running Degrees of Belief are shown in Figure 30.

MARTIN. No signs of a rapprochement, I'm afraid. I understand that, when next we meet, the ball will be in your court, Claudia.

CLAUDIA. Yes, I hope to show you all that there is more to the Dedication of the Sonnets than meets the unsuspecting Stratfordian eye.

JAMES. Perhaps, in the meantime, we can have a rapprochement over cocktails.

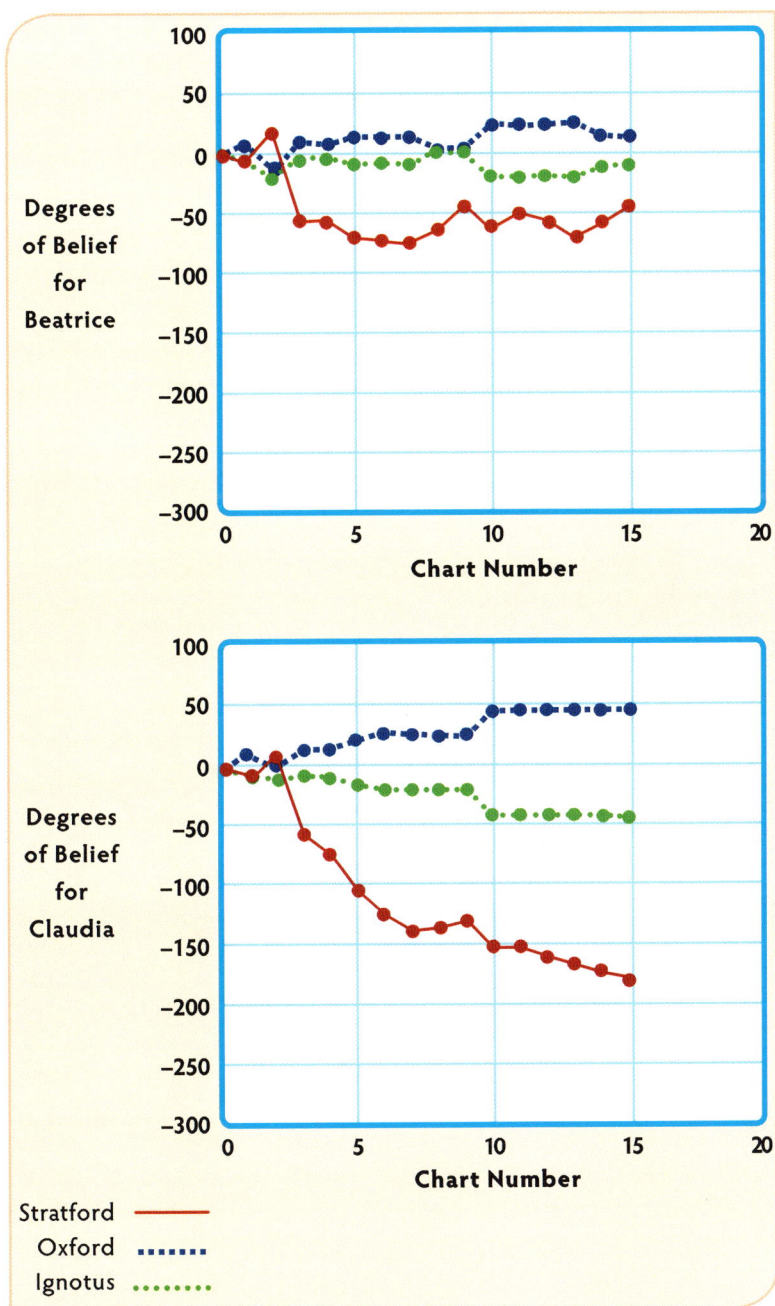

Figure 30. Running Degrees of Belief for Beatrice and Claudia, based on Charts 1 through 15.

NOTES

1. McCrea (2005), 105.
2. Booth (1977), 466–473.

Reader's Chart

The reader is invited to enter his or her own estimates of the weights in the following chart:

Chart 15, Scene 21: Sonnets— "Will"	Evidence Analysis	Stratford No-Compact Theory	Oxford Compact Theory	Ignotus Compact Theory
Reader: Date:				
S1: The poet is named "Will" or uses the name "Will"				
S2: The poet is not named "Will" and does not use the name "Will"				
Post Probabilities				

James' Study at the *Hacienda*

Introduction to the
Dedication to the Sonnets

The Sonnets are mysterious—but their Dedication is more so.

JAMES. We have now had a very brief overview of the sonnets. Thank you both, Beatrice and Claudia. I gather that there is an enormous literature of analysis, interpretation, and exegesis of these enigmatic poems. Most of it based on the assumption that they were written by Stratford, but more recently some are based on the assumption that they were written by Oxford. However, Claudia, I understand that you intend to focus our attention on the curious Dedication, which I have taken it upon myself to reproduce:

TO.THE.ONLIE.BEGETTER.OF.
THESE.INSVING.SONNETS.
Mr. W.H. ALL.HAPPINESSE.
AND.THAT.ETERNITIE.
PROMISED.
BY.
OVR.EVER-LIVING.POET.
WISHETH.
THE. WELL-WISHING.
ADVENTURER.IN.
SETTING.
FORTH.

T.T.

As I recall, the initials 'T.T." are those of the publisher, Thomas Thorpe. Are we to understand that Thorpe was the author of the Dedication?

CLAUDIA. You have touched on a crucial question, James. It seems that almost everyone has assumed that to be the case. However, I suggest that we put that question on hold until we have examined the contents of the Dedication. If we can understand what is hidden in the Dedication, then we can address the question: "Who did the hiding?"

BEATRICE. Are you asking us to start off with the assumption that there is a message hidden in the Dedication?

CLAUDIA. Let us say that I am asking you to entertain that possibility. If we find no hidden message, then our game is over. If we do find one, we have to first decide whether the apparent message can have arisen by chance, and therefore has no real significance. If we find that it *cannot* be attributed to chance, we are then left with the puzzle of trying to comprehend the nature and significance of the message.

Let me begin by saying that although Elizabethan authors wrote many books, and many collections of essays and poems, and although many of those publications began with a dedication, none of those dedications bears any resemblance to the one before us.

Much of what I have to say is based on the work of John Rollett [1], who was the first person to unravel two of the messages hidden in the Dedication. In the course of his research, Rollett found that Thorpe had incorporated dedications in several of his other publications—but they bear no similarity whatever to the Dedication of "Shakespeare's Sonnets." (See, for instance, [2].) It took Rollett many years to make the discoveries I hope to present to you in an hour or so. If some of the steps do not seem obvious, it is because they are not obvious.

BEATRICE. But why on Earth would a publisher or an author, or whoever, wish to hide a message in a dedication? Why not come out and say what he had to say?

MARTIN. A very good question, Beatrice. But it is just part of the great question we asked at the outset—If the author was not Stratford, why the mystery? Why didn't the author announce his authorship when the sonnets were published, and when the plays were performed? As I recall, we agreed at the outset that we would table that question. If we end up with a strong case for the identity of the author, that could provide a solid basis for a subsequent project, aimed at answering the question—Why the mystery? But—to use a parliamentary term—"Why" is not part of our remit.

CLAUDIA. After a number of false starts, Rollett focused on two features of the layout of the Dedication:

1. There is a period after every word, and
2. The text is displayed as three trapeziums, of lengths six lines, two lines, and four lines.

He later saw a coincidence that the name "Edward de Vere" has three parts, of lengths six letters, two letters, and four letters.

After some research, Rollett learned of a type of cryptogram called an *innocent letter code*. This is the procedure of embedding the words of a secret message in what seems to be an innocent message. The "key" might be *extract every tenth word*, or *extract the fifth word, then the seventh word, and keep repeating this procedure,* etc.

Rollett finally (following the clues of the layout, and the letters in de Vere's name) guessed that the key was to extract the sixth word, then the second word, then the fourth word, and cycle this sequence through the entire Dedication. This is called an "acrostic" cypher. The result turns out to be:

THESE SONNETS ALL BY EVER THE FORTH

Rollett initially saw no significance in "EVER," or in 'THE FORTH." It was only after he learned of *de Vere* as a candidate for the mantle of Shake*Speare that he realized that EVER may be an acrostic for VERE or shorthand for E. VERE.

As far as I know, Rollett never proposed an interpretation of "THE FORTH." Some ideas have been put forward, but there is no consensus, as far as I can tell.

BEATRICE. If that is all that is hidden in the Dedication, I do not find it very impressive.

CLAUDIA. No—it is not all that is hidden in the Dedication. It is just the beginning.

However, since this is part of the evidence that some scholars think relevant to the Authorship Question, I wonder if there is a way for us to compare notes on it. What are your thoughts, Martin?

MARTIN. If we count every symbol or letter or combination of letter between two periods as a "word," then there are 30 words in the Dedication. The 6-2-4 procedure extracts just 7 words from those 30. We can ask how many ways there are of extracting 7 items from 30, and the answer is 30*29*28*27*26*25*24, which is approximately 10 billion. However, if we stipulate that the order of the words should be the same as in the original sequence, we must divide this by 1*2*3*4*5*6*7 which is approximately 5,000. So the number of ways of extracting 7 words and keeping them in the same order is approximately 2 million.

But we must then consider how many of these 2 million combinations form a comprehensible (and hopefully relevant) message. I would guess there are either none or very few, but I'll be very generous and say that there might be 100. Then the probability that a random rearrangement of 7 words (retaining their order) leads to a comprehensible message is 1/20,000.

CLAUDIA. I guess that we could proceed to set up a chart and try to evaluate the significance of this piece of the Dedication. However, there are several more aspects to the Dedication that bear on the Authorship Question. I think it makes more sense to view them as a whole, rather than individually, so I suggest that we postpone our evaluation of the Dedication until we have looked at the other ingredients. I think you will find the overall picture fascinating.

JAMES. You are telling us that you want to hold your fire until you see the whites of our eyes?

CLAUDIA. Not exactly—But yes.

JAMES. That means that we have to hold our fire, too.

Lunchtime: Let us break bread together. And perhaps a small libation before the breaking of the bread.

NOTES

1. Rollett (1997a, 1997b, 1997c).

2. Bond (2009), 16.

James' Study at the *Hacienda*

Examining the
Dedication to the Sonnets

Is there more to the Dedication than meets the eye?

JAMES. Claudia, I think you said that our discussion this morning, concerning the Dedication to the Sonnets, was "just the beginning." Can you tell us what comes next?

CLAUDIA. We referred to the work of John M. Rollett [1] this morning. He was the first person to unravel the acrostic cypher in the Dedication, leading to: *THESE SONNETS ALL BY EVER THE FORTH.*

However, it occurred to Rollett that the Dedication might also contain the kind of cryptogram that we met in relation to the Stratford monument [2]. He therefore examined the text to see if it contained a message that had been concealed by the *ELS* (Equidistant Letter Sequence) procedure. As you may recall, the procedure is to take the sequence of letters in the overt message, enter them into a rectangular grid, and then look to see if one can recognize any words in any of the columns, reading either top to bottom, or bottom to top.

The first step is, of course, to count the number of letters. This is found to be 144. That immediately got Rollett's attention, since one can fit that number of letters into several "perfect grids."

Listing only those that have six or more letters both horizontally and vertically, we arrive at the following seven possibilities: 24 × 6; 18 × 8; 16 × 9; 12 × 12; 9 × 16; 8 × 18; and 6 × 24. (For grids of width or height 2, 3, or 4 letters, most words would need to be chopped up into very small pieces.)

Rollett began to examine these grids in order. There was nothing obvious in the 24 × 6 grid. However, when he organized the letters in the 18 × 8 grid, something caught his attention.

Using the same kind of display that we saw in discussing the Inscription on the Monument, he found this:

T	O	T	H	E	O	N	L	I	**E**	B	E	G	E	T	T	E	R
O	F	T	H	E	S	E	I	N	**S**	V	I	N	G	S	O	N	N
E	T	S	M	R	W	H	A	L	**L**	**H**	A	P	P	I	N	E	S
S	E	A	N	D	T	H	A	T	**E**	**T**	E	R	N	I	T	I	E
P	R	O	M	I	S	E	D	B	**Y**	**O**	V	R	E	V	E	R	L
I	V	I	N	G	P	O	E	T	W	**I**	S	H	E	T	H	T	H
E	**W**	E	L	L	W	I	S	H	I	N	G	A	D	V	E	N	T
V	**R**	E	R	I	N	S	E	T	T	I	N	G	F	O	R	T	H

There, broken up into three pieces, we see

WRIOTHESLEY

(in three pieces: WR—IOTH—ESLEY).

BEATRICE. An unusual name—but what is special about it?

CLAUDIA. You may recall that "William Shakespeare" (whoever he was) burst on the London scene with two long narrative poems, *Venus and Adonis* (in 1593) and *Rape of Lucrece* (in 1594).

Both poems have dedications that begin as follows:

To The Right Honourable, Henry Wriothesley,
Earl of Southampton, and Baron of Titchfield.

BEATRICE. So Shake*Speare had an author–patron relationship with the Earl of Southampton. Doesn't this explain why Stratford would weave his name into the Dedication of the Sonnets?

CLAUDIA. It might—if Southampton really was his patron. But there is no evidence of such a relationship between Southampton and Stratford—no letters, no gifts, no commendatory verses (as we saw back in Scene 8), and no such dedications in any of his plays.

JAMES. Presumably we shall need to look into the possibility that those eleven letters could have turned up by chance.

MARTIN. Yes, indeed. That is something that I am willing to take on. I can report back to you Monday morning. But is this one surname all that is hidden in the Dedication?

CLAUDIA. Not at all—There is much more! Bond has found a remarkable combination of messages in these 144 letters [3]!

Examining the 18 × 8 grid more closely, we find

T	O	T	H	E	O	N	L	I	E	B	E	G	E	T	T	E	R
O	F	T	H	E	S	E	I	N	S	V	I	N	G	S	O	N	N
E	T	S	M	R	W	H	A	L	L	H	A	P	P	I	N	E	S
S	E	A	N	D	T	H	A	T	E	T	E	R	N	I	T	I	E
P	R	O	M	I	S	E	D	B	Y	O	V	R	E	V	E	R	L
I	V	I	N	G	P	O	E	T	W	I	S	H	E	T	H	T	H
E	W	E	L	L	W	I	S	H	I	N	G	A	D	V	E	N	T
V	R	E	R	I	N	S	E	T	T	I	N	G	F	O	R	T	H

which contains the sentence

TO ESPIE OFT WRIOTHESLEY WIT NEED NOT HERE TRIE

This is a somewhat archaic and somewhat roundabout way of saying

> *To see Wriothesley often in these sonnets is easy if you use your wits.*

BEATRICE. Possibly. Is there anything else secreted in that Dedication?

CLAUDIA. Yes. Let us look at the grid with 15 columns and 10 lines (not a perfect grid).

T	O	T	H	E	O	N	L	I	E	B	E	G	E	T
T	E	R	O	F	T	H	E	S	E	I	N	S	V	I
N	G	S	O	N	N	E	T	S	M	R	W	H	A	L
L	H	A	P	P	I	N	E	S	S	E	A	N	D	T
H	A	T	E	T	E	R	N	I	T	I	E	P	R	O
M	I	S	D	B	Y	Y	O	U	R	E	V	E	R	L
I	V	I	N	G	P	O	E	T	W	I	S	H	E	T
H	T	H	E	W	E	L	L	W	I	S	H	I	N	G
A	D	V	E	N	T	U	R	E	R	I	N	S	E	T
T	I	N	G	F	O	R	T	H						

We find

HENRY

—Wriothesley's Christian name!

BEATRICE. Maybe Stratford did have a patron—Southampton—and perhaps he was simply incorporating the name of his patron into the Dedication.

CLAUDIA. Possibly. But there is yet more to be found in these 144 letters. When the text is arranged in a grid with 25 columns, one finds

T	O	T	H	E	O	N	L	I	E	B	E	G	E	T	T	E	R	O	F	T	H	E	S	E
I	N	S	V	I	N	G	S	O	N	N	E	T	S	M	R	W	H	A	L	L	**H**	A	P	P
I	N	E	S	S	E	A	N	D	T	H	A	**T**	E	T	**E**	R	N	I	T	**I**	E	P	R	O
M	I	S	E	D	B	Y	O	V	R	E	V	**E**	R	L	I	V	I	N	G	**P**	**O**	**E**	**T**	W
I	S	H	E	T	H	T	H	E	W	E	L	**L**	W	I	**S**	H	I	N	G	A	D	V	E	N
T	V	R	E	R	I	N	S	E	T	T	I	N	G	F	**O**	**R**	T	H						

LET ROSIE LIP POET APE OWN

The interpretation of these words is rather subtle, and I suggest that we postpone it until we have decided whether or not these apparent messages are due simply to chance.

JAMES. This does all seem pretty subtle! My head is spinning. I think we should adjourn soon. Is there anything else in this Dedication that we should know about?

CLAUDIA. Yes—remarkably enough, there is one more message. But it is in Latin!

The simplest grid—and probably the first one that an astute reader might examine if he suspected a hidden message—is the 12 × 12 grid.

T	O	T	H	E	O	N	L	I	E	B	E
G	E	T	T	E	R	O	F	T	H	E	S
E	I	N	S	V	I	N	G	S	O	N	N
E	T	**S**	M	**R**	W	H	A	L	L	H	A
P	**P**	**I**	N	**E**	S	S	E	A	N	D	T
H	**A**	**T**	**E**	**T**	E	R	N	I	T	I	E
P	**R**	**O**	M	**I**	S	E	D	B	Y	O	V
R	**E**	V	**E**	**R**	L	I	V	I	N	G	P
O	E	T	W	I	S	H	E	T	H	T	H
E	W	E	L	L	W	I	S	H	I	N	G
A	D	V	E	N	T	V	R	E	R	I	N
S	E	T	T	I	N	G	F	O	R	T	H

In the first five columns, we find

PRO PARE VOTIS EMERITER

Reading horizontally, we can also discern ***EVER***, a word that we found in the Inscription to the Monument (Scene 16) and in the acrostic cypher in this Dedication (Scene 23), and which turns up frequently in the Sonnets (for instance, in Sonnet 116). We can pick up the interpretation of these words during our next meeting.

JAMES. Thank you, Claudia. You have given us a lot to think about. But the next step will be for Martin to advise us whether these words and sentences are here by design, or simply chance occurrences.

MARTIN. Yes, this will keep me busy over the weekend. While you are all exploring the Nineteen Mile Drive and Point Lobos, I expect to be engrossed in numerology! I hope I have something definite to report to you on Monday.

JAMES. Thank you, Martin. We have had a busy day. Now Claudia and I want to take you both to our favorite fish restaurant in Pacific Grove.

NOTES

1. John M. Rollett (1997a, 1997b, 1997c).
2. Scene 16.
3. Jonathan Bond (2009).

James' Study at the *Hacienda*

Assessing the Apparent Messages in the Dedication to the Sonnets [1]

Numerology, if treated respectfully, can be respectable.

JAMES. I'm afraid we gave Martin a difficult assignment on Friday—to provide us with some probability estimates concerning the apparent secret messages in the Dedication to the Sonnets.

How did you fare, Martin?

MARTIN. Claudia informed us that John Rollett [2], Jonathan Bond [3], and perhaps others claim to have discovered several messages secreted in the Dedication. My ideal result would have been to present you with an overall assessment that those messages were real (not due to chance), and significant (in that they made sense, and carried an intelligible message).

However, I soon realized that that was far too grand a goal to set myself as a weekend assignment. I have had to be much more modest, but I think I still have something interesting to share with you.

BEATRICE. Are you going to have some kind of probability estimate for us?

MARTIN. Yes, I shall. I have been able to investigate two very small pieces of the puzzle.

CLAUDIA. The names *Henry* and *Wriothesley,* I suppose.

MARTIN. You guessed right. They are the two words that first attracted Rollett's interest—after he had discovered the sentence linked to the 6-2-4 layout of the Dedication.

I believe that I can give you a useful and reliable "lower limit" to the significance of the hidden messages by calculating the probability that these two words might have appeared by chance.

BEATRICE. Is it possible to explain this to us, without using any higher mathematics?

MARTIN. I shall try to explain the line of argument without all of the details. Let us take the name HENRY first. One can begin by calculating the probability that a given sequence of five cells will contain the letters H,E,N,R,Y. This is about $5 \cdot 10^{-7}$. One can then calculate the number of ways of selecting a sequence of 5 cells in all the admissible grids. This is approximately 4,000. In this way, we find that the probability of finding HENRY by chance somewhere (up or down) in one of the possible grids to be approximately 0.002. The details are given in Appendix E.

We can carry out a similar calculation for the probability of finding the name WRIOTHESLEY by chance. This is a similar calculation, but more complicated to take account of the possibility that the name might have been broken up into either two or three parts. The details are given in Appendix F. We finally arrive at an estimate of the probability of finding the name WRIOTHESLEY by chance. It is found to be $7 \cdot 10^{-6}$.

Multiplying the probability of finding HENRY by chance by the probability of finding WRIOTHESLEY by chance, we arrive at the probability of finding both parts of the name by chance. It is found to be $1.5 \cdot 10^{-8}$.

CLAUDIA. But HENRY and WRIOTHESLEY are just two of the words in those messages. What we need to know is the probability that all of those messages might have occurred by chance.

MARTIN. That would be a much more complicated calculation. You would need to have some way of deciding whether or not a given sequence of letters comprises a sensible message. Let me say only that the probability of finding all of those messages by chance would be infinitesimal!

What we can say with conviction is that our probability estimate of 1.5 10^{-8} is a *highly conservative* estimate of the probability that the Dedication contains one or more significant messages.

Now we need to see what impact this result has on the status of each of our three candidates.

Would you like to suggest a chart, Claudia?

CLAUDIA. This is a tricky question, but a crucial one I think. If we try to focus on the content of the apparent messages, then we shall be debating "Why should Oxford be referring to Wriothesley?", "Why should Stratford be referring to Wriothesley?, and "Why should some unknown person be referring to Wriothesley?" I would anticipate that the answers to these questions would be highly speculative.

However, there is another approach that I suggest: *Is there, or is there not, a hidden message in the Dedication?* As far as I am aware, the only times that the author names any names is in his dedications to his first two poems—which are (intriguingly enough) dedicated to "Henry Wriothesley, 3rd Earl of Southampton." So *Wriothesley* is certainly a name that is relevant to the Authorship Issue. From this line of thought, it seems that Martin's calculations yield a sensible estimate of the probability that there *is* a hidden message in the Dedication.

This then leaves us with the questions of whether or not any hidden messages are to be expected on the basis of our three standard hypotheses. And I think these are questions we can address in a more or less sensible manner, for the following reason:

Hidden messages, especially those that name names, are perfectly compatible with the two hypotheses that allow for what we tactfully call a "compact"—which somebody else might term a "conspiracy." But I would claim that hidden messages are incompatible with any hypothesis that does not provide for the possibility of a compact.

Let me try to express these thoughts in the form of a chart:

Chart 16, Scene 24: Sonnets—Dedication	Evidence Analysis	Stratford No-Compact Theory	Oxford Compact Theory	Ignotus Compact Theory
S1: The Dedication contains one or more hidden messages				
S2: The Dedication contains no hidden message				
Post Probabilities				

Bearing in mind that the name *Henry Wriothesley* has a special—maybe unique—role in the Authorship Issue (since it is the only name explicitly named in the Shake*Speare corpus), I think it is reasonable to adopt Martin's results in filling out the first column. So my entries in the Data column would be:

Chart 16, Scene 24: Sonnets— Dedication	Evidence Analysis	Stratford No-Compact Theory	Oxford Compact Theory	Ignotus Compact Theory
Claudia				
S1: The Dedication contains one or more hidden messages	1			
S2: The Dedication contains no hidden message	1.5×10^{-8}			
Post Probabilities				

Now we come to the entries for our three hypotheses—and this is where the terms *Compact* and *No-Compact* become crucial. We agreed early on that our basic hypothesis concerning Stratford is the orthodox assumption that he wrote what he wrote, that he did not try to hide the fact, and that nobody else tried to hide the fact. In short, there is no compact (aka *conspiracy*) involved or implied in the *Stratford* hypothesis. Hidden messages are compatible with hypotheses that allow for a compact, but they are incompatible with any hypothesis that explicitly rules out the possibility of a compact.

This leads me to the following entries for the next column:

Chart 16, Scene 24: Sonnets— Dedication	Evidence Analysis	Stratford No-Compact Theory	Oxford Compact Theory	Ignotus Compact Theory
Claudia				
S1: The Dedication contains one or more hidden messages	1	0		
S2: The Dedication contains no hidden message	$1.5 \cdot 10^{-8}$	1		
Post Probabilities				

On the other hand, we have agreed to explicitly allow for the possibility that both the Oxford and Ignotus hypotheses may involve a compact. This does not tell us exactly what weights to enter in the OX and IG columns, but it does tell us that the entries for S1 should be non-zero.

Oxford and Southampton (aka Wriothesley) were both noblemen. Furthermore, each of them was at one time a ward of Lord Burghley. So—independently of what one might read into the sonnets, etc.—they were no doubt acquainted. On the other hand, Ignotus may or may not have been a nobleman who may or may not have been acquainted with Southampton. This line of argument would, I think, justify us in giving more weight to S1 (or, equivalently, less weight to S2) for the Oxford hypothesis than for the Ignotus hypothesis. So, focusing on S1, I suggest entering W for Oxford and W/10 for Ignotus.

Chart 16, Scene 24: Sonnets—Dedication	Evidence Analysis	Stratford No-Compact Theory	Oxford Compact Theory	Ignotus Compact Theory
Claudia				
S1: The Dedication contains one or more hidden messages	1	0	W	W/10
S2: The Dedication contains no hidden message	$1.5\ 10^{-8}$	1	1	1
Post Probabilities				

All that remains is to decide what number to adopt for the probability that Oxford (and, by implication, Ignotus) would have entered—or caused to be entered—a secret message in the Dedication. That is to say, what number should we adopt for W?

But I have been carrying on for a long time. What are your thoughts, Beatrice?

BEATRICE. I agree in general with your line of thought, and I have no objection to the figures you enter in the *Evidence* column. Martin vouches for the accuracy of those figures.

However, you have made two crucial assumptions concerning the hypotheses columns. You argue that the existence of one or more hidden messages would be incompatible with the hypothesis we have labeled *No-Compact*. If we had foreseen this issue early on, we might have decided to also consider the option *Compact* in relation to Stratford. This would have allowed for the possibility that the gentleman from Stratford-upon-Avon may have been involved in some political or financial machinations that he chose to, or was required to, keep quiet about. But, of course, that is not part of the orthodox Stratfordian position. Since our *Stratford No-Compact* hypothesis is supposed to represent the orthodox position, I have to agree that secret messages are incompatible with that hypothesis.

It also seems to me that you are on pretty solid ground in arguing that our two "compact" options, *Oxford Compact* and *Ignotus Compact*, allow for the possibility of secret messages. Any self-respecting conspirator would expect to have that privilege as a basic requirement in his line of business.

This leaves us with only two decisions to make—the weights we assign to the statements in the Oxford and Ignotus columns. I personally do not see why the weight for S1 (keeping the weight for S2 fixed) should be less for Ignotus than for Oxford. We know nothing about their secret goings-on. So my format would be the following:

Chart 16, Scene 24: Sonnets—Dedication	Evidence Analysis	Stratford No-Compact Theory	Oxford Compact Theory	Ignotus Compact Theory
Beatrice				
S1: The Dedication contains one or more hidden messages	1	0	W	W
S2: The Dedication contains no hidden message	$1.5 \ 10^{-8}$	1	1	1
Post Probabilities				

This leaves both Claudia's and my charts with this uncertain quantity W. I suggest that, before we agonize too much on that question, we can ask Martin how much difference it would make to our final outcome if we were to choose W = 0.1 or W = 0.01, or W = 0.001, etc.

MARTIN. That is not a difficult question to answer. Just give me two or three minutes to run a few calculations. . . . The answer is very interesting—and perhaps a little surprising. I find that, for both Beatrice's and Claudia's charts, the end result is quite insensitive to our choice of W. I am going to enter W = 0.01, but the end results would be substantially the same had I adopted W = 0.001, or W = 0.0001, etc.

Chart 16, Scene 24: Sonnets—Dedication	Evidence Analysis	Stratford No-Compact Theory	Oxford Compact Theory	Ignotus Compact Theory
Claudia				
S1: The Dedication contains one or more hidden messages	1	0	0.01	0.001
S2: The Dedication contains no hidden message	1.5×10^{-8}	1	1	1
Post Probabilities		5×10^{-9}	0.91	0.09

and

Chart 16, Scene 24: Sonnets— Dedication	Evidence Analysis	Stratford No-Compact Theory	Oxford Compact Theory	Ignotus Compact Theory
Beatrice				
S1: The Dedication contains one or more hidden messages	1	0	0.01	0.01
S2: The Dedication contains no hidden message	$1.5 \ 10^{-8}$	1	1	1
Post Probabilities		$5 \ 10^{-9}$	0.5	0.5

Beatrice's suspicion was absolutely correct—it makes virtually no difference what value we adopt for W.

Where does this leave our scoreboard, James?

JAMES. Beatrice's and Claudia's probabilities convert to the following Degrees of Belief:

for Beatrice,

> DB(Stratford) = -83 db
>
> DB(Oxford) = 0db
>
> DB(Ignotus) = 0 db

and for Claudia,

> DB(Stratford) = –83 db
>
> DB(Oxford) = 10 db
>
> DB(Ignotus) = -10 db

These are shown in Figure 31.

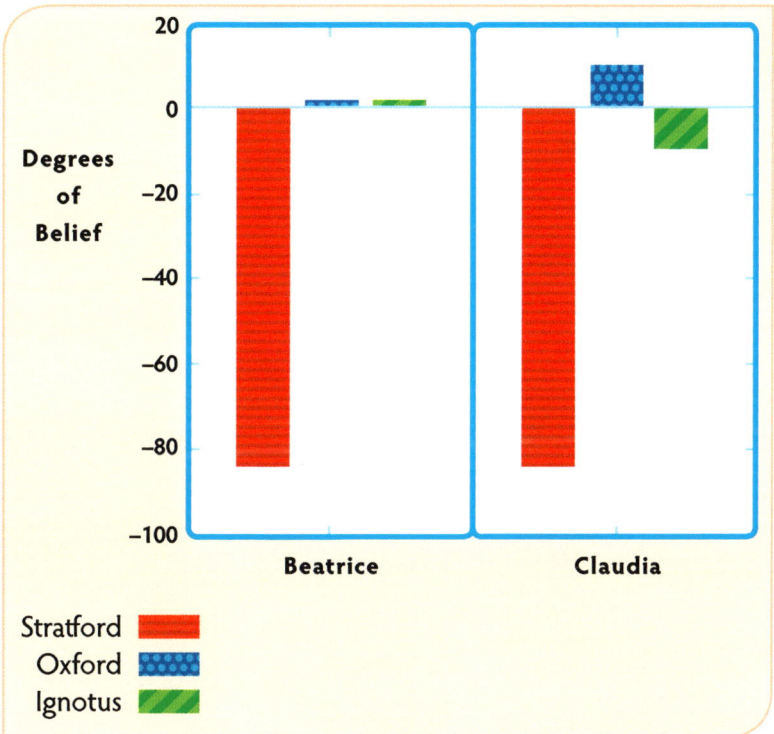

Figure 31. Degrees of Belief for Beatrice and Claudia, based on Chart 16.

I am afraid I am bringing bad news for anyone rooting for Stratford. Here are what I believe will be our final scores:

Beatrice's new running probabilities are:

RP(Stratford) = 10^{-13}

RP(Oxford) = 0.92

RP(Ignotus) = 0.08

and Claudia's are:

$$RP(\text{Stratford}) = 8\ 10^{-27}$$

$$RP(\text{Oxford}) = 1 - 5\ 10^{-6}$$

$$RP(\text{Ignotus}) = 5\ 10^{-6}$$

In terms of *Degrees of Belief,* these figures become

for Beatrice,

$$DB(\text{Stratford}) = -128\ \text{db}$$

$$DB(\text{Oxford}) = 11\ \text{db}$$

$$DB(\text{Ignotus}) = -11\ \text{db}$$

and for Claudia,

$$DB(\text{Stratford}) = -261\ \text{db}$$

$$DB(\text{Oxford}) = 53\ \text{db}$$

$$DB(\text{Ignotus}) = -53\ \text{db}$$

The complete trend is shown in Figure 32.

A wide spread in your two sets of estimates, but both are pretty decisive, as far as Stratford is concerned. The difference is that Claudia heavily prefers Oxford over Ignotus, but Beatrice is not quite so sure on that point.

Well Beatrice, I think you can see why I was not impressed with your initial guess of odds of only one hundred to one!

However, there are other questions that we could address. We have not even asked "Who was the enigmatic *Mr. W.H.*"? Let us meet tomorrow to sort out what we do know and what we still do not know.

But let us have a more relaxing venue tomorrow—maybe a picnic by the coast.

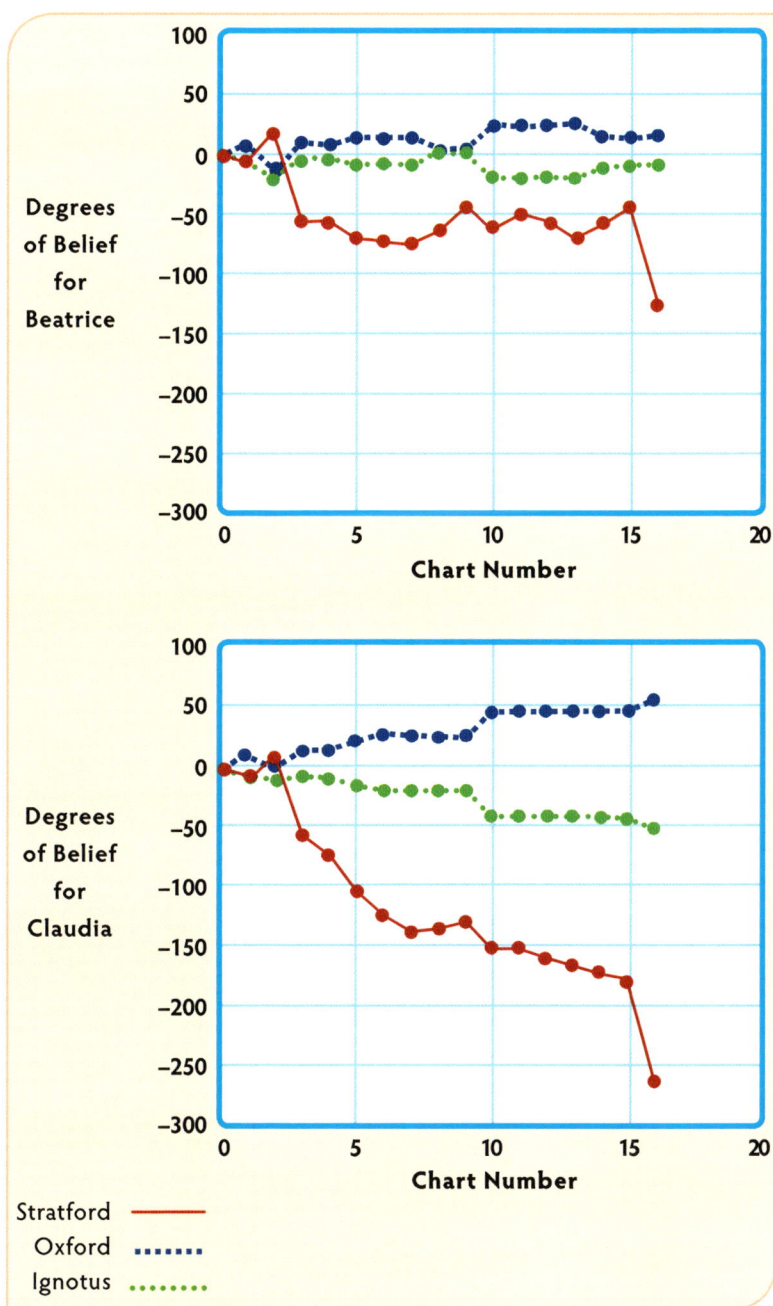

Figure 32. Running Degrees of Belief for Beatrice and Claudia, based on Charts 1 through 16.

NOTES

1. The calculations presented in Appendices E and F, which are incorporated in this scene, were carried out by the author in collaboration with Professor Martin Hellman (Emeritus Professor of Electrical Engineering at Stanford University), who is an expert in modern cryptography. They were also reviewed by Dr. Jeffrey D. Scargle (a member of the scientific staff of the NASA Ames Research Center) who is an astrophysicist distinguished for his contributions to statistics and probability theory.

2. Rollett (1997a, 1997b, 1997c).

3. Bond (2009).

Reader's Chart

The reader is invited to enter his or her own estimates of the weights in the following chart:

Chart 16, Scene 24: Sonnets— Dedication	Evidence Analysis	Stratford No-Compact Theory	Oxford Compact Theory	Ignotus Compact Theory
Reader: Date:				
S1: The Dedication contains one or more hidden messages				
S2: The Dedication contains no hidden message				
Post Probabilities				

A Picnic Table at Point Lobos

An Estimate of the Situation [1]

Logical thinking can lead to surprising conclusions.

JAMES. The last three or four sessions were pretty demanding, so we thought we owed it to ourselves to find somewhere more relaxing and refreshing for today's meeting. Claudia has kindly packed us a picnic, and I have a surprise bottle of wine. We all thought that Multepulciano is produced only in Italy. Well, during the Vintners' Meeting in Napa, a vintner from Alexander Valley gave us each a bottle of Montepulciano from his own winery. He claims it is every bit as good as the Italian original. We can check out his claim today.

Now to business—We have been grappling with the question of whether there are any hidden messages in the Dedication to the Sonnets. Thanks to Martin, we learned during our last meeting that the answer is a resounding *Yes!* Or, at least, *Yes to a high probability!*

So I now suggest that we review the Dedication and the ciphers. What were they all about? Who actually composed the Dedication? Who was the intended recipient of the assembled sonnets? Who was the enigmatic "Mr. W.H."?

BEATRICE. But before we get to that, can you or Martin help me understand the results of our exercise? We have gone through about sixteen evaluations, as I recall. Apart from the last one, which led to a very small probability for Stratford, none of the them individually seemed particularly dramatic. Yet we end up with some pretty small probabilities, and some pretty big numbers for our degrees of belief.

I have enormous difficulty comprehending such big numbers. Martin—Can you give me some way to understand Claudia's final odds of about 10^{26} to 1 against Stratford?

MARTIN. I'll try. Suppose that somehow we are given a sphere the size of the Earth, and suppose that we could fill this with ping-pong balls, each about one inch in diameter. They are all white, except for one, which is black. The black one could be anywhere inside that sphere the size of the Earth. Now suppose that, without any information to guide you, you select one of those balls from anywhere inside that sphere the size of the Earth. The probability that you will have selected the black one will be much the same as Claudia's estimate that Stratford was Shake*Speare!

Pretty long odds, I would say!

BEATRICE. I find it very, very hard to believe that the evidence we have reviewed—or any reasonable extension of that evidence—could lead to such an incredible result. Are you sure there is no error in our calculations?

MARTIN. The calculations are quite straightforward. There is no error in the calculations. If you wish to change the results, you will need to persuade Claudia to change the numbers in her charts. And don't forget that your own entries led to a strong case against Stratford. Not as big as Claudia'a, but pretty strong all the same.

BEATRICE. How big a pile of ping-pong balls to match my conclusion?

MARTIN. You would have a much easier time. You would have to find the right ball in a pile that is only 800 yards across! It contains only ten million million ping-pong balls! However, we should not forget that we have not used all the evidence available to us.

CLAUDIA. What have we forgotten?

MARTIN. We have actually used only a small fraction of the evidence secreted in the Dedication to the Sonnets. We found that examination of the ELS procedure reveals the names *EVERE, Henry,* and *Wriothesley.*

BEATRICE. But what else is there?

MARTIN. There are actually four messages:

> *THESE SONNETS ALL BY EVERE THE FORTH*
>
> *TO ESPIE OFT WRIOTHESLEY WIT NEED NOT HERE TRIE*
>
> *LET ROSIE LIP POET APE OWN*
>
> *PRO PARE VOTIS EMERITER.*

JAMES. That last sentence caught my attention, Martin. I asked the Chair of the Classics Department at Bradford University what he could make of it. He recognized the words as Latin, but found them very puzzling. Here are his suggestions for what the sentence may mean:

> *For a peer: according to the vows/wishes/prayers; deservedly.*

Jonathan Bond—who is admittedly not a Latin scholar, but who studied Latin in his so-called "public" school in England—proposes the following possibilities:

> *For my dear companion, vowing to be well-deserving;*
> *As here revealed, praying to earn your friendship; and*
> *Devoutly promising to be a well-deserving father.*

The four proposed translations are all different, but they all involve the ideas of friendship and commitment.

MARTIN. Very interesting, James. Concerning

LET ROSIE LIPS POET APE OWN,

some scholars think that *Wriothesley* may have been pronounced *Roseley*. The word *rose* certainly turns up a lot in the sonnets. The combination *Rosie Lips* occurs only once in the entire Shakespeare corpus—in the famous Sonnet (116) that begins *Let me not to the marriage of true minds* . . .

I gather that the term *poet-ape* was coined by—or at least used by—Sir Philip Sidney, around 1581, in referring to hack poets. So the author could conceivably have been saying:

> *Well, Wriothesley, see what a so-called "hack poet" can do, when he tries!*

JAMES. I guess that we shall never know exactly what the author had in mind, but it certainly seems that the Dedication is full of very clever word games. Frankly, I cannot grasp a probability of one part in 1 followed by 26 zeros! On the other hand, I cannot conceive that these sentences (one in Latin) are due purely to chance! How many monkeys would it take hammering away at typewriters, and for how long, to produce a document like this?

You are a statistician, Martin. Does this document seem at all surprising to you?

MARTIN. Indeed it does. I find it extraordinarily sophisticated. I also sense that the author had a great sense of humor. It would have taken months of intense effort to come up with this complex a document. He must have taken great pleasure in the process, or he never would have done it.

JAMES. I see that we have now moved on to the speculation stage. So now we can speculate about two key questions:

Who composed the Dedication? and
Who was the mysterious Mr. W.H.?

CLAUDIA. Following up Martin's comments, that it must have taken extraordinary skill and patience to generate this complicated a document, I think we can safely set aside the usual assumption that the Dedication was composed by Thomas Thorpe. Even if he had the skill (and knowledge of Latin) to produce this document, and even if he could devote months to the task, it would have been unforgivably impertinent of him to give away secrets concerning two noblemen—Oxford and Southampton. It is obvious to me that the Dedication was composed by Oxford himself. To refer to it as "Thorpe's Dedication" is silly!

BEATRICE. You are probably correct that Oxford was playing a game at which he was very skilled, and which he obviously enjoyed playing. But I also suspect that part of his motivation was that he was trying to impress someone—presumably his friend *Rosey!* Perhaps he was also throwing out a challenge to some of his competitors—such as Jonson—to find the messages he had so cleverly concealed.

JAMES. I have to agree with your proposed answer to the authorship of the Dedication. That leaves us only with the puzzle—Who was *Mr. W.H.?*

MARTIN. Now the analysis is behind us, perhaps you will allow me to do some speculating. "Mr. W.H." has to be the person Oxford was trying to impress. I think that Beatrice hit the nail on the head—Oxford had probably written most of his sonnets for Southampton, and he was probably trying to either further impress him, or perhaps just amuse him, with this extraordinary *tour de force*—the Dedication.

CLAUDIA. Yes, but the dedicatee is addressed as *Mister*, not as *My Lord!* Would that not be impudent?

JAMES. I don't think so. Oxford was twenty-three years older than Southampton, and he was higher in the chain of noble command. It is also conceivable that the Dedication was composed while Southampton was in the Tower, when he had been stripped of all of his titles, and was then just *Mr. Henry Wriothesley.*

BEATRICE. All very clever—but probably also very wrong. The initials are the wrong way round!

MARTIN. Well, of course, we do not know the original version of the Dedication, as it went to Southampton. It happens that neither of those letters—*W* and *H*—is used in any of the grills. For all we know, the original version, which went to Southampton, had them in the reverse order—as *Mr. H.W.*

BEATRICE. So who reversed the order, and why?

MARTIN. Southampton himself! If he did not provide the sonnets to Thomas Thorpe, whoever did would certainly seek his concurrence. Presumably Southampton gave the green light, but he may have imposed one condition.

BEATRICE. Namely?

MARTIN. That the initials be reversed to hide the fact—or at least make the fact less obvious—that he was—as so many people have suspected—the *Fair Youth* of the sonnets.

JAMES. That all seems very plausible. And that is probably the most we can hope for, in addressing these two questions.

BEATRICE. But tarry a little—there is something else.

CLAUDIA. That sounds ominous. What do you have in mind?

BEATRICE. The reference to *Our Ever Living Poet!* The phrase *Ever Living* was applied only to someone who had passed away. If Oxford was the author of the Dedication, he was presumably living when he composed it. Then how can he refer to himself as

Ever Living?

JAMES. Well done, Beatrice, you have given us something else to think over! However, it is lunchtime. Let us take a few deep breaths of the sea air, admire this beautiful scenery, and open a bottle of Montepulciano—Alexander Valley style!

NOTE

1. This scene also is based on Bond (2009).

SCENE 26

A Private Deck at the Highview Inn

Final Thoughts

All's well that ends with champagne.

JAMES. Since we began our meetings here at the Highview Inn, this seems an appropriate place to end them. I had planned and expected that this would be simply a celebration, so I reserved this private dining room. However, Beatrice pointed out this morning that we have missed an important question concerning the Dedication to the Sonnets. We seemed to have a clear picture of who composed the Dedication (Oxford) and who was the intended recipient (Southampton). But Beatrice noticed that the poet is referred to in the Dedication as *Ever Living*. She pointed out—quite correctly I believe—that the term *Ever Living* was used only in reference to someone who was deceased.

So now we have a new question to address: Do we have to go back to Thomas Thorpe as the author of the Dedication, or is there some other way to resolve this puzzle?

MARTIN. I have done a little reading about Oxford. We know that the sonnets were not published during his lifetime. Many scholars see them as deeply personal, concerning his complex relationships with the Fair Youth—believed to be Southampton— and the Dark Lady—believed to be Anne Vavasour. She was one of the Queen's ladies–in-waiting, and the Queen was not amused when Vavasour bore Oxford a son (later christened Edward). Oxford was sent to the Tower, as also were Vavasour and her baby—but probably not to the same chamber.

Oxford may have thought that it would be ungentlemanly for him to publish these intimate poems, which of course it would have been. But if he bequeathed the collected sonnets (with a suitable dedication) to Southampton, it would be entirely up to Southampton to decide whether to publish them, lock them away in a safe, or simply destroy them. And—by the way—since Southampton would be receiving the collected sonnets after Oxford had passed away, it would be entirely appropriate for Oxford to refer to himself as "ever-living."

CLAUDIA. That is a possible explanation. But somehow I do not find it completely satisfying. I wonder whether there is some other piece to the puzzle. When we were talking about the marriage of William Shakspere to Anne Hathaway, we looked to see if there was something odd about their wedding, and we found that there was. This raises the question—What do we know about the death of Oxford? I have done some homework, too, and I find that—as seems to be the case with much of Oxford's life—his death is yet another mystery.

He is reputed to have died on June 24, 1604, and to have been buried on July 6 in the Church of St. Augustine in Hackney (where Oxford lived after his marriage to Elizabeth Trentham in 1591). However, an eerie silence surrounds his death: No one mentions his death in any letters; He died intestate; The cause of his death is unknown; There is no record of a funeral; There were no elegies or epitaphs; His grave has never been found; and, most curious of all: The Earl of Southampton was arrested, with several of his friends, that same day [1]. Southampton's papers were seized and he was interrogated. According to the French ambassador, King James went into a panic and posted his Scots guards around his quarters. However, Southampton and his friends were released the next day.

Of course, there are no state records to explain what went on. It is just another puzzle apparently related to the mysterious Earl of Oxford. All we can say without fear of contradiction is that either Oxford died in 1604 or he did not. If he did die in 1604, he had written the words *ever living* in anticipation of his death. If he did not die in 1604, he wrote those words because he was in some way dead to the world.

Since we became interested in this project from reading a review of Bill Bryson's book, you might be interested in what he has to say about the demise of Oxford. It is very brief: He simply informs us that *Edward de Vere incontestably died in 1604* [2]. Unfortunately, Bryson does not give us a citation for the evidence on which this pronouncement is based. If I had to give weights to that assertion,

Plate 9. Anne Vavasour in a painting attributed to Robert Peake the Elder. Vavasour was one of the Queen's Ladies of the Bedchamber and the Queen was not amused when Vavasour gave birth to a son, courtesy of the Earl of Oxford. She and her newborn baby (later named Edward de Vere) were sent to the Tower, as also was Oxford. Vavasour is the leading candidate for the identity of the "Dark Lady" of the Sonnets. [Chiljan, 2011, Plate 23, Cobbe Collection, Hatchlands Park, UK]

based purely on the evidence of Bryson's scholarship, I could not give it better than even odds of being correct.

MARTIN. That is all fascinating, Claudia. However, you were willing to indulge yourself in speculation concerning the marriage of Stratford. Could you not also indulge yourself in some speculation concerning the death or vanishing of Oxford?

CLAUDIA. Only if you insist. My wild speculation is that Oxford made some rash move around that time. While in his cups, he may have voiced Catholic sympathies, and/or he may have expressed his preference for seeing someone from the Tudor line upon the throne of England. Even worse, he may have expressed such sympathies to a correspondent in France or Spain—forgetting that such correspondence would probably be intercepted by James' version of MI5.

That might have been enough to get James worried about the possibility of a *coup d'etat*. In those days, a *coup d'état* could also lead to a *coup de tête*! It would have been natural to suspect that Southampton would be part of such a plot, but apparently he was cleared. On the other hand, Oxford may have been considered to be something of a loose cannon, who should be either done away with or placed somewhere where he could cause no further unrest. Robert Cecil may have persuaded James that he could sleep peacefully at night if Oxford was simply relocated to an out-of-the-way part of England (or possibly elsewhere) where he would be held incommunicado. Who knows—*The Tempest* may in fact be autobiographical! Maybe that was the only way that Oxford could let people know his fate. According to Paul Streitz [3], one researcher has suggested that Oxford may have spent what remained of his life on Mersea Island, off the coast of Essex [4]. This could explain a tongue-in-cheek use of the term *Ever Living*. However, concerning *The Tempest*, Roe makes a stronger case that its setting is Vulcano, off the north coast of Sicily [5].

BEATRICE. Honestly, Claudia, it is that kind of fantasizing that gives conspiracy a bad name!

JAMES. Don't be too hard on her, Beatrice, we did ask Claudia to speculate, after all.

Our efforts to identify Shake*Speare may have answered one question—Was Stratford really Shake*speare?— but it obviously leads to many more puzzles, which may be just as difficult to solve—or perhaps more so. We were either wise or lucky that we set ourselves just the one limited question to address!

With your consent, I am happy to declare that our project is now concluded. I hesitate to say that our mission has been

Plate 10. Queen Elizabeth in a portrait by Nicholas Hilliard, circa 1575. She holds a red rose, the symbol of the House of Tudor. Early in his career at Court, de Vere was a favorite of the Queen, who referred to him as her "Turk." In 1581, after Anne Vavasour bore him a son, de Vere became persona non grata at Court. He returned to court in 1583 and in 1586 Elizabeth ordered that de Vere—who was in dire financial straits—should receive a pension of 1,000 pounds per year. It is believed that references to the "Moon" and "Cynthia" in the Sonnets refer to Elizabeth. Sonnet 107 is believed to refer to the Queen's death in 1603. [http://en.wikipedia.org/wiki/ File:Elizabeth1_Phoenix.jpg]

accomplished, since we should not take ourselves—or our deliberations—too seriously. Let me instead use Leoncavallo's great line at the end of Pagliacci:

La Commedia e' Finita!

But I am curious—Assuming that the author was in fact Oxford, what would it take to convince orthodox scholars of that fact?

MARTIN. For anyone with a mathematical turn of mind, the evidence we have already found in the Dedication to the Sonnets should be more than enough.

BEATRICE. However, I do not know any orthodox Shakespeare scholar who has a mathematical turn of mind, so that is a non-starter.

CLAUDIA. Maybe it will be enough to show that Paul Roe was on the right track in uncovering his remarkable evidence that Shakes*Speare had spent time in Italy.

BEATRICE. I doubt it. It would probably take a box full of manuscripts in Oxford's handwriting. And even then, the discoverer would probably be denounced as a huckster, a charlatan, and a fraud. But what are your thoughts, James?

JAMES. I am reminded of the famous remark by Max Planck, the founding father of quantum mechanics:

New scientific truth does not triumph by convincing its opponents and making them see the light, but rather because its opponents eventually die, and a new generation grows up that is familiar with it.

Maybe the same is true of literary theories.

But I am also curious to know what impact, if any, this project has had on each of you.

Beatrice—Do you plan to give a seminar on the Authorship Question at Marin State University?

Claudia—Will this be the plot or a sub-plot in your next novel?

Martin—Do you plan to write an article, *A scientific approach to non-scientific problems?*

BEATRICE. A seminar? No time soon! You thought that I was closed-minded? I am a free spirit compared with most of my colleagues. But perhaps I can inject some small parts of the puzzle into some of my seminars, and see if any of my students sniff the bait and rise to it.

CLAUDIA. Maybe my detective will, quite by chance, come across some incredibly important state secret. To avoid an untimely demise, he creates an alter ego and—to all the world—becomes that person, so that he can live peacefully thereafter.

MARTIN. A fascinating idea for a plot. It has also been fascinating to see that a Bayesian approach can be brought to bear on a non-mathematical—indeed, a non-scientific—problem. But will it play in Peoria? Luckily, intelligence officers are like engineers—they are interested in whatever works! So it just might play in Peoria, if the audience could be drawn from the intelligence community!

JAMES. Yes, I think you are onto something, Martin. Scientists do not have a dog in this fight, so they may be willing to follow the scent and see—or sniff—where it leads. On the other hand, most scientists—like most other professionals—are pretty conservative, and it is not easy to get them interested in a truly new idea—unless it is patentable, of course.

CLAUDIA. It seems to me that you are suggesting that a person will change his mind only if there's some incentive to do so. This fits in with my experience: People tend to believe what they want to believe. I can quote Bertrand Russell [6] on this issue:

> *If a man is offered a fact which goes against his instincts, he will scrutinize it closely, and, unless the evidence is overwhelming, he will refuse to believe it. If, on the other hand, he is offered something which affords a reason for acting in accordance to his instincts, he will accept it even on the slightest evidence.*

Tell me, Beatrice, what would you say to one of your colleagues if the Shakespeare Authorship Question ever does come up?

BEATRICE. That is a big IF. It is highly unlikely that any of my colleagues will ever raise that question. We have made progress on this question largely because we have been meeting *in camera*—including some very pleasant *camere*.

I have been able to forget that I am a professor of English literature, who is supposed to know all about Shakespeare. If the Department Chair were to learn that I had been studying the Shakespeare Authorship Question, would she invite me to give a seminar on that topic? Not a chance! She would rather suspect that I had been keeping bad company!

CLAUDIA. Well, perhaps you have! But honestly, Beatrice, we have all been impressed with your willingness to be involved in this project. It is not every professor who would be willing to study a subject when the study might prove that he or she has been barking up the wrong tree—so to speak—for all of his or her career.

JAMES. I agree. It must at times have been a difficult experience for you, Beatrice. But Thomas Jefferson would have approved. He once wrote "here we are not afraid to follow truth wherever it may lead." Congratulations! It is not easy to change horses in midstream, or to change dogmas in mid-career!

We—in our smug presumed wisdom—wonder how any men (or women) could possibly have been so foolish as to believe that the Earth was flat. Maybe in a hundred years' time, men and women will wonder how otherwise sensible people could possibly have imagined that the works of Shake*Speare were written by a butcher's apprentice from a small town in Warwickshire!

BEATRICE. Surely you jest, Dr. Munroe!

JAMES. Of course, Professor Quinn! Yet many a true word is spoken in jest. Perhaps we can see what great revelation is to be read in a glass of champagne!

CLAUDIA. But now that we have got to know you both so well, we do hope that we shall see you here again soon.

MARTIN (taking Beatrice's hand). Not very soon, I'm afraid. I am taking Beatrice off for a vacation in Provence. We leave on Monday.

CLAUDIA. Vraiment! What is the French for "Still waters run deep"?

BEATRICE. I don't know off-hand—But I'll do some research and send you an email from Avignon.

CLAUDIA. And what happened to your plans for an Aegean cruise?

BEATRICE. A lady always has the prerogative to change her mind—or to have someone change it for her.

JAMES. You know, I was once afraid that we might come to blows. But—if I am not deceived—we seem to have come to an embrace, instead. Now we have two good reasons to pop the champagne: A toast to the Mysterious Bard (who is not quite as mysterious now as he was a few months ago) and *Bon Voyage* to Beatrice and Martin!

MARTIN. Thank you James, but I have promised Beatrice *un Tres Bon Voyage*.

NOTES

1. Paul (2004).
2. Bryson (2007), 190.
3. Streitz (2001), 128.
4. Barton (2003).
5. Roe (2011), 265.
6. Russell (1918).

APPENDIX A

Bayes' Theorem

Bayes' Theorem [1] defines the way in which the compatibility of new information with the hypothesis influences our assessment of the hypothesis. It involves the converse relationship: Is the hypothesis H such as to lead us to expect that the new information N is likely, or is it such as to lead us to expect that it is unlikely? If H leads us to expect N, and we actually receive the new information N, that should increase our confidence in H—and vice versa.

We use the notation $P(A|B)$ to denote the probability that the proposition A is true on the basis of knowledge that the proposition B is true. We adopt the usual convention that the measure of probability extends over the range zero to unity:

$P(A|B) = 0$ if A is impossible given B, and

$P(A|B) = 1$ if A is certain given B.

The notation AB stands for the logical product of the two propositions A and B. Then AB is true if and only if both A and B are true. The product rule of probability theory [2] states that

$$P(AB|C) = P(A|BC)\, P(B|C), \qquad (A.1)$$

Since $AB = BA$,

$$P(AB|C) = P(B|AC)\, P(A|C). \qquad (A.2)$$

Hence

$$P(A|BC) = \frac{P(B|AC)}{P(B|C)} \, P(A|C). \qquad (A.3)$$

This is usually referred to as Bayes' Theorem.

A change in notation clarifies the significance of this theorem. In writing

$$P(H|NZ) = \frac{P(N|HZ)}{P(N|Z)} \, P(H|Z), \qquad (A.4)$$

the symbols have the following meaning: H is a hypothesis under consideration, Z represents the "baseline" or "zero-base" information, and N represents a new item of information. Then $P(H|Z)$ is the "prior probability" and $P(H|NZ)$ is the "post probability;" $P(N|Z)$ is the probability that N is true, based only on the baseline information Z; and $P(N|HZ)$ is the probability that N is true, evaluated on the assumption that the baseline knowledge Z and the hypothesis H are both true. The quantity $P(N|HZ)$ is referred to as the "likelihood" of N, referred to the hypothesis H, for given information Z.

We see that if N is likely to be true on the basis of Z alone, knowledge that N is true will not greatly increase the probability of H. On the other hand, the probability of H will be increased significantly if N is unlikely on the basis of Z alone, but likely on the basis of both Z and H.

If N is highly unlikely on the basis of Z and H, the fact that N is true would make H much less likely.

NOTES

1. Jaynes (2003), 89, 112.

2. Jaynes (2003), 24.

Derivation of
The Basin Procedure

We now derive equations for what we term the "BASIN" procedure, since it is based on BAyeS' equation and uses an INterface. This procedure was derived for application to astrophysics, in which field one must draw a sharp distinction between observation and theory [1]. It is the task of an observer to reduce his observations into a summary that a theorist can compare with his theory, and it is the task of a theorist to compare that summary with one or more theories. The observer does not deal directly with the theories, and the theorist does not deal directly with the observations. This summary of the observational data comprises the "interface."

We propose that it is helpful to adopt a similar structure in our study of the Authorship Question. In place of the astronomical observer, we can introduce an "analyst" who analyses the evidence. The analyst divides his information into several "items." An example of an item would be information relevant to the lameness issue discussed in Scene 5. As in that example, we introduce, for each item, a complete list of statements such that—logically—one and only one of the statements must be correct. We denote such a set of statements by S_n, $n = 1, \ldots, N$. It is the task of the analyst to assign probabilities to each of the statements on the basis of the data that he has examined. We denote these probabilities by $P(S_n|D)$, where "D" denotes "data."

As in astrophysics, we introduce a "theorist" for the Authorship Problem. The theorist must first decide upon a complete set of hypotheses, which we denote by H_k, $k =1,...,K$. (In our Authorship Problem, there are just three hypotheses—that the author was Stratford, Oxford, or Ignotus.) For each item, the theorist is required to assign probabilities to the same statements S_n, $n = 1,..., N$, for each of the hypotheses. We denote these probabilities by $P(S_n|H_k)$.

A basic requirement is that the probabilities $P(S_n|D)$ are independent of the hypotheses, and the probabilities $P(S_n|H_k)$ are independent of the data. A further basic requirement is that, for each item, the probabilities $P(S_n|D)$ constitute a complete representation of the data.

Since one and only one of the statements S_n must be true, it follows that

$$\sum_{n=1}^{N} P(S_n|D) = 1 \qquad\qquad \text{(B.1)}$$

and

$$\sum_{n=1}^{N} P(S_n|H_k) = 1, \text{ for } k = 1,..., K. \qquad\qquad \text{(B.2)}$$

It also follows that, since one and only one of the statements S_n must be true,

$$P(H_k|D) = \sum_{n=1}^{N} P(H_k S_n|D), \qquad\qquad \text{(B.3)}$$

where the term in the summation on the right-hand side is the probability that *both* H_k and S_n are true, based on the data D.

By the product rule of probability theory, this equation may be rewritten as

$$P(H_k|D) = \sum_{n=1}^{N} P(H_k|S_n, D)\, P(S_n|D). \qquad \text{(B.4)}$$

However, according to our assumptions, the connection between the hypotheses and data occurs only via the statements S_n, so that we may ignore the term D in the first term on the right-hand side of the equation (B.4). This equation therefore becomes

$$P(H_k|D) = \sum_{n=1}^{N} P(H_k|S_n)\, P(S_n|D). \qquad \text{(B.5)}$$

We may now use Bayes' Theorem to express the first term on the right-hand side of Equation (B.5) as follows

$$P(H_k|S_n) = \frac{P(S_n|H_k)}{\sum_j P(S_n|H_j)}\, P(H_k|-), \qquad \text{(B.6)}$$

where the expression $P(H_k|-)$ denotes the initial (or "prior") probability of H_k (before taking account of the data).

By combining equations (B.5) and (B.6), we obtain

$$P(H_k|D) = \sum_{n=1}^{N} \left(\frac{P(S_n|H_k)\, P(S_n|D)}{\sum_j P(S_n|H_j)\, P(H_j|-)} \right) P(H_k|-). \qquad \text{(B.7)}$$

This equation enables us to calculate the probability of each hypothesis H_k, based on the evaluations of the statements S_n made by the examiner and by the analyst.

We now suppose that the hypotheses have been evaluated on the basis of two datasets, which we write as D_1 and D_2, which we assume to be independent. We first note that

$$P(H_k|D_1D_2) = \frac{P(H_kD_1|D_2)}{P(D_1|D_2)}. \qquad \text{(B.8)}$$

By an argument parallel to that leading to (B.5), we see that

$$P(H_k|D_1D_2) = \sum_j P(H_k\, D_1|H_jD_2)\, P(H_j|D_2) \quad \text{(B.9)}$$

and

$$P(D_1|D_2) = \sum_j P(D_1|H_jD_2)P(H_j|D_2). \quad \text{(B.10)}$$

The first term on the right-hand side of Equation (B.9) may be expressed as

$$P(H_k\, D_1|H_jD_2) = P(H_k|D_1H_j\, D_2)P(D_1|\, H_j|D_2). \text{ (B.11)}$$

However, it is obvious that

$$P(H_k|D_1\, H_j\, D_2) = \delta_{k,j}, \qquad \text{(B.12)}$$

since knowledge of D_1 and D_2 is irrelevant for an assessment of the hypothesis if information about the hypothesis is provided directly. Furthermore, our specification of the sense in which D_1 and D_2 are taken to be independent implies that

$$P(D_1|H_jD_2)=P(D_1|H_j).\qquad\text{(B.13)}$$

If we now note from Bayes' Theorem that

$$P(D_2|H_j) = \frac{P(H_j|D_2)}{P(H_j|-)}\,P(D_2|H_j)\,,\qquad\text{(B.14)}$$

we find from Equations (B.8) ,..., (B.14) that

$$P(H_k|D_1D_2) = \frac{P(H_k|D_1)P(H_k|D_2)[P(H_k)]^{-1}}{\sum_j P(H_j|D_1)P(H_j|D_2)[P(H_j)]^{-1}}\,.\qquad\text{(B.15)}$$

We can then prove by induction that

$$P(H_k|D_1...D_U) = \frac{P(H_k|D_1)...P(H_k|D_U)[P(H_k)]^{-(U-1)}}{\sum_j P(H_j|D_1)...P(H_j|D_U)[P(H_j)]^{-(U-1)}}\,.\qquad\text{(B.16)}$$

It is clear that the sum of these probabilities is unity, and that the final estimate is independent of the order in which datasets are combined.

If the initial probabilities are all equal, Equation (B.7) simplifies to

$$P(H_k|D) = \sum_{n=1}^{N} \frac{P(S_n|H_k)\,P(S_n|D)}{\sum_j P(S_n|H_j)}\,,\qquad\text{(B.17)}$$

and Equation (B.16) simplifies to

$$P(H_k|D_1...D_U) = \frac{P(H_k|D_1)... P(H_k|D_U)}{\sum_j P(H_j|D_1)... P(H_j|D_U)}.$$ (B.18)

NOTE

1. Sturrock (1973).

Summary of
the BASIN Procedure

We now summarize the procedure (developed in Appendix B) for evaluating hypotheses when the implications of the data are uncertain, and the implications of the hypotheses are also uncertain. We address this question by defining an "INterface" between the hypotheses and the data, and applying BAyeS' Theorem to each side of the interface.

We need to start by identifying a complete set of hypotheses H_k, $k = 1,\ldots, K$, and assigning their prior probabilities $P(H_1|-)$,$\ldots$, $P(H_K|-)$. For each item of data D, we need to introduce a set of statements S_n, $n = 1,\ldots, N$, which can be evaluated either on the basis of the hypotheses, or on the basis of the data. It is necessary to estimate both sets of probabilities, $P(S_n|H_k)$ and $P(S_n|D)$, and then combine these estimates so as to end up with the post-probabilities $P(H_k|D)$.

We adopt the simplifying assumption that the initial probabilities $P(H_k|-)$ are all equal $[P(H_k|-) = 1/K]$. Then we may use Equation (B.17):

$$P(H_k|D) = \sum_{n=1}^{N} \frac{P(S_n|H_k)\, P(S_n|D)}{\sum_{j} P(S_n|H_j)}, \qquad \text{(C.1)}$$

We need to be able to combine results from several items of evidence, say $D_1,\ldots,D_U$. The relevant procedure is Equation (B.18):

$$P(H_k|D_1\ldots D_U) = \frac{P(H_k|D_1)\ldots P(H_k|D_U)}{\sum_j P(H_j|D_1)\ldots P(H_j|D_U)}. \qquad (C.2)$$

In words, this means that, for each hypothesis, we multiply all the post-probabilities, and then normalize the set of products so that they sum to unity.

In applying these formulas, it is convenient to begin by giving "weights" $W(S_n)$ to any set of statements. The probabilities may then be derived from the weights by dividing each weight by the sum of the weights:

$$P(S_n) = \frac{W(S_n)}{\sum_k W(S_k)}. \qquad (C.3)$$

That is to say, the probabilities are the weights, normalized to sum to unity. This is simpler than specifying the probabilities *ab initio*, since it avoids the necessity of ensuring that the probabilities sum to unity.

Concerning
the Sequence *EVERE*

After counting the number of times each letter occurs in the text, we can draw up the following table, where the columns show:

1: Letter

2: Number of such letters available

3: Number of letters left to choose from

4: Probability of finding that letter in that cell

E	26	220	0.1182
V	11	219	0.0502
E	25	218	0.1147
R	9	217	0.0415
E	24	216	0.1111

Hence we find that the probability of finding EVERE in a group of 5 cells is given by

$$P_5 = \frac{26 \times 11 \times 25 \times 9 \times 24}{220 \times 219 \times 218 \times 217 \times 216} = 3.137 \ 10^{-6}$$

We now need to compute how many ways there are to enter this sequence in a single column.

In the following table, the columns show:

1: Number of cells per row

2: Corresponding number of rows (rounded for convenience)

3: Number of ways of selecting 5 contiguous cells out of any column. (This is the number of rows – 4.)

4: (Number of columns) × (Number of ways of extracting 5 contiguous cells from a column)

10	22	18	180
11	20	16	176
12	18	14	168
13	17	13	169
14	16	12	168
15	15	11	165
16	14	10	160
17	13	9	153
18	12	8	144
19	12	8	152
20	11	7	140
21	10	6	126
22	10	6	132
23	10	6	138
24	9	5	120
25	9	5	125
26	8	4	104
27	8	4	108
28	8	4	112
29	8	4	116
30	7	3	90
31	7	3	93
32	7	3	96
33	7	3	99
34	6	2	68
35	6	2	70
36	6	2	72
37	6	2	74
38	6	2	76
39	6	2	78
40	6	2	80
41	5	1	41
42	5	1	42
43	5	1	43
44	5	1	44

The sum of the numbers in Column 4 is 3,922. However, we must allow for the possibility that the letters are to be read either from top to bottom, or from bottom to top. Hence the number of ways of selecting five contiguous cells in a single column, considering all possible grills of widths 10 to 44, and allowing for reading in either direction, is 7,844.

We now calculate the number of possible 5-cell sequences times the probability of finding EVERE in any one sequence.

This is $7,844 \times 3.14 \ 10^{-6} = 0.0246$.

Hence the probability of finding the sequence EVERE, read either downward or upward, is approximately 0.025.

Concerning the Name *HENRY*

We first count the number of times each letter occurs in the text. The columns show:

1: Letter

2: Number of such letters available

3: Number of letters left to choose from

4: Probability of finding that letter in that cell

H	10	144	0.0694
E	23	143	0.1608
N	13	142	0.0915
R	19	141	0.1348
Y	1	140	0.0071

The probability of finding all 5 letters in a given set of 5 cells is (to good approximation) the product of the above values, which is found to be $4.7 \cdot 10^{-7}$.

However, we now need to take account of all the ways that the author could have selected a sequence of 5 cells. There are 10 rows in that grid, so one can fit 5 letters as a sequence in a given column in 6 ways—starting with the top cell, the second cell, etc., down to the sixth cell. Hence the probability of finding HENRY in any given column of 10 cells is $6 \times 4.7 \ 10^{-7}$, which is $2.8 \ 10^{-6}$. But remember that we are willing to have this word read from top to bottom or from bottom to top. This increases the probability by a factor of 2, giving us a probability of $5.6 \ 10^{-6}$.

We next take account of the fact that the grid has 15 columns, so the probability of finding HENRY (either up or down) somewhere in that grid is $15 \times 5.6 \times 10^{-6}$, which is $8.4 \ 10^{-5}$. This is the estimate for a single grid with 10 rows. However, we could fit the name HENRY into a grid with only 5 rows. If we consider grids with 5 rows or more and 5 columns or more, we find that there are 21 possible grids that meet these requirements.

Taking this factor into account, we find that the probability of finding the name HENRY by chance is $21 \times 8.4 \times 10^{-5}$, which is approximately 0.002.

APPENDIX F

Concerning the Name *WRIOTHESLEY*

We first count the number of times each letter occurs in the text. The columns show:

1: Letter

2: Number of such letters available

3: Number of letters left to choose from

4: Probability of finding that letter in that cell

W	4	144	0.0278
R	9	143	0.0629
I	14	142	0.0986
O	8	141	0.0567
T	17	140	0.1214
H	10	139	0.0719
E	23	138	0.1667
S	10	137	0.0730
L	6	136	0.0441
E	22	135	0.1630
Y	1	134	0.0075

The product of those probabilities is found to be 5.58×10^{-14}. This is the probability of finding the sequence WRIOTHESLEY in 11 cells by chance.

We next consider the possibility that the letters WRIOTHESLEY might have been organized in just two columns, with results shown in the following table. The columns contain the following:

1: Number of letters in one column

2: Number of letters in the other column (these two numbers must sum to 11)

3: Number of ways one can arrange the letters in column 1 in a column with just 8 cells (this is 9 minus the number)

4: Number of ways one can arrange the letters in column 2 in a column with just 8 cells (this is 9 minus the number)

5: Product of the numbers in columns 3 and 4

3	8	6	1	6
4	7	5	2	10
5	6	4	3	12
6	5	3	4	12
7	4	2	5	10
8	3	1	6	6

The number of ways that one can arrange the 9 letters in 2 columns is the sum of the numbers in column 5. This is found to be 56.

However, since one may need to read a sequence either from top to bottom or from bottom to top, we must multiply this number by 4, to obtain 224.

There are $^{18}C_2$, i.e. 153, ways of selecting two columns out of 18. With this factor, we find that there are 34,272 ways of entering 11 letters in the grid, using only 2 columns of the grid.

We now repeat these calculations on the assumption that the letters are distributed in 3 columns. Now restricting the options to 2 or more letters per column, the possible arrangements are found to be:

2	2	7
2	3	6
2	4	5
2	5	4
2	6	3
2	7	2
3	2	6
3	3	5
3	4	4
3	5	3
3	6	2
4	2	5
4	3	4
4	4	3
4	5	2
5	2	4
5	3	3
5	4	2
6	2	3
6	3	2
7	2	2

We now proceed as before, calculating the number of ways of entering 11 letters in 3 columns of 8 cells each as follows:

2	2	7	7	7	2	98
2	3	6	7	6	3	126
2	4	5	7	5	4	140
2	5	4	7	4	5	140
2	6	3	7	3	6	126
2	7	2	7	2	7	98
3	2	6	6	7	3	126
3	3	5	6	6	4	144
3	4	4	6	5	5	150
3	5	3	6	4	6	144
3	6	2	6	3	7	126
4	2	5	5	7	4	140
4	3	4	5	6	5	150
4	4	3	5	5	6	150
4	5	2	5	4	7	140
5	2	4	4	7	5	140
5	3	3	4	6	6	144
5	4	2	4	5	7	140
6	2	3	3	7	6	126
6	3	2	3	6	7	126
7	2	2	2	7	7	98

In this table, columns 1 to 3 list the number of cells occupied by letters. Columns 4 lists the number of ways of arranging the number of letters listed in column 1 in 8 lines, etc. Column 7 lists the products of the numbers in columns 4 to 6. The total number of ways of arranging 11 letters in 3 columns is the sum of the numbers listed in column 7, which is found to be 2,772.

Allowing for the up–down ambiguities (a factor of 8), this becomes 22,176.

The number of ways of selecting 3 columns out of 18 is $^{18}C_3$, i.e. 816.

With this factor, the number of options becomes 18,095,616.

If we add the number for the two-column case, we get 18,129,888.

Combining this with the basic factor of 5.58 10^{-14}, we estimate the probability of finding the name WRIOTHESLEY by chance in the 18 × 8 grid to be 1 10^{-6}.

However, there are six other "perfect grids" that have 6 or more columns and 6 or more lines: 24 × 6; 16 × 9; 12 × 12; 9 × 16; 8 × 18; and 6 × 24. Assuming that analyses of these grids give a similar result, we estimate the probability of finding the name WRIOTHESLEY in one of the 7 grids to be 7 10^{-6}.

References

Barton, John, 2003, Prospero's Island, *The Shakespeare Oxford Newsletter*, 2 (Winter).

Bierce, Ambrose, 1911, *The Devil's Dictionary* (Doubleday and Co., New York).

Bond, Jonathan, 2009, *The de Vere Code: Proof of the True Author of Shake-Speare's Sonnets* (Real Press, Canterbury, UK).

Booth, Stephen, 1977, *Shakespeare's Sonnets* (Yale University Press, New Haven, Connecticut).

Bryson, Bill, 2007, *Shakespeare: The World as Stage* (Harper Collins, New York).

Chiljan, Katherine, 2011, *Shakespeare Suppressed: The Uncensored Truth about Shakespeare and His Works* (Faire Editions, San Francisco).

Condon, E. U., & Gillmor, D. S., 1969, *Scientific Study of Unidentified Flying Objects* (Bantam Books, New York).

Durning-Lawrence, Sir Edwin, 1910, *Bacon Is Shakespeare* (The John McBride Co., New York).

Friedman, W. F., & Friedman, E. S., 1957, *The Shakespearean Ciphers Examined* (Cambridge University Press, Cambridge, UK).

Good, I. J., 1950, *Probability and the Weighing of Evidence* (Griffin, London).

Hakluyt, Richard, 1600, *Principal Navigations, Voyages, Traffiques, and Discoveries,* Volume 3 (George Bishop, Ralph Newberie, & Robert Barke, London).

Howson, C., & Urbach, P. 1989, *Scientific Reasoning: The Bayesian Approach* (Open Court, La Salle, Illinois).

Hume, David, 1777, *An Enquiry Concerning Human Understanding* (edited by L. A. Selby-Bigge, The Clarendon Press, Oxford, UK).

Jaynes, Edwin T., 2003, *Probability Theory: The Logic of Science* (edited by G. L. Bretthorst, Cambridge University Press, New York).

Jeffreys, Harold, 1931, *Scientific Inference* (Cambridge University Press, Cambridge, UK).

Looney, J. Thomas, 1920, *"Shakespeare" Identified as the Seventeenth Earl of Oxford* (Frederick A. Stokes Company, New York).

McCrea, Scott, 2005, *The Case for Shakespeare* (Praeger, Westport, Connecticut).

Michell, John, 1996, *Who Wrote Shakespeare?* (Thames & Hudson, London).

Ogburn, Dorothy, & Ogburn, Charlton, 1958, *This Star of England* (Coward-McCann, New York).

Paul, Christopher, 2004, A monument without a tomb—The mystery of Oxford's death, *The Oxfordian*, 7, 7.

Price, Diana, 2001, *Shakespeare's Unorthodox Biography: New Evidence of an Authorship Problem* (Greenwood Press, Westport, Connecticut).

Roe, Richard Paul, 2011, *The Shakespeare Guide to Italy: Retracing the Bard's Unknown Travels* (HarperCollins, New York).

Rollett, John M., 1997a, Secrets of the Dedication to Shakespeare's Sonnets, *The Oxfordian*, 2, 60.

Rollett, John M., 1997b, The Dedication of Shakespeare's Sonnets; Part 1: Mr. W. H. revealed at last, *Elizabethan Review*, 30, 93.

Rollett, John M., 1997c, The Dedication of Shakespeare's Sonnets; Part 2: These. sonnets.all.by.,,,., *Elizabethan Review*, 30, 107.

Rollett, John M., 1999. Secrets of the Dedication to Shakespeare's Sonnets, *The Oxfordian*, 2, 60–75.

Roper, David L., 2008, *Proving Shakespeare: The Looming Identity Crisis* (Orvid Books, Cornwall, UK).

Shaw, George Bernard, 1906, *The Doctor's Dilemma* (first produced on 20 November 1906 at the Royal Court Theatre, London, UK).

Sobran, Joseph, 1997, *Alias Shakespeare* (The Free Press, New York).

Streitz, Paul, 2001, *Oxford: Son of Elizabeth I* (Oxford Institute Press, Darien, Connecticut).

Sturrock, Peter A., 1973, Evaluation of astrophysical hypotheses, *Astrophysical Journal*, 182, 569.

Sturrock, Peter A., 1994, Applied scientific inference, *Journal of Scientific Exploration*, 8, 491.

Thomas, Sidney, & Cox, Jane, 1985, *Shakespeare in the Public Records* (Public Record Office, Her Majesty's Stationery Office, London).

Vendler, Helen, 1997, *The Art of Shakespeare's Sonnets* (Harvard University Press, Cambridge, Massachusetts).

Whittemore, Hank, 2005, *The Monument* (Meadow Geese Press, Nyack, New York).

Wolfendale, A., 2008, Profile, Sir Arnold Wolfendale, FRS, *Astronomy and Geophysics*, 49, 4.

Ziman, John, 1968, *Public Knowledge, Essay Concerning the Social Dimension of Science* (Cambridge University Press, New York).

Ziman, John, 1978, *Reliable Knowledge, an Exploration of the Grounds for Belief in Science* (Cambridge University Press, New York).

Ziman, John, 2000, *Real Science, What It Is and What It Means* (Cambridge University Press, New York).

17431336R00183

Made in the USA
Charleston, SC
11 February 2013